Thanks for
letting me be P○
of your entrepreneur's
journey

-20

Dwight

Praise for *Trajectory: Startup*

"I look to invest in founders with big ideas and a track record of hitting their milestones. Dave Parker and *Trajectory: Startup* provide a helpful roadmap for entrepreneurs on how to go from idea to that first VC pitch."
—Steve Case, Chairman and CEO of Revolution and cofounder of AOL

"Dave has a genuine heart for the startup ecosystem globally and genuine care for founders. While many mentors create whiplash with their feedback, Dave pushes the founder to ask the critical questions of their business model, team, and themselves. Just like in his book, these provoking questions lead founders to the heart of what makes a great idea and a great company. Highly recommended!"
—Bridgette Beam, director of startup and developer programs at Facebook

"Dave has been an integral part of our accelerator bootcamps over the past few years. In addition to delivering workshops in line with the latest startup trends including business models exit strategies he also throws in thought provoking questions encouraging the startup founders to think with a holistic mindset. Dave's vast experience across industries and the fact that he wears two hats as an investor and entrepreneur himself, he can relate to the different founders' concerns and challenges."
—Albert Malaty, managing director at Flat6 Labs Cairo

"As a first-time entrepreneur, I was grateful to have had Dave's mentorship from the beginning. He helped me refine my product, pitch, and go to market strategy in the earliest stages of my idea. With his help we were able to create a new industry vertical and successfully exit after one round of funding. The amount of mistakes Dave helped me avoid are too numerous to count . . . if we all could just 'choose to learn from [others'] mistakes,' the successful entrepreneurial journey could be accessible to more people."
—Anna Steffeney, former founder and CEO of Leave Logic and
Vice President of Digital Ventures & Transformation at Unum

"I've watched Dave's contribution to founders' early stage efforts from a front row seat. His advice is to the point and actionable. *Trajectory: Startup* is what you require to get your idea to the next level."
—Rodney Sampson, executive chairman and CEO of Opportunity Hub

"Brilliant! Dave Parker does something the others writing about starting up have not done. He reveals the what, the how and the WHY about each step in the process. This book will become the startup's bible, referred back to again and again. You must read this book, especially if you are in the startup process, and especially if you can't describe your 'product/market fit.'"
—Dave Berkus, super angel investor, venture capitalist,
and creator of the Berkus Method

"Few people have both the startup experience and ability to turn that experience into practical lessons for others. Dave Parker is one of those few. This book deserves to join the small pantheon of must-read books for founders and those supporting them."

—Dane Stangler, senior advisor for Global Entrepreneur Network and former VP of research and policy at the Ewing Marion Kauffman Foundation

"Dave is a strong supporter of the community and women in tech—I know from personal experience. He was one of the first mentors that didn't make me feel dismissed about my idea. And like he says, " every idea is crazy, right before it works!" If you never get to work with Dave in person, this book is a good proxy."

—Jill Angelo, cofounder and CEO of Gennev

"If there's anything I've learned from building a successful business, it's that having a playbook you can trust matters—*a lot*. Fortunately, Dave's superpower is simplifying the complex, and after decades of building, investing in, and studying a vast array of businesses, Dave has transformed his lessons into an easy-to-follow guide."

—Mandela Schumacher-Hodge Dixon, CEO of Founder Gym

Trajectory: Startup

Trajectory: Startup

Ideation to Product/Market Fit

A Handbook for Founders and

Anyone Supporting Them

Dave Parker

Matt Holt Books
An Imprint of BenBella Books, Inc.
Dallas, Texas

BenBella Books, Inc.
10440 N. Central Expressway
Suite 800
Dallas, TX 75231
www.benbellabooks.com
Send feedback to feedback@benbellabooks.com

BenBella is a federally registered trademark.
Matt Holt and logo are trademarks of BenBella Books.

Printed in the United States of America
10 9 8 7 6 5 4 3 2 1

Library of Congress Cataloging-in-Publication Control Number: 2020046007
ISBN 9781953295071 (print)
ISBN 9781953295149 (ebook)

Editing by Shawn Carkonen
Copyediting by Scott Calamar
Proofreading by Greg Teague and Lisa Story
Text design and composition by PerfecType, Nashville, TN
Cover design by Andrew Means
Printed by Lake Book Manufacturing

Distributed to the trade by Two Rivers Distribution, an Ingram brand
www.tworiversdistribution.com

Special discounts for bulk sales are available.
Please contact bulkorders@benbellabooks.com

To my family—Brandon, Carson, Drew, and Lauren.
I don't know if you'll follow my entrepreneur journey
given the crazy ups and downs you've seen, but I know you'll
follow your own and I'll always be very proud of you!

To my wife, Kathryn. It's been quite an adventure.
Thanks for being my first editor and my partner in life.

CONTENTS

Acknowledgments	xiii
Foreword	xv
Introduction	1

PART ONE: CONTEXT MATTERS 13

Chapter 1: Why Are You Doing This?	19
Slide Zero: Starting with Your Why	21
Chapter 2: What Do You Need to Do?	31
It Starts with the Market	32
Don't Forget the Product	33
Selling into the Market	33
Chapter 3: How Are You Going to Do It?	37
Startups 101	45
Chapter 4: Why Do Startups Fail or Succeed?	49
Chapter 5: Startup Economics	61
The Venn of Business Models	62
Two Perspectives—Founder and Investor	64
How Investors Make Money	72

PART TWO: DOING THE WORK 75

Chapter 6: Ideation, Research, Competition, Markets, and Scorecard	77
Ideation	78

Researching Your Idea   92

Competitive Landscape   98

Markets   98

Scoring Yourself   103

Next Steps   117

Chapter 7: Customer Development, Pivoting, Awkward Cofounder Discussions, and Telling Your Story   119

Customer Development   120

Pivoting   129

Awkward Cofounder Discussions   130

Telling Your Story   134

Deliverables   135

Chapter 8: Value Propositions, MVP, Features, and Costs   137

Value Propositions   138

Minimum Viable Product (MVP)   141

Chapter 9: Marketing, Sales, Revenue Models, and Pricing   151

Marketing   153

Sales   167

Pricing   170

Chapter 10: Preparing to Pitch, Fundraising 101   177

Preparing to Pitch   187

How to Value a Startup   193

Dos and Don'ts of Fundraising   198

Launching/Milestones   201

PART THREE: BREAKING DOWN BUSINESS MODELS   203

Research Results   204

Chapter 11: Business and Revenue Models   209

The Fourteen Revenue Models   212

Services/Fee for Service   213

Commerce   218

Subscription 219

Metered Services 220

Transaction Fee/Affiliate/Rentals 220

Productize a Service 221

Combinations 223

Marketplace 223

Lead Generation 224

Gaming 225

Advertising/Search 226

New Media 226

Big Data 228

Licensing 229

Summary—The Fifteenth Model? 229

PART FOUR: GO/NO GO 231

Chapter 12: Increasing Your Odds of Success 233

Chapter 13: Startup Business Mechanics and Compensation 237

Choosing a Startup Lawyer 237

Compensation 240

Chapter 14: Building the Community You Want to Be Part Of 243

Epilogue 249

There Is So Much More to Cover 249

Failing Smart and Starting Over 249

Addendum/Resources 253

About the Author 255

ACKNOWLEDGMENTS

If you want to go fast, go alone. If you want to go far, go together.

—African proverb

Startups are a team sport, and I've been a part of some great groups of people. Writing a book isn't a solo effort either, so let me give a few shout-outs to an amazing crew that made this possible.

For the UP Global team and Startup Weekend Community, thanks for being an inspiration at every turn and showing me my tribe in the startup community regardless of location or language!

To Andrew Means, my friend and designer extraordinaire. We started designing software products together and, now, he's supported me with the book cover and illustrations.

To my friends who did my pre-read, thanks for providing critical feedback and an eye into your unique areas of expertise: Chris, Barrington, Dan, Brett, and Matt. To Marc Nager, thanks for creating a movement and bringing me in to join.

FOREWORD

Having had a front-row seat at the emergence of startup communities around the world over the past two decades, several people have been instrumental in shaping the early-stage landscape for entrepreneurship support globally. Dave Parker is one of them, embodying the #Givefirst ethos and supporting thousands of entrepreneurs as a leader, mentor, founder, and investor.

I met Dave through my involvement with Startup Weekend. As a board member, I worked with the CEO, Marc Nager, to recruit experienced leaders to help what was then a small event company emerge into a global organization that is now part of Techstars. Dave joined as the senior vice-president of Programs and People, playing a crucial role in scaling the organization and merging it with Startup America, a combined initiative with support from the White House and Steve Case as the chairman. The combined entity, UP Global, went on to have a meaningful impact on hundreds of thousands of entrepreneurs and to help shape startup communities in some of the most unlikely places. Today, that organization and its programs thrive as a part of Techstars, solidifying our shared vision of the connection between startup communities, accelerators, and investors in creating more meaningful ventures around the world.

Dave played a pivotal role in shaping the programs, growing a grassroots organization, and building early-stage entrepreneurship support. However, there continues to be a void between the time after Startup Weekend and before a startup is ready for an accelerator program like Techstars. During that phase, there are fundamental questions to be answered, and *Trajectory: Startup* fills that gap, post-inspiration and pre-accelerator. Dave helps explain how to validate your idea and develop a plan for your startup to make money. And a critical piece of that is getting investors, mentors, or critical hires interested in your company.

As a VC, while I meet with thousands of entrepreneurs, we only invest in a small percentage of the companies we see. That's just the math of venture capital. We say no or "not now" to many startups. A considerable percentage of those companies never follow up with us, fail to provide regular updates, and seldom have a disciplined approach to answering the critical questions we need answered before we invest.

We say "not now" when we see an exciting team and idea, but it's too early for us to invest. There are many things these entrepreneurs need to accomplish before we would invest, and the tempo of my life as a VC means that I can't consistently and exhaustively provide a road map of the tasks we would like to see accomplished before the next meeting or serious consideration. For that reason, few VCs provide precise feedback.

Some of the critical tasks for startups include your go-to-market planning and execution. Understanding how you will make money. Managing your cash burn. And many others.

Dave has written the handbook for startup founders to help you with the *what* and the *how*. He enables you to answer questions such as: How do you get to product/market fit? What should you do? How should you do it? He pushes you to get to these milestones, explains how you should communicate your progress with potential investors, and outlines an approach for regular updates. You don't have to create everything from scratch, and this book can help get you down the path.

Ultimately, a considerable percentage of startups fail. You can increase your odds of success if you "kill bad ideas fast," as Dave outlines in the book, rather than "fail fast." Think of yourself as the first investor in your startup and apply the same discipline to your business that other investors will. Prioritize your resources and your time. Don't follow your hunch; instead, follow the data.

Finally, this book is also useful for community builders, managing directors in an accelerator, and early-stage investors. While the company's team will still need to do the work, hit the milestones, and find product/market fit, you can use this book to help them see that path faster and get to the scaleup stage of their business.

Good luck on your journey!

Brad Feld
Partner, Foundry Group
Cofounder, Techstars
September 2020

INTRODUCTION

Don't waste the next 24,960 hours of your work life on a dumb-ass idea. That's eighty hours of work. Every week. For the next six years of your life. You can't get that time back. Ever. And according to the statistics, 75 to 90 percent of startups will fail. You shouldn't be a statistic!

I know the math doesn't apply to you. For that matter, I knew the math never applied to me. We're a hardy bunch of souls, a tribe, who believe we can defy the odds and sometimes gravity. In a group of one hundred, you will look around the room and feel sorry for the rest of the group. You know you will be in the top 10 percent.

We are all slightly delusional. We don't lack for confidence, and we know every idea is crazy, right before it isn't. Indeed, here's to the crazy ones!

Should you leave your day job to pursue your startup? For some, it's not really an option. Say, market conditions change and your job is gone. For others, it's fear of job loss that pushes you to pursue your own idea. For many, it's a compelling idea that you must pursue. Some people even talk of it in terms of a calling, destiny, or mission.

Why do startups fail? There are a lot of reasons, and we'll dig into them in the chapters that follow. But the number one reason is that the founder or founding team builds a product that no one wants to use or buy. What that means is that the product doesn't solve a problem or isn't fun to use. It also means that your customer isn't willing to pay enough for the product to cover the cost of building and selling it plus a reasonable profit. The math means you won't have a company. Ultimately, a profit (or a path to profit) matters because you need to get paid and your investors want a return on their investment.

1

Founders are the target audience for this book. I'll be helping you, the founder, better understand your *why* early in the book. We'll then transition to *what* and *how* to validate your idea, understand if it can make money, and build out a monthly and quarterly set of deliverables to give you a go/no-go decision process about whether to continue or pivot to a new idea or market.

If you're not a founder but in the startup ecosystem as a fan, angel investor, or venture capitalist (VC), I'll set out a framework that helps you nudge the founder into making regular progress against a meaningful set of goals in order to validate or invalidate their idea. You don't have to enable them or patronize them. Don't tell them "it will be great" when you know it's not going to be great.

This book is also for:

- Those considering joining a startup
- Organizational leaders of
  - Accelerators, those organizations that provide programming and capital to help launch startups in their local markets
  - Startup studios and incubators with their own ideas they want to turn into products and scale into the market
- Investors who want to understand which business models produce the best returns and VCs directly supporting early-stage startups
- Legal and other professionals who want to know how to effectively judge ideas before taking on new clients
- Students who want to learn a startup framework to apply to their idea or an academic project

The failure statistics are so staggering because many startup founders didn't know their idea was doomed from the very beginning. They may have a great vision to build a complex product but not enough cash to get to the vision.

How do you know if your idea justifies leaving your day job? By doing your homework and getting early customer feedback and validation before you make the jump. But let's break down "a product no one wants" into its two parts: a) it's not useful, doesn't solve a problem, and isn't fun and engaging; and b) no one wants to pay for it. So you need to address both concerns before you launch a company.

Your idea may be unique. But how you make money isn't unique. I will outline the fourteen successful revenue models used in both technology and service companies to grow their businesses. You aren't likely to invent a new revenue model. This data comes from a five-year project researching 2,500 companies in CrunchBase.

You're going to need to learn the basic unit economics of your business. There's going to be a cost to build or deliver your product or service, and a cost to sell it. And you'll need to price it correctly so there's a profit left over at the end. If the basic "back of the napkin" math doesn't work, a complex spreadsheet won't work either. I'll walk you through both of those mechanics. Because even extreme grit won't save your idea or company if you don't have a path to positive unique economics.

If you are starting a service-based business, such as consulting, editing, legal, commercial landscaping, etc., there's good news. You don't have to worry about your product finding product/market fit (PMF) because other people are out in the market selling those services today. Your potential customers know what your service offering is and are used to buying it from someone already. The questions are how you will price it and how will you sell it.

However, if you're launching a product company, especially a new product that has never been sold before, you're going to have to convince your potential customer they should buy the product and use it.

> The life of any startup can be divided into two parts—before product/market fit and after product/market fit.
> —Marc Andreessen

Remember the world before the internet? Before the smartphone? Before *Game of Thrones*? Our world is defined by epochs we know well, a period of time in history typically marked by notable events. Startups are the same. There's everything you need to do to get to product/market fit before a whole new world opens up with amazing opportunities and challenges.

"Product/market fit (PMF)" and "traction" are two terms used by early investors and venture capitalists to refer to early-stage startup companies. But these buzzwords lack a standard accepted definition. Sometimes they are defined by what you, as the founder, don't have. This becomes an elusive goal that's always around the next corner.

From the founder's perspective this usually means something you don't yet have, some mystical property required, yet undefined, prior to funding. Many of your initial investor meetings will conclude with a rejection due to your company's lack of traction. But what is it, and how do you get it? I'll answer that question in depth throughout the book, but in its simplest terms, PMF is completing a series of milestones that validate your assumptions about a business idea and having a hypothesis for how you will make money. This includes soliciting feedback from your target customers to help you refine your idea and inform your product decisions. Early users who show a willingness to pay for the product with cash or their time as a consumer will help you achieve launch.

In October 2020, the short-form streaming platform Quibi announced they were closing six months after launch. The company had a famous executive team including CEO Meg Whitman, former CEO of eBay, and Jeffrey Katzenberg, DreamWorks Animation CEO. They had raised and spent $2 billion. Even $2 billion can't force product/market fit, you still need to deliver a product people want.

Trajectory is a force that you leverage, but it requires a formula. Apollo 13, both in real life and in the movie, mirrors startup life (though, hopefully, no one will be risking death at your budding company). After the lunar craft explosion aboard Apollo 13, the NASA team had to do the calculations to use the moon's gravity to get the craft and crew back to their ultimate target of Earth. Similarly, your startup will need:

- A goal
- A ship (even if it's broken)
- A plan with a clear set of actions that you can adjust as you go

Your target is to build a successful company that generates cash flow. That cash flow creates enterprise value (the amount a company is worth if you were going to sell) so that the company can be sold, go public, or pay back investors in the form of dividends. Along the way, you'll face a great number of challenges that could end your company's life.

Your ship is the problem/solution/product you are building. It's a complex machine that requires a team to build and manage. Pick the wrong market, you lose. Build and distribute the wrong feature at the wrong time, you lose. Run out of cash, you lose.

Your plan will include a set of actions you can use to validate your problem/solution/product. You'll then gather data, do the math, and make the calculations to achieve your goal of consistent cash flow. But your startup will be dealing with limited resources, so you'll have to make the most of what you have. It's like that famous scene from the *Apollo 13* movie where the engineers dump a bunch of materials found onboard the spacecraft onto a table and then have to figure out how to fix the ship using only those objects.

Does attitude matter? Of course, as does passion. But attitude and passion aren't enough. If you miss some of the actions, your course will be off by a few degrees and you'll miss the target. Yes, you can passionately fail! Every startup has many different phases of growth and challenges.

Pre-PMF, you're in search of a product or service that customers want enough to pay for. You'll also need to worry about surviving and having a company that you can scale, or grow in a predictable and forecastable fashion. Post-PMF, you'll need to worry about growth, your organization, (fixing) culture, and much more.

If you were 100 percent sure your company was to succeed, you would start with culture, because attracting a team and customers to an exceptional culture is amazing. Also, if you're a jerk, working on culture will make you less of a jerk and that's good for recruiting the team and meeting investors. Culture doesn't just happen. You're going to need to work on it as you run toward your Minimum Viable Product (MVP). Be deliberate about how your team works together, because that will become institutionalized. Some people believe that culture is set early in startups, usually at around twenty-five employees. Culture matters, but a viable company comes first, otherwise you have a club (or a nonprofit). For now, know that your values and the values of the team will begin to set your culture. But build a viable company first.

All startups are difficult, whether you're dealing with software, services, or products. There are countless examples of companies that failed because customers were unwilling to pay for their products. That's the market at work—it will either accept or reject your product or service. But how you go to market can dramatically change your outcome, so let's begin with the first four items you need to address:

1. Start with the market
2. Identify the problem you are solving
3. Build the right team
4. Create a product that solves that problem

Some VCs put the team first on this list, but generally the preference goes to the market. Why? Because if you're in an exceptional market, even a mediocre team could do well. But if you're in a lousy market, it's unlikely that even a great team will succeed in a big way. That's why getting to revenue and hopefully early PMF within six months is so important. If you're building a more complex product (such as an enterprise software product, geared for an organization rather than individuals) you might have a hard time getting a complete product built in that period, but you should be able to find some form of validation in that time. If you have an idea for an app or hardware, we'll start with validation and narrow the scope to get your MVP out the door. It's all about refining your trajectory and increasing your odds of success. If you can't get validation in six months, you may want to find a new idea.

As a five-time founder, I've loved all my ideas. But not all of them were worth the time I invested in them. In fact, three of the companies sold, and two closed. This book is an effort to help founders evaluate ideas early and judge if, and it's a big if, they are worth your time and effort, let alone a second mortgage on your house. At the start, you're the largest investor in your company, so you'll need to decide early if it's worth your investment, beginning with your time.

Remember, passion is important but not sufficient. The **market** matters. Both the **idea** and the **execution** of the idea matter. But you can execute well on a bad idea and still fail. And if you launch into a bad market, it's like being a great surfer on a small wave—the outcome will just be "meh."

How I Got Here

In addition to having five of my own startups, I've been a VC, an entrepreneur-in-residence (EIR) for a venture fund in Silicon Valley, the leader of an accelerator program for five cohorts in Seattle with the Founder Institute, the Senior VP of Programs (Startup Weekend, Startup Week, Startup Digest, and Startup Next) for UP Global, as well as the mentor and advisor to dozens of companies through Techstars Seattle. I've also chaired the Washington Technology Industry Association's Startup Program supporting the local community. All these experiences have given me the opportunity to study thousands of ideas and work with hundreds of teams at the earliest startup stage. Some of these companies were at the beginning of the process, just pitching an idea for the first time at a Startup Weekend, while others were further along. All these programs have their benefits. But the founders and teams that get the most trajectory from an accelerator have brought more mature ideas into the program.

Startup Weekend is an amazing event where you get to join a group of one hundred or more people pitching startup ideas on Friday night, then recruit a team of designers, developers, business managers, and marketing experts to validate the idea, build a prototype and showcase a demo on Sunday evening. Marc Nager and Clint Nelson scaled Andrew Hyde's original concept with a lot of work and the team of Franck Nouyrigat, Ashley Nager, and Adam Stelle. I was fortunate to join this remarkable group of people in 2009 as a mentor, and in 2013 I joined as a team member to scale the organization and its programs. The first task was to fix the Startup Next program. It was originally designed to fill the gap between Startup Weekend and accelerators. But it wasn't working, and our customers weren't completing the program and were leaving too early. We had what is called "exceptional churn."

To fix this, I worked with Matt French and Peter Marculans to better understand the market, our competition, and what our customers needed—i.e., *customer development*. Customer development is the term used for interviewing your target customer to gather feedback on your idea, product, and features. We quickly tested a new MVP and iterated until we thought we had a program that scaled. This process, which is detailed in this book, is the same one you'll follow for your own startup. Following our adjustments, the organization was sold to Techstars in 2015 and became Techstars Community Programs. Startup Next then became Startup Boost, a community program operating in more than twenty-five cities worldwide today.

I'll admit an addiction to startups, both my own and others'. I've met with founders in Hungary, Japan, Brazil, Egypt, and many other countries. It was those experiences as well as my own as a startup founder, investor, and board member that inspired me to write a series of blog posts @dkparker.com and, subsequently, this book. It has been a cathartic way for me to process my own learning, capture some of the lessons from both the bad and good decisions I've made, and to help aspiring founders.

A founder once asked me an innocent question: "Can I have a copy of your financial model template?" Now, I'm all about community and helping, but they were doing a business-to-consumer (B2C) marketplace, and my model was a business-to-business (B2B) subscription, two entirely different things. But the question intrigued me and sent me on a strange quest to discover how many model templates would be needed to cover 80 percent of all startup ideas. It also led me to investigate how many startup ideas exist (tech and services), whether new business models come around often, how they have changed over time, and which are most likely to succeed and why.

Like Sam and Frodo reaching the edge of the Shire, I didn't intend to embark on a grand adventure. It was just a query to help some Seattle founders with their startups. Or so I thought. But as I dug deeper, I found it wasn't just the financial model I needed to study, but the components of the broader business model as well. In the end, that simple question about a financial model turned into a five-year study of more than 2,600 funded companies. And I'm using my conclusions to help you:

- Create value with your product or service;
- Decide on primary and secondary revenue models from the list of fourteen that are right for your business idea;
- Deliver value and make money using your positioning, marketing methods, and sales model; and
- Capture value.

In the following chapters, I will break down each of these items into their individual parts.

Looking Back and Forward

Knowing what you know now, what advice would you give your younger self about launching a startup? That's the question I asked myself when embarking on this effort. My goal is to help you avoid the mistakes I made so you can navigate your way from ideation to a successful scaling of your company in less time. Learning from experience is important, but that doesn't mean you need to repeat common mistakes many founders make in their early days.

Maybe you're the person who is full of ideas but never gets something launched. Maybe you're the person with one precious idea that you hold on to tightly until it fails. Or maybe you're the person who wants to apply a more rigorous scientific process to your startup idea before taking the plunge. I want to convince you that the third way is the one most likely to lead to success. I want you to ask the hard questions *before* you spend your savings or mortgage your future on an idea that you could have discovered to be flawed from the beginning had you taken a more disciplined approach.

Being an entrepreneur isn't about taking unprecedented risks or rushing into battle to fight bravely and die young. It's about using data to mitigate your risks and make more informed decisions. Much of the data is already there; you just need to know where to look for it. You aren't likely the first person to venture on this quest. In addition to a killer idea and amazing execution, it will take some extreme grit and some luck as well, depending on how you define "luck." Not everything is in your control; in fact, very little is, other than your work ethic and attitude. So, to help you lower your risks and sharpen your business idea, here's what we'll cover in this book:

- Part One—Context Matters: Why startups fail, what makes a unicorn, and what you should know about your journey as a founder. Why are you going to pursue a startup? And if the why is correct, what will you do and how will you do it?
- Part Two—Doing the Work: Tasks and tools to guide your decision about whether to pursue, pivot, or drop your idea, including deliverables and resources at the end of each chapter.
- Part Three—Breaking Down Business Models: Analysis of fourteen revenue models as well as the conversion metrics and market trends of each.
- Part Four—Go/No Go: Increasing your odds of success, your go-to-market approach, working with financial models and revenue forecasting, startup mechanics, and the importance of adding to the startup community.

You can read the book faster than you can do the work. Remember, this is not homework, it's your business (and if it feels like homework, you may want to reconsider your idea). Do the work and it will speed your time to launch. Defer the work and it will slow your trajectory. I estimate the work can be done in four to six months. While it's possible to finish faster, I've found most founders need about six months because it isn't always a linear path. You'll be making some iterations along the way, and this will require you to go back to your previous steps. The process is also designed to create customer data that will inform your decisions in future chapters. So, if you don't do the customer interviews, and you build the wrong features as a result, you'll likely waste a tremendous amount of time and delay a successful outcome for many more years.

What's Ahead for You?

Over the next few months, you'll need to do some personal development to be ready to launch your startup. For example, recruiting a cofounder is similar to selling your first customer. If you don't have those skills, you'll need to develop them to be successful. Being a CEO of a startup means acquiring skills at each step of your entrepreneurial journey. If you're technical, you'll need to learn marketing.

If you're good at business, you'll need to learn to be more technical. In all cases, you're going to need to learn to be the product manager. (And a note to engineers and programmers: writing more code is not the answer to the questions outlined in the following chapters.) You will never have enough resources in a startup. Never enough cash, never enough talent, never enough time. That means you will need to cover tasks no one else can cover, at least in the short term. For example, you're not likely to have a CFO at the startup stage, so you'll have to learn QuickBooks until you can hire someone to do that for you. And if you're the smartest person in the room, find a new room.

Block out some regular time each day to focus on your startup idea. If you don't currently use calendar blocking, I suggest you make it a habit starting today. (You can find a calendar blocking template at www.GetTrajectory.com/startup/links.) The idea is to schedule time for your startup just as you make time for your family, day job, exercise, etc. And this includes weekends. Nothing great was ever achieved without a cost, and your cost right now is time. Assume this effort will cost you twenty hours a week, every week, for six months. If you have only ten hours a week, it will take you twelve months instead of six to deliver on these tasks.

All the data shows that humans are not good at multitasking. And even if you think you're the exception, blocking time for major tasks like research, building a website, or learning Google Ads will require a significant amount of hours, so pick your productive time slots and then stick to your schedule. How much time will it take? That depends. Too many founders are looking for a silver bullet, that one right thing to say or formula to follow to unlock an investor's wallet and get the big branded check to fund your company's growth. For some of you, in the time you have taken waiting to find a technical cofounder, you could have enrolled in an online course and learned to code. Stop wasting your time being a wantapreneur.

You and your company are on a journey, and it's going to require sacrifices. Kids' soccer games missed, time not spent on hobbies or vacation. Not all of the potential outcomes are venture scale, the type of company that could produce a 10–20X-plus return for an investor. Not all companies are going to be unicorns, the term coined by Aileen Lee of Kleiner Perkins Caufield & Byers (also known as just "Kleiner") that describes a business valuation of more than $1 billion, post-money, or after the last round of funding. These companies are as rare and mythical as the fantasy animal, hence the name. Everyone wants a great valuation for their company, but the internal and external factors will determine the value. It's true that a few companies have raised huge sums of money, and even gone public, without ever turning a profit. I hope that will be you, but for most of us mere mortals, we'll have to grow our business with the cash we invest and generate from sales. Plan on that, and if it rains pixie dust, all the better.

The first question you need to answer is how your company is going to make money, so we'll start there. This includes addressing questions like: Do you need funding? What are your funding options, ranging from bootstrapping to fundraising? And is your idea venture scale? Now, let's get to work!

PART ONE

Context Matters

If you don't know where you are going, you'll end up someplace else.

—Yogi Berra

In the world before Google Maps I was an Eagle Scout. One of the things we learned was how to prepare for a hike, and that included understanding how to use a map. To do that, we first needed to know where we were starting from and where we were going. We also needed to know how the lines on the map represented the terrain and learned to look to the map's legend to find these details. This helped us make sense of the map. I'm trying to give you a better legend for your startup map.

With Google Maps, you need to know where you are, where you want to go, and your destination. What route will you choose for how you want to get there—the slow way, the toll road? Finally, what vehicle are you using—a bike, public transportation, a train? These same factors will determine the outcome and timeline of your startup:

- Where you're starting is your context, your *why*.
- Where you're going is your vision.
- The waypoints are the steps to get to that vision. The first major milestone is getting to PMF. You can choose the toll road, if you have the cash to pay. You can go the long way, but I wouldn't recommend it.
- The vehicle you choose is the final choice. You can go alone, but as you add the team, you'll gain momentum.
- You'll also need fuel, in the form of time and cash. Otherwise, you'll just have a dream and a map with no way to get to your destination.

Think of it this way: There are two trains to get to where you want to go. One is the local and one is the express. How quickly do you want to get to your destination?

There isn't a secret formula for startup success. There are just too many variables to consider. But knowing the legend will help by giving you the best practices in advance. Don't worry, you'll learn plenty of lessons from experience, and there's no need to make the journey harder than it is. As founders, we all bring different experiences to the entrepreneur's journey. Yet, we all start with some form of inspiration. Personal motivations may range from a desire for greater personal freedom to changing the world to making money or solving a problem. This sets us on a path to learning and rounding out our skill set or finding cofounders who bring different skills to the company.

As a founder, you're executing an idea. But the founder comes before the startup. There is work to do before you commit to leaving your day job and starting a company, let alone taking on outside investment.

At Startup Weekend we used the chart on the following page to help our audience place themselves in their journey. We called it the Entrepreneurs Journey or EJ.

As a startup, you're building a team, a product or service, and a company. This usually requires a long commitment of resources and time. As renowned author and entrepreneur Steve Blank says: "You're an organization seeking a scalable business model." In the early days of your startup, the pre-PMF phase, you'll find revenue, but you won't yet be able to accurately predict or forecast growth. As you hire more team members and grow your customer base, you'll see some of the fruits of your

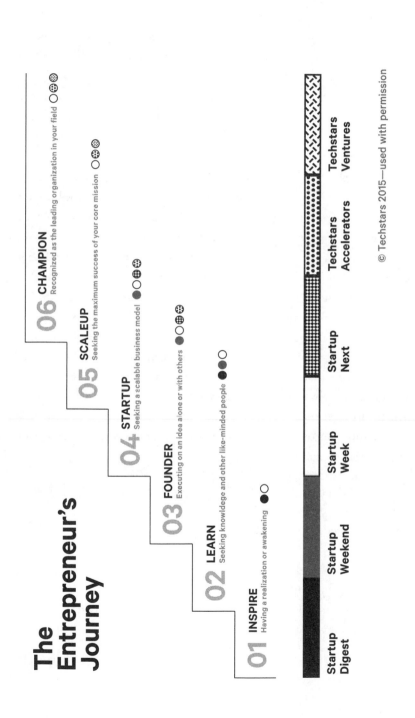

The
Entrepreneur's
Journey

01 INSPIRE Having a realization or awakening ●○

02 LEARN Seeking knowldege and other like-minded people ●●○

03 FOUNDER Executing on an idea alone or with others ●○⊕⊛

04 STARTUP Seeking a scalable business model ●○○⊕⊛

05 SCALEUP Seeking the maximum success of your core mission ○⊕⊛

06 CHAMPION Recognized as the leading organization in your field ○⊕⊛

Startup
Digest

Startup
Weekend

Startup
Week

Startup
Next

Techstars
Accelerators

Techstars
Ventures

© Techstars 2015—used with permission

labor in increased value or an expanded geographic footprint. Getting to PMF is your first major milestone because it means you have a real company.

During the scaleup stage of your company, you'll have an entirely different set of challenges to deal with, starting with adding more people. Along with expanding your team, you'll also need to think about your company culture, running a board meeting that doesn't suck, and many other details. Though do note that culture is the one topic that spans from startup to scaleup. You can fix it at the scaleup stage if you mess it up early, so don't stress about this one right now. But first things first. We'll get to these topics in *Trajectory: Scaleup*, the second book in the series.

The champion phase comes when your business has grown and you have assembled a team to fill all critical roles. For a champion, it's more than the business at this point, it's about giving back to the community and the team that helped you reach your success. Perhaps you'll decide to be a mentor or an investor or both. Either way, don't rush to be a champion too soon. Go get a company sale or exit (or two) under your belt first. Besides, you can give back in other ways at earlier stages. You can run a business meetup group to help fellow founders or volunteer at community entrepreneur events to stay engaged as you grow, but you don't need to lead the community before you have a successful exit. The point is, you're not alone in this journey. We tend to get focused on our own ideas and projects and forget there are people around us at similar stages working on completely different and noncompetitive ideas. Help each other where you can.

The part in the entrepreneurial journey where I want to bring some clarity is the murky stage after the moment of inspiration strikes and before you leave your day job, up to PMF. Specifically, the book is for:

- Founders and aspiring founders who want to confirm if an idea is worthwhile before leaving a day job;
- Potential cofounders who want to join a startup or are looking for other cofounders;
- Corporate innovators looking to put some structure to corporate goals as well as meet potential like-minded employees;
- Students who want to learn a process and structure for identifying and refining good ideas as well as rejecting bad ones.

Just know that your first idea may not be the idea you'll ultimately launch. Killing bad ideas quickly is smart, failing fast is dumb.

The Side Hustle

What's the difference between a side hustle and a startup? Most side hustles are using your non-working time (away from your day job) to make extra income. Hopefully, it's using your highest-value skill set. For example, driving for Uber is a side hustle, but you are trading hours for dollars. That's still good, but it won't scale past the rate Uber allows you to make because there are only so many hours in a day. If you're a designer with a day job who makes logos after hours, great. Same if you're knowledgeable about products and resell on Etsy or eBay. A startup is about using your skills to make a product that scales so you can trade product for dollars, not hours for dollars.

Elizabeth Yin from Hustle Fund (@dunkhippo33) had a great tweetstorm on the topic of leveraging your time.

> **Elizabeth Yin @dunkhippo33**
>
> 1) First, let's go back to the ancient days. For much of the 1800s and 1900s, there was limited technology. Human-work directly turned into product or service outputs.

> 2) If I were say in a factory, and I made widgets, my salary would be tied to the sale of those widgets. And even assuming those widgets sold like hotcakes, if I could hand-make 1 widget/hr, my hourly wage COULD NOT BE MORE than the price of that widget. Right?

She goes on to outline the different ways people leverage their time, starting with a SaaS (software as a service) company making marketing automation software for hippos. They charge five dollars a month. In the beginning it's not interesting, and they have only a handful of clients. But if the hippos like it and it starts selling like hotcakes, suddenly, a small team can have an effective hourly rate of more than $1,000.

Her other example is spending ten hours making a video that can be watched by ten people or ten million people. The payoff is based on the audience. Contrast that to cutting hair where you can only do so many haircuts a day. When you can't leverage your time, your salary is capped.

Startups are a slog and can be incredibly difficult. Like any marathon, to succeed, you need to be prepared. It's like an adventure I had last summer when I completed a 150-mile bike ride with over 10,000 feet of vertical climbing. Several months before the ride, I set out some rigorous training goals with my riding partner Tim. The ride went well because of the preparation, but the training wasn't glamorous, it was work. Yet the preparation changed the outcome, just as it will for your startup.

As a founder, you're thinking about many things at once. And you may be eager to start scaling your team, working on building a great culture, or a dozen other important steps. But spending time on topics like these before deciding on PMF is like debating the color of the file folders you'll have in your office—it just doesn't matter. Because without PMF, it's unlikely you'll raise significant capital, and your company won't last.

Is now a good time for a startup? I'm an optimist: the glass is always half full for me. There are always opportunities and there are always challenges and reasons to wait. This process will help you personally de-risk some of the assumptions and be more confident about the timing of your launch.

Why you and why now? Are you the right person to execute this idea? Have you put together a team that can help you pull it off? Is now the right time? Are there external factors that point to the correct timing? These are the questions I will help you answer as we move through the process.

Why Are You Doing This?

You need to start with your *why* because this is going to be hard. Companies don't miraculously appear as successes overnight. Many have been going for seven or more years before you've even heard of them or they announce a major fundraising round. You may know DocuSign, the digital signature company. It was founded in 2003. But before it was DocuSign, it was DocuTouch in 2000. The company went public in 2019. You guessed it, a sixteen-year overnight success story!

The problem they were solving started with Tom Gonser's first company, Net-Update, a platform that would automate the real-estate transaction process, and one specific problem they were addressing, the signature process. There had to be a better way, and online just made sense, but they were way in front of the market. They knew their why, but the market was nascent, and no one had done it before.

As of this writing, DocuSign exited as a unicorn that has boomed in the post-COVID-19 world and has a market cap of more than $36 billion.

Eugenio Pace was looking to leave a big tech company and start his own venture. We met in the spring of 2011 when he came through the Founder Institute program that I was running in Seattle. FI is a great program to help founders gain velocity. But thirteen weeks is a short amount of time, unless you have a well-formed idea with a clear market. Halfway through the program, founders need to make a go/no go decision and incorporate and continue or drop out. The decision comes after an evening of presenting your research and progress from the first six weeks in the form of a pitch to mentors. Eugenio's mentor feedback: get a new idea. He dropped the program and looked for a different idea.

In 2013 he launched Auth0, an identity-management software platform that allows you to connect your authenticated profile with other online services. It sits in the background as a service used by *The Economist* and News Corp. Though he and his cofounder were seven thousand miles apart, Auth0 grew to be a leader in the identity management market. Their last round of funding pushed the company's value to over $1 billion.

You Are Here!

You are at the start of your journey. The challenge for many of us entrepreneurs is that we believe we can see the future. But there's a fine line between vision and delusion.

I use the following chart to make a point about the difference between where you are today at launch versus where you will be at scale. You'll notice there is a great deal of ink (and time) between today and scale. Along the way, there will be ups and downs, personal and corporate challenges, economic booms and busts, and other outside factors. There will be people who think you're crazy for leaving that

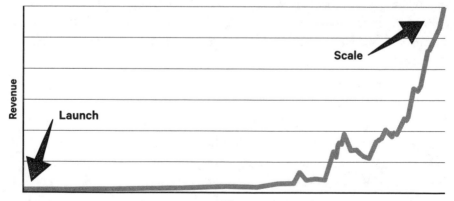

good job, and people who support you through everything. Embrace that latter group—you're going to need them on your entrepreneur's journey.

Vision, Mission, Values, Goals, and Objectives

Some startups figure out their vision, mission, and values at the beginning. Others do it years later or take some time in the future to retool their first attempt. If you're going to have cofounders in your company, it's important to at least discuss and create a rough draft of your vision, mission, and values early to ensure some level of alignment with the founding team.

Putting off this process won't doom your startup. Not every business needs these items framed and on the wall from day one. Besides, they are likely internal to the founding team, and if it's really what you believe, it won't matter what is on the wall. But if you do have them, they are more likely to guide your business forward. Here's an outline of what each term covers:

- Vision—Describes what the company wants to be in the future state, the top of the mountain.
- Mission—Guides your daily activities and what your company does now.
- Values—Outlines your core beliefs or your company DNA. As the founder, this is an extension of your core beliefs. Values define your culture.
- Goals—Details what you need to accomplish to implement your strategy.
- Objectives—Includes specific actions with timelines.

But before we get to these items, let's start with you.

SLIDE ZERO: STARTING WITH YOUR WHY

There are a lot of product or business ideas you could pursue, but should you? What if it's not a great idea? This is something all founders must grapple with. I started my first business in 1998. Since then, I've been fortunate to work with hundreds of startups and founders. This includes a number of my own companies as well as working as a VC, and consistently as a mentor.

The data says 75 to 90 percent of startups fail, so how can you mitigate your risk? After all, a startup isn't about throwing caution to the wind, it's about understanding the best way to manage your risks and navigate the startup process. That makes this book a map for mitigating the risk and getting you to ask yourself hard questions as you go through a deliberate process.

I'm sure you are like me; I love my own ideas. I admit it. It's human nature. But I don't fall in love with my ideas anymore. I've learned that ideas are not things until you act on them. Many startup founders keep an idea in their heads for years yet never act. They are scared to share the idea because they worry someone will steal it. But that just doesn't happen. Ideas die from a lack of exposure, not overexposure. After mulling it over for months or years, they'll see a product or service on the market and say, "I had that idea!" But an idea without execution is just an idea. I've had a few good startup ideas as well as my share of bad ones. The difference is how I look at those ideas today versus how I looked at them early in my startup career. I wish I had a pre-release copy of *The Lean Startup* by Eric Reis or some of the other blogs and resources available today for my first startup. I would have learned a lot about customer validation, MVP, and getting a product launched.

You need to get your idea out in front of your potential customers earlier—even before you start your "Build-Measure-Learn" process outlined in *The Lean Startup* or before you launch your Minimum Viable Product (MVP) to help you better frame your idea. So when you start the process of building your product and company, you've already done some of the work required to know what customers want.

Don't get me wrong, customers matter. Having a transformational product matters. Having great design matters. And there are countless books and resources on the topic of products. What I'm trying to impart is how you make money, create business models, and sell your product at a margin that recoups all your costs and delivers a great return to you and your investors. But customer validation isn't enough. The problem is that some ideas are huge but can't be done yet. In some cases, the technology isn't ready. In other cases, the market isn't ready. And of course, some ideas are small and not worth pursuing (even if you have great passion for an idea). Finally, some ideas will get favorable customer validation, but the economics won't allow you to get the product to market profitably. In other words, your product could succeed, but your business will likely fail.

I've had both failures and successes in my career. Sometimes my startup timing was good, sometimes it wasn't. The company I launched in 1998 was sold in 2002 after surviving the tech bubble and 9/11. I launched another company in 2006, and when the Great Recession started in 2008, we went from good customer growth in September to zero revenue in October of that same year. Here's what I learned: When you fail, you own it. When you succeed, the team gets the credit. Get used to it, because that's the role of a leader. John Kennedy popularized the quote that sums it up nicely: "Success has many fathers, but failure is an orphan."

If you're launching a startup for the glory, you're likely in the wrong place to succeed. You're going to need to build a team. Startups aren't a solo sport. In the beginning, you won't have much to compensate your team, just a vision, hopefully good leadership, and a sense of contributing to something greater than yourselves. Because you don't have cash, you'll need to learn to get good at the other intangible things. Remember, wisdom is the ability to learn from other people's experiences instead of having to learn everything yourself.

Here are some general numbers for startup math:

- Eighty hours a week—average time spent on a new startup.
- Between 4.7 and 7 years—average time from VC funding to an exit.
- Twelve years—time from startup incorporation to angel funding to VC (source: Venture Source).
- One hundred million—number of startups founded every year. 1.35 million tech startups.
- Fifty thousand—number of companies funded by angels every year (source: Gust). 1,500 get funded by venture capitalists.
- Seventy-five percent—number of startups that fail (source: the *Wall Street Journal*).

Because these stats are from different sources, there are some discrepancies in how the details reconcile. The meta point, however, is the same. You're going to spend a lot of time on your idea, building a product or service, and growing your company. You need to make sure the idea is worth it.

Given the commitment of time, and to tilt the odds more in your favor, I've created a framework that you can follow. This is especially designed for those of you who haven't yet left your day job. This process should help you prove whether your idea is a good one before you make the jump. Can you do it faster? Maybe, depending on your resources and ambition. Can you do it slower? Yes, but time is your most valuable resource (though you may not feel that way yet). So, we'll focus first on what makes a good idea by asking the following questions:

- Can you make money with the idea? This seems silly to even have to ask, but many ideas are a solution looking for a problem or a market.
- Is the idea fundable? You may raise venture capital, or you may not, but you should understand what makes a fundable company—and you should have the mindset of an investor yourself.
- Are you truly passionate about the idea or will you be bored in a year or two?

A successful startup isn't defined by whether it gets venture funding. Yet many people who have never raised capital or done a startup define success that way. Don't be one of them. Instead, think of it this way: a successful startup either creates cash flow in the form of profit or it creates an asset that can be sold to another company or taken public.

If you're going to create cash flow instead of a large exit, or if your timeline doesn't match with your investors, you may want to look at other funding options like bootstrapping, where you grow the business through cash flow. Let me give you an example. A consulting company, law firm, or services company creates cash flow. Most of the value for the services rendered is paid back to the people who do the work. Adding new clients requires adding staff. The business scales linearly with process improvements along the way that increase profitability. A law firm will "drain the coffers" at the end of each year because it's a pass-through entity. When a consulting company sells, it usually has a price range of .75–1.5 times on trailing twelve months' revenues, so a $5 million consulting business will sell for around $5 million assuming 35 percent gross margins and 10 percent net profits.

Services businesses are intrinsically people dependent. This means that the average service business will require a transition. Or, to translate that into mergers and acquisitions (M&A) speak, it will include an earnout. An earnout is part of the pricing of the transaction earned over time, which is usually two to three years. That means the buyer is going to use the profit from future years' sales to pay for the company they purchased from you. Congratulations, you've sold your company, but you have to stay to get paid.

By contrast, a product company can "make money while you sleep." You don't have to hire people proportionate to your customer base. The customer base can grow disproportionately or in a nonlinear way. But you will have to build a product first. So, the investment will be greater in a product business than a services business. Software businesses are examples of this. They make the software version once, then it's used (or installed) thousands of times and customers pay to continue using the product.

This contrast between service and product businesses isn't a good or bad judgment. It's simply a question of what your company uses as a comparison. For example, let me contrast the two models and two customer profiles here:

	Product	Service
B2B	Salesforce.com	Consulting
B2C	Games (Candy Crush)	For-Profit Education

Product businesses, which grow revenue without scaling people, create disproportionate value compared to services. Compared with the .75–1.5X revenue for services, recurring revenue subscription software businesses can be valued at 7–12X (or more) forward-looking revenue (or forward twelve versus trailing twelve). Market conditions are also a factor because of the predictability of the revenue and the gross margin associated with the business. So, if you're going to spend the time, begin with the end in mind.

On occasion, I hear founders say they are building the next (fill in unicorn name here). Except they aren't building a product company, and they aren't focused on a massive market like Uber. What they are really saying is that they want their valuation to compare to the unicorn. Yet their business isn't actually anything like the company they are using for comparison. That just makes you look naïve as a founder!

Let me be clear about what I'm *not* saying here. Very few people can launch a startup with an idea and progress as planned through a company exit all while focusing on optimizing around exit valuations. Yes, you need to focus on building a great product and giving customers great value. But you shouldn't be naïve about exit valuations either. Those who claim to have navigated their way deliberately through the process are likely rewriting history. You are not building a company to "flip." A single tech founder doing this is just a great story line you might find in the HBO series *Silicon Valley*, #nothotdog Season 4.

During the next several years, on average six to eight, you're going to face some major obstacles to your startup. Some will involve your business, some won't. It's called life. Outside factors have a way of pressing in on us and testing our resolve. Categorically, they will shape up to something like this:

- Financial—Do you have enough cash to get the product launched and show early traction?
- Market Conditions—When I started one of my companies early in 2008, I had no idea the Great Recession was around the corner. Just like those who started in January 2020 didn't see COVID-19 coming.
- Competition—Your competitors aren't going to be standing still through your process, especially if you get traction and success.
- Personal—Let's face it, "life happens" and sometimes life is hard.
- Time/Boredom—It takes a long time to grow a company, so make sure you really love the product and the market.

What do you want to get out of your startup? To answer that, start with *why* you want to pursue this idea and company. This concept is based on Simon Sinek's book *Start With Why*, which came from a Seattle TEDx talk called "How great leaders inspire action" that has been viewed more than thirty million times. In the video, Sinek outlines his Golden Circle, starting at the center of three rings:

- Why you do what you do
- How you deliver
- What you do or what you make

His point is that most businesses and individuals do the opposite: they start by explaining what they do and lack the why and the how. So what is your why? Why do you want to build a startup? Here, I have to start with the negative: If your why is to become a billionaire, you should probably put this book down right now. That goal is an abstraction, and like many out-of-reach goals, your brain will have a difficult time connecting the goal with the efforts required to reach it. There are some great books that focus on you and your why, and, in the Addendum/Resources section at the end of the book, I have included a link to my website, which has some recommended titles. This book focuses on getting you ready for fundraising. But if your why is wrong you can still screw this up.

Setting Goals

In addition to knowing your why, you're going to need to set practical goals and milestones to measure your progress over the next few months. There are a lot of options for doing this. I'm a big fan of objectives and key results (OKRs). John Doerr's book, *Measure What Matters*, outlines the OKR process that was started at Hewlett-Packard, and which he introduced to Google. OKRs are a great process for managing a team and growing a company. However, you don't yet have product/ market fit, so you don't need to worry about implementing an OKR methodology or system until you do. Get PMF and then you'll have a company where all of that will matter.

What I've discovered personally and professionally is that there are two types of goals:

1. SMART goals, which were pioneered as a system from General Electric. SMART stands for:
   - **S**pecific—well defined, clear to anyone working on the project
   - **M**easurable—understand what "completed" or "achieved" means
   - **A**greed Upon—when you're working on a team, the individual goals need to lead to a team accomplishment
   - **R**ealistic—within the time and resources available
   - **T**ime based—reasonable timelines based on the work required, usually broken down into quarters
2. Stretch goals, which are those you don't know how you will hit, and don't yet have resources or technology to hit. But despite being beyond your current reach, you still need to document them for future use.

SMART goals can push people to "think small," which can be a good thing. In a corporate job, you're seldom rewarded for having outrageous goals. For example, I have a friend who would put items on her to-do list that were already completed just so she could check them off. That's human nature. As Simon Sinek says in his To-Do List = Dopamine video, checking something off our list gives us a hit of dopamine, which is yet another reason to write down your goals. We want to know we are accomplishing some of our goals on a regular basis. This is important because stretch goals alone will become de-motivating to the team since you will never see progress in a reasonable amount of time. Even so, you need to have stretch goals so you can pull back from your day-to-day duties and focus occasionally on the horizon line.

Having these two sets of goals will free your mind and keep you focused on your primary, pressing tasks while still helping you build a vision of where you want to go with your product and company. Think of them as base-camp goals, or what you need to do in preparation to make the summit. In short, you will need both sets of goals to meet the needs of the startup. You as an individual may be motivated enough by the stretch goal and your vision, but that vision is not generally as clear as you believe it to be at the early stages of a company.

Sorry to break the news to you, but the product or solution that is likely clear in your head—including market conditions, what your company looks like at scale, and what product features you release—can sound like a jumbled mess when you try to explain it to your team, your potential investor, or your mom. (It's OK, we'll work through the process and break down the complex items into actionable steps that will help you get to launch.) When I explain this conclusion to entrepreneurs, they usually have one of two reactions. Some look at me like I'm stupid for not understanding the sentences they have just spent thirty minutes dumping on a table. Or, those with more self-awareness ask me how to better explain their idea so that they can recruit a team, get customers, or attract investors.

Entrepreneurs are amazing. Every idea is crazy, **right before it works**. They defy odds to launch companies that didn't exist before. They need big goals to do that, sometimes change-the-world goals. You will need to make sure your idea is one you want to pursue for a long time. It seems that founders have two competing forces within themselves: the dogged determination to find a way no matter what, and the ability and self-awareness to accept feedback, including knowing when to say *when* and close a business down.

Does this Zen-like character exist in the wild? Or is it a learned set of character-istics? Angela Duckworth examines this in her book, *Grit,* in which she shares many stories of people who have shown determination to succeed. As a founder, there will be many things you'll need to say no to in order to launch your company. And there will be lot of things you'll need to avoid at all costs. It's worth taking the time to think about your goals now. You, too, may be surprised by what you discover.

As you've probably noticed, I'm a reader. I read via Audible, Kindle, and physical books. I love to read, and I love to give credit where it's due. I always strive to share quotes accurately and attribute them to the correct person. Carol Dweck, the author of *Mindset,* is one of my favorite writers. In her writing, she stresses that your mindset determines how you take on the challenges of your new product and company. As you answer the question of why you are doing this venture, always consider your motivation and mindset. Why are you going to do a startup?

- Solve a problem
- Create jobs for yourself and friends/family
- Create cash flow or an asset that you can sell at some point in the future
- Change the world
- Get away from your boss
- Because it's really cool to do a startup!

As you go through the process of refining your goals and vision, you will also identify skills you'll need to improve upon. That skill set will range from simply competent to expert. You have the rest of your life to train yourself, so identify them and use some of your previously unproductive time to your advantage.

Be Epic!

For every great story, there is a hero. And in your story, that hero is you. You are faced with a challenge and a journey. The journey has many choices, and that challenge can lead to a tragic failure or an epic success. Some heroes have a guide, and that's my role in your journey. I have my own scares, and I get a little twitchy from time to time based on those failures and scares. Your story needs to be an epic success.

To be heroic and legendary, you need to be remembered, and hopefully for doing something remarkable with your business, your team, and your community. When you're launching an early-stage startup, you're under everything: understaffed, underfunded, and the product is usually underwhelming. It starts with you.

What Do You Need to Do?

Now that you've started to outline your why, you need to get to work confirming that the problem you're solving matters to customers. This process is what you need to do to validate the idea.

Building a company is more than just building a product. I know that sounds like heresy to some engineers and product managers. Sorry to bring you the bad news. Occasionally, you'll see someone on *Shark Tank* with an invention, or the more mature version, a product line. An invention by itself isn't a company.

Product/market fit is when you've built a product that your customer has validated through increasing usage or by paying for the product. Your specific metrics are defined by the revenue model (how you make money), not by vanity metrics, which are things like registered users and page views versus active users and engagement. PMF is defined as: *the degree to which a product satisfies a strong market demand. When your customer sells your product for you. And when they would be disappointed if they couldn't use the product.*

As Wikipedia also points out, some people define it as a minimum viable product (MVP). MVPs represent a product that has a useful set of features that allows the user to see the current or future benefit of the product. But product/market fit is more than an MVP—it's addressing the market's demand for the product early, then growing the product concurrently with the demand and capturing value for the product. Marc Andreessen, of the venture capital firm Andreessen Horowitz, explains it this way: "Product/market fit means being in a good market with a product that can satisfy that market."

IT STARTS WITH THE MARKET

Whichever definition we use, the main point is this: PMF starts with the market, not the product. And not even an amazing team can transform a bad market into a great one. Or, as Wealthfront CEO Andy Rachleff puts it, "When a great team meets a lousy market, market wins. When a lousy team meets a great market, market wins. When a great team meets a great market, something special happens."

Let's face it, most untapped billion-dollar markets don't exist—yet. And if they did, companies like Amazon or Google would already be there. Remember, Airbnb had a nascent market of unoccupied space in people's homes, not unreserved hotel rooms.

UberCab's 2008 pitch deck, since posted on Medium, originally thought the entire market for ride sharing was only $4.2 billion (and growing). And Facebook's initial market was confined to college campuses, not all campuses (such as high schools) and definitely not everyone in the world. In other words, these companies were only looking at the initial or launch market for their ideas, not the broader market potential. Venture capitalist Mark Suster calls this the ability to focus on the base camp, and sell the story of the summit. Investors care about the summit, the total growing market size; founders need to care about both the base camp and how to reach the summit. If you're building a huge company, your idea exists before the billion-dollar market does. Innovation comes before the market is ready and matures (hopefully) along with the market.

In a post on A16z.com, Tren Griffin described venture investing in a business as an "effort to build a stool with three legs: people, markets and innovative products." In making his point, he quotes Don Valentine, an early investor in Apple, who said, "The marketplace comes first, because you can't change that, but you can change the people." If you have the right market, you can build products for that market with the right team.

Products that create incremental improvements won't win a nascent market. Nascent markets, when developed, have blockbuster value and create unicorn-size companies. PMF without a massive market will still give you a great return.

You can't assess your market on a hunch. You need data, and that requires research.

DON'T FORGET THE PRODUCT

The ability to build a product doesn't necessarily qualify you for PMF. The customer also has to hear about your product and be compelled by your value proposition, or the concise description of your product or service that they could repeat, so that they could purchase or use the product. The value proposition should call them to act on your marketing. And to get to that point, your product must be memorable. It needs a hook people will remember and talk about with their friends or coworkers, creating word-of-mouth marketing. If you're building a mobile app, say, the hook is the defining feature that makes it sticky or fun to use. An MVP may be enough to prove you can build something but not enough to get your customers' attention. For that, you're likely going to need a kick-ass product (KAP).

What features do you need to launch to show a viable alternative to current options in the market? What is the product road map that shows a large business customer where you are going in the future? While customer development interviews are useful for defining your KAP, they don't generate a single "aha" moment; instead, they offer a composite view of what customers want your product to deliver, or what Clayton Christensen, in his book *The Innovator's Dilemma*, has called "the job to be done."

SELLING INTO THE MARKET

How do you know if you have product/market fit? Often, founders use anecdotal statements or vanity metrics to determine if PMF exists or not. Be careful here that you are really tracking the unit economics that matter. For instance:

- Website traffic is great—but only if visitors convert to customers.
- Downloads and reviews on an app store are awesome—but don't mean as much if customers won't pay.
- Early revenue is great—but only if it leads to profitability and retention.

Revenue isn't always the key indicator, but in most cases, it is. We'll break down each of the revenue models later. Unicorns can get away with not making money initially because they have meteoric customer growth. If you don't have that growth, you'll need a faster path to profitability.

As your product offering matures, you'll begin to more accurately forecast and predict revenue. This will likely start with web or app store traffic, some sort of form completion to gather user info, product use, and frequency of visits. When you see a customer come through your marketing effort, qualify on your website, and complete the sales process without you knowing them personally or "touching" them, then you're close to PMF. Or, if you have a low price point and don't require a salesperson to close the deal, you're close to PMF when you get an order from someone you don't know living in a different city from your own.

I was pitched by a company that was part of a "lab" or "studio" model, which is an incubator backed by a venture capital firm. They had customers and revenue, but all the customers on the list were part of the same venture portfolio. Though they were "customers," they were friendly customers, and this skewed their perspective. The company didn't really have a good idea of their actual target customer profile because their employees were coerced by their venture fund to become customers to help the fund. For a restaurant or franchise, this is like customers reacting to word of mouth from the credibility of a friend, instead of your outbound marketing or sales efforts. In this case, you'll want to do your best to track down the source of the referrals to thank them.

Signs of PMF Trouble

Think of it this way: If no one is buying or downloading your product, or if your churn, the percentage of customers that quit using your service monthly, is high and customers are leaving or not paying for your product or service, you don't have PMF. Sean Ellis, the founder of Growth Hackers, has a helpful way to find out if you're in that camp. He memorialized a survey of product/market fit (the Sean Ellis test and SurveyMonkey template) that asks existing users/customers a simple question: How would you feel if you could no longer use this product? Users could choose from the four following answers:

- Very Disappointed
- Somewhat Disappointed
- Not Disappointed (it really isn't that useful)
- Not Applicable (I no longer use the product)

Based on the survey question above, PMF success is defined as having greater than 40 percent of the respondents being very disappointed if they couldn't continue to use your product. When you find out if the customer cares, you can dig deeper into why. And if the results throw a bucket of cold water on your idea, use the feedback to develop a better product.

This measurement looks backward on the process. How can you see PMF looking forward? It's hard. But in the B2B market, it's likely the tipping point of increasing lead volume at the top of the funnel, decreasing sales cycle time, and increasing average contract value. For B2C, it's new user growth, or an increase in daily, weekly, and monthly active users (DAU/WAU/MAU) as you bring on new user cohorts. Your final test will be retention (low activity churn) and stickiness (increasing the customer lifetime value). One measure isn't enough for determining PMF, but the compounding effect of all three is a solid sign.

PMF Playbook

Let's face it, if we had a playbook to follow, we'd spend less time floundering around looking for the best solution. Other founders and companies have done this before. Some have told their own stories, maybe even captured some best practices. My goal is to give you a playbook. Not everything in the book will apply to your business, but you should have tactical approaches to compress your time to launch.

If you're a business services company, like commercial landscaping or an accounting firm, you don't need to worry about PMF because other people and companies are providing a similar service and the market already exits. Though your market may be limited to a local or regional geography, you'll still need to price your service competitively, deliver quality work, and have someone sell it, but at least you know the market is there.

But if you're launching an innovative new product, or even creating a new category, you're in a sprint to prove customers actually want the product and that your idea is worth the investment of time and money. To get to PMF in this case, you're going to have to address a number of topics that we'll outline in the following chapters, listed in no particular order:

- Know the market (including competition) and the customer profile.
- Have a problem/solution hypothesis.
- Understand the value proposition and key marketing messages.
- Know your product features and product road map.
- Understand marketing methods and selling models.

- Build a plan for monetization that exceeds the cost of building and selling the product so you can create a return that could be funded by investors.
- Track site traffic, bounce rates, pages per visit, and other metrics.
- Track customer lifetime value (LTV) and at least estimate customer acquisition cost (CAC). LTV is hard to calculate early, but you need a hypothesis or at least a guess.
- Understand a budget for building and selling the product.
- Survey your customers to monitor your churn.

Ironically, you can answer many of these topics before you leave your day job, build an MVP, or release the product into the wild. If you don't yet know how to get to product/market fit, don't stress. This book is going to walk you through the mechanics, including validating your idea through customer development, testing your value proposition, writing a specification, building a budget for your MVP, and starting a marketing plan.

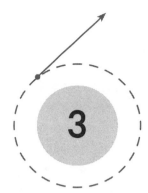

How Are You
Going to Do It?

We always overestimate the change that will occur in the next two years and underestimate the change that will occur in the next ten. Don't let yourself be lulled into inaction.

—Bill Gates

Entrepreneurship is a legitimate career choice. But to succeed at being a founder you'll need to corral many resources and skills to launch a company from scratch. It's going to take action and planning. Starting with you! How fast you work on your idea during the next few months will determine how quickly you get to the destination.

Once you declare your intention to launch a startup, people will be watching, including future team members, prospective investors, and customers. If you announce but don't take any action, they won't believe you're serious. You're going to want the most direct route you can afford—and the toll road might not be an option yet.

In the startup world, we have all kinds of events, some high value and some low value. Some of these are designed to inspire people to consider a startup as a career choice. That includes those who don't yet know what idea they want to pursue, just that they want to be their own boss and follow a dream. I am all for that! Just make sure the dream is something you really want to pursue so it doesn't become a nightmare instead. To avoid that, let's look at some resources and address what is "stage appropriate" for where you are today.

If you're looking for inspiration, you can find it in your local startup ecosystem. Startup Grind, which hosts events in 500 cities and 125 countries worldwide, is designed to educate, inspire, and connect entrepreneurs. These events have a moderator with a speaker or founder talking about their personal journey. Another early-stage startup event is 1 Million Cups, which came out of the Kauffman Foundation in Kansas City. Startup Weekend, which is in 120 countries and 625 cities, is another. It's organized like a pickup basketball game for startups.

At this stage, it's all about investing in yourself, testing your idea, learning, and applying that learning to improving your concept or even developing a new one. MBA entrepreneur programs fit this category as well. Those programs are great, if you have the time and budget. But going back to college for a couple of years can be tough if you have a family and a job. And considering most founders are thirty-five or older, that's not always an option. Founder development is the process of helping early and first-time founders like you learn from repeat founders, mentors, entrepreneurship programs, and investors. In addition, you'll need to get your company properly positioned before you can access outside capital.

Don't misunderstand: I know you may have an acute need for money to fund your startup idea. Again, your need for money is not correlated with your ability to raise it. Sorry to be the bearer of bad news. However, if you do the necessary up-front work, you will be more likely to find capital—it just might not come from a TV show like *Shark Tank* or a VC.

To get funded, you'll need to show you can hit your milestones. Further funding will be based on your continued ability to launch your product and grow your customer base. In the following chapters, I've broken these milestones down so you can systematically work through them by yourself or with your potential cofounder or team as you develop your idea. The process will confirm whether you have a solid idea, and whether you have talked with enough potential customers to have validated your idea. In most cases, this is before you incorporate, spend money on trademarks, or even divvy up any equity. And for many of you, it's before you leave your day job.

As you work through the book's deliverables over the next four to six months, you will learn to define and refine your idea, understand how to make money, and how to make an informed decision about whether to leave your day job or not. If you are at the idea stage and don't yet have a cofounder, this process could take six months. If you already have a team and an MVP, you can likely get through the tasks in a much shorter period. To that end, you will find many task lists to complete in the following chapters. I can't emphasize enough how important it is to get through the entire checklist. Shortcuts won't help you in the long run.

As a founder, you have to do things that aren't always easy or fast. But you need to do the work and check it off. Here's an outline of the work ahead in Part Two:

- **Ideation, Research and Competitive Analysis, and Markets**
  - **Ideation**—What makes a good idea anyway? (Hint: Passion alone isn't enough.) Are you looking to scale your idea into something that is fundable or to create a lifestyle to support you and your family? There is a lot to learn about what makes ideas either good or bad. And don't believe the quote "Ideas don't matter, only execution matters." That implies you have a good idea in the first place! You want to solve a big problem in a non-obvious way.
  - **Research and Competitive Analysis**—How do you research other companies and learn from their successes and failures? How do you focus on your customers first? Before you start your company, you need to know which current features meet or exceed the market's needs as well as the current pain your customers are feeling.
  - **Markets**—How should you think about your target customer and target market? Is it big enough? How will you get to it, and do you have the runway needed to succeed? I'll break down how to calculate your markets in Chapter 6.
- **Customer Development, Pivots, Awkward Cofounder Discussions, and Telling Your Story**
  - **Customer Development**—This is the process of systematically interviewing potential customers for feedback that will inform your product priorities and decisions. This is a method you will take forward and use for every idea and company you launch, so it pays to become an expert in customer development.

- ○ **Pivoting**—This is the decision point. Should you pursue this idea and project, pivot in another direction with the same market, or put this idea to rest and go after a new one? What happens when outside factors, like COVID-19, create massive headwinds or in some cases tailwinds for the business? You will have to respond to market conditions.

- ○ **Awkward Cofounder Discussions**—These founder interview questions cover commitment, equity, and the contribution of time and capital you need to have *before* you incorporate. It will never get easier to have these conversations, and it's important to do it early since 73 percent of teams split equity in the first thirty days without knowing the journey they face. Don't set yourself up for problems later.

- ○ **Telling Your Story**—It's not a pitch deck at this point, but a structure for telling your story and making sure you cover the basics.

- **Value Propositions, Testing Your Hypothesis, Product Features, and Benefits**
  - ○ **Value Propositions**—After collecting customer feedback, you should start getting your value propositions clearly laid out. This step helps you develop, clarify, sharpen, and effectively deliver your story to target customers.

  - ○ **Testing Your Hypothesis**—A hypothesis is just an educated guess until you have actual data to confirm or refute it. This process will help you outline a method to test messaging, advertising, and conversion ratios so you can get the data needed to inform your theory.

  - ○ **Product Features and Benefits**—This is when you begin to identify the features and benefits of your product for both the launch and the scale of your startup. Scale and vision are great, but you have to survive long enough to get to scale. Narrowing your focus for launch is key because you have only so much in terms of resources, time, engineering, and capital. Remember, constraints are good thing because they force you to set priorities.

- **MVPs, Product Development, Product/Market Fit, Making Money, Revenue Models, and Pricing**
  - ○ **Minimum Viable Product (MVP)**—Here, the emphasis is on viable not minimum! What are you required to ship to provide a useful solution to

your customer? What one thing do you want to prove with your MVP? What could cause your product to fail?

o **Product Development**—Product development and specifications outline what's required for an engineering team or offshore development company to build your MVP. This will include design. It may be as simple as a PowerPoint deck that looks like a mobile app or website, or as complex as an enterprise software solution.

o **Product/Market Fit**—You'll reach product/market fit when you have mapped your minimum viable product to the customer needs that you have discovered and have fulfilled that value promise. This step will help you know when you've hit that point.

o **Making Money and Revenue Models**—You need a path to positive-unit economics. We'll cover the three parts of a business model: creating, delivering, and capturing value. There are fourteen revenue models, and each will be outlined in order of difficulty to help you select the right model for your startup so you make money. Your startup is unique, but your revenue model isn't. Part Three will cover all the revenue models in greater detail.

o **Pricing**—This step covers how you should price your product and how often you should change that pricing.

• **Fundraising Fundamentals, Pitch Prep, Revenue, Product Cost, Marketing 101, Sales, and Launch**

o **Fundraising Fundamentals**—This covers sources of capital and how to access them.

o **Pitch Prep**—Outlines what to include in an effective pitch deck.

o **Revenue**—What will your customers pay for your product? And what other key metrics should you be tracking? These questions are important to answer, but don't get lost in vanity metrics. Instead, follow a set of key metrics for each of the revenue models so you can learn how to get traffic to the site and capture registered users and people who will pay you for your product. These are the same metrics investors will want to see when you ask for cash.

o **Product Cost**—This step covers the cost to build your product, and the cost of selling it, while also returning a profit to you or your shareholders.

Many products can be made; this helps you decide whether it *should* be made.

o **Marketing 101**—You need to start building a customer list and target customer(s) before you ship your product. This section will help you nail down the basic tasks required even if you've never been schooled in the dark arts of marketing.

o **Sales**—There are four ways to sell your product, and you'll need to pick your best option and begin testing it. You can build a great product, but if you can't sell it, you're going to have a problem.

o **Launch**—Product launch represents the previous few months of work toward getting something in front of your customers. Based on the complexity of your product, this may be a simple version 1.0 of a more robust product offering. In any case, you'll have a road map to launch that you'll follow based on customer feedback.

In Part Three, we will break down business and revenue models into their parts.

• **Fourteen Revenue Models**—Though your startup idea is hopefully unique, your plan to monetize it almost certainly won't be. Each of the following revenue models have key metrics—the drivers or key performance indicators—that I'll break down by model. Combination revenue models are also possible. Here they are from easiest to hardest:

1. Services or Fee for Service
2. Commerce
3. Subscription
4. Metered Services
5. Transaction Fee/Rental
6. Productize a Service
7. Combinations
8. Marketplace
9. Lead Generation
10. Gaming
11. Advertising/Search
12. New Media
13. Big Data
14. Licensing

In Part Four, we'll face some go/no-go decisions. Is your idea worth pursuing? How do you increase your odds of success and build a community you want to be a part of?

- **Maximize Your Success.** Increasing your odds of success after the launch, including hacks that can speed your process.
- **Select the right business structures.** This is US centric but addresses incorporation types and impact.
- **Build a community you want to be part of.** Build your company first but give back to the community that will support you.
- **Epilogue or what's next?** Exiting well or closing down?

I'm not trying to crush your business dream before you get it launched. I do want to help you identify what makes a good dream, a good idea, and a good business. You should still dream big because that will be the thing that carries you through the startup process and challenges to come—and there will be challenges. But you shouldn't take the next four years of your life to figure out if your idea sucks! You can do that in the next six weeks or six months and recoup those potentially lost years while you're hopefully still young enough to work on the next big idea. In the conclusion of his book *The Lean Startup*, Eric Ries writes about innovation, what we can build, and the differences between the Industrial Revolution and management of 150 years ago: "The lean movement stands for the principle that the scientific method can be brought to bear to answer the most pressing innovation question: How can we build a sustainable organization around a new set of products or services?"

Along with helping you think realistically, I also want to provide you with some tools for evaluating whether you should or should not move ahead with your startup idea—specifically, testing the macro and microeconomics of your idea. (Don't worry, we won't dig into economics at the academic level, just the practical level.) So, if you do decide to build the product, you'll understand what it means to both you and your team before you lease office space or start writing code.

I have two options as an author: I can tell you the truth or I can focus only on the positives. Many authors want to highlight just their accomplishments and successes, some with a bit of revisionist history thrown in for posterity's sake. However, we all learn more from our failures than our successes. You have to choose to learn from those mistakes. It's not easy, but it's worth it. Some people recast failure as learning opportunities. Let's be clear, though: failure is painful and expensive. If you can avoid it, you would want to know early.

Not all the sections of the book will be relevant to your idea, specifically when I cover the economics section of revenue models or how to build a Minimum Viable Product. So, focus on the parts most relevant to your idea and skim the rest. If you're not building a tech startup, you can still benefit from being tech enabled or following tech best practices, specifically in tracking your marketing efforts and conversion metrics. You can also apply tools and technology to help deliver your product and keep your margins higher. Google Analytics, proper website setup, search engine marketing, and search engine optimization still apply to you, even if you're operating a local services business. You'll also benefit by reviewing the sales and business development section. There is no secret formula to launching a startup; however, there are best practices, and I've tried to outline as many as possible so you don't have to learn from trial and error (though you'll do some of that, too).

I often ask founders: Would you rather discover you have a bad idea in six months or six years? (Spoiler alert: no one says the latter.) You may be able to get through the content of this book in a few days, but it's going to take you more time to "get out of the building," as Steve Blank says, to meet with prospects and get customer validation.

A few years ago, a former team member from my first startup asked to meet for coffee so he could explain an idea. To be clear, I'm not the final judge and jury on his or any other person's idea. But during the meeting, it became clear he hadn't considered a number of topics for his startup. At the end of the meeting, I commented that "at least you still have your job at Microsoft" and you can get answers to some of these overlooked questions before you leave your job. To which he responded that he had already quit and was working on this idea full-time.

I strongly suggest you answer the questions outlined here before you leave your day job. That isn't because your day job isn't worth leaving; that's a different issue. If you're doing a startup to escape a job you hate, you need to be extra critical in your analysis. However, if you're pursuing a startup because it's a compelling idea and you're passionate about it, that's great. Passion, though, is just one of the requirements for making a startup work. And the problem with passion is that it's easy to have when things are going well yet difficult to maintain when things are going poorly. Besides, passion is more likely a delusion at this stage.

Now, passion is important, but you must temper it with realism and hard data. At the beginning of your journey, there is nothing but a big future and endless possibilities ahead of you. You and your cofounder(s) can see the future as if it already exists. But you haven't done the work yet, or even figured out if the customer wants the product or if you can build it for a reasonable price. You're in that euphoric stage, kind of like a first date when the person, at least in your imagination, is perfect. Until they start talking and you realize you can't wait for the date to be over.

STARTUPS 101

Understanding your startup begins with understanding the world in which it will function and, hopefully, grow. You're only in business if you make money. You don't always have to make money right away, but you need to have a plan for how to do so. You also need to understand the fixed and variable costs associated with the business such as:

- Compensation expenses
  - Salary
  - Bonus
  - Payroll taxes
  - Benefits
- Contract services (1099 staff for product development)
- Professional services
  - Legal
  - Accounting
  - Tax
- Marketing
  - Contractor services
  - PR
  - Search
  - Website
  - Trade shows
- Other operating expenses
  - Rent
  - Utilities (internet, phone)
  - Insurance

SHOULD YOU PAY YOURSELF A SALARY?

Not all investors think you should pay yourself a salary, and in the early days it's not likely that you'll have compensation other than drawing down your personal savings or creating personal credit card debt. You can track that contribution and it will be rolled into your contribution at the time of incorporation, but if you're thinking that when you raise investment capital you'll be paid back for accrued salary, you'll likely be wrong. As I mentioned early, your investors want to pay for your future growth not for your past, and that includes accrued salary expenses for the founders. Expenses might be considered, depending on the investor, but don't plan on it.

You should have a path to a livable wage—but it won't be a great wage for a while, because you have a significant percentage of the company's stock. You don't get both. If you want a great wage, get a job.

Regarding a salary, as you raise each round of funding you should be able to pay yourself in similar stairstep. A pre-seed round might get you close to 50% of market for a similar role (at a similar size and stage of company, not compared to CEO of a large company). By an A round of funding, you should be closer to market rate.

Your early employees will have a small percentage of stock ownership and they will be paid a salary closer to a market rate.

These items will end up being in your "chart of accounts" when your accountant sets up QuickBooks or a similar online accounting package.

- Setup Costs
  - Cost to incorporate and get a business license
  - Legal costs
- Cost of goods
  - Cost to build a product
- Sales Costs
  - Marketing
  - Sales
  - Distribution

There is also opportunity cost, which is the income you could be earning elsewhere if you weren't working on your startup. It won't be in your chart of accounts, but it's something you need to think hard about. OK, those are a lot of cost items. And it can get more complicated as the revenue models become more complex. In the commerce model, the product has a cost, and you have a price. Subtract the cost from the price and you have your gross margin. In the case of a software subscription, the costs to build are then amortized over (hopefully) many customers and over a period of time, like three years. This is what makes it difficult to pick a cost of delivering the product.

You'll hopefully have revenue through one of the following methods:

- Product sales
- Subscriptions
- Metered service fees
- Transaction fees
- Services sales (billable hours or project based)

But top-line revenue alone isn't the best way to compare your ideas or how investors will compare you to other investments. My first company was in the software distribution business selling Microsoft licenses. This was a high-dollar volume item, but with low margins. A $10 million distribution business isn't the same as a $10 million subscription business with high gross margins. Gross Profit (GP) is a dollar amount and Gross Margin (GM) is a percentage.

- GP = Net Sales – Cost of Goods Sold
- GM = ((Net Sales – Cost of Goods Sold) / Revenue)
  The profit is the amount left over after you pay expenses

I've met with a number of founders to review their investor pitch deck. Surprisingly, many leave off a competition slide, something I expect every founder to at least acknowledge in their presentation. Once, when I asked about a particularly well-funded startup competitor, I got a blank stare. This founder didn't know there was already a competitive company in the same product category and market—and that this company had already raised more than $40 million from a brand-name venture capital team.

I understand that Amazon.com doesn't focus on competitors, it chooses to be customer obsessed instead—and at scale this is part of what drives them. But as you'll be reminded throughout the book, you are currently at the launch stage of your company, not the scale stage. You'll first need to understand how you fit into the market, and that starts with research and paying attention. You should never be surprised about your competition in front of potential investors, an employee, or a cofounder.

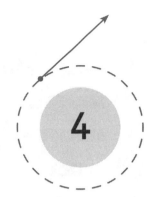

Why Do Startups Fail or Succeed?

"It's not about the idea, it's about execution" is a half-truth.

Failure is painful. If you're building a company to any size, you're bringing people with you. Those people will have families and mortgages, and you will feel responsible for them. But here's the silver lining: You will learn more from failure than success. You can also learn from others' failures, so you don't have to go down the same dead-end alleys they did. Startups fail for all kinds of reasons. Because the statistics are so staggering, it's worth taking a chapter to study some of these reasons. The one most often quoted is that the company ran out of cash. Though that does qualify as a "Well, duh!" reason, it's actually second on the list.

Since January 2014, CB Insights has conducted postmortems on startup failures several times each year. (You can find a URL to the complete survey at www .dkparker.com/books/trajectory-startup/.) On the next page is a graphic showing the top twenty reasons startups fail according to their research.

Each company can select multiple reasons for failure, so the list is over one hundred in total and can be a bit of a mixed bag, but there is a common thread. I'm

BASED ON ANALYSIS OF 101 STARTUP POSTMORTEMS
Top 20 Reasons Startups Fail

Reason	Percentage
NO MARKET NEED	42%
RAN OUT OF CASH	29%
NOT THE RIGHT TEAM	23%
GET OUTCOMPETED	19%
PRICING / COST ISSUES	18%
USER UN-FRIENDLY PRODUCT	17%
PRODUCT WITHOUT A BUSINESS MODEL	17%
POOR MARKETING	14%
IGNORE CUSTOMERS	14%
PRODUCT MISTIMED	13%
LOSE FOCUS	13%
DISHARMONY AMONG TEAM / INVESTORS	13%
PIVOT GONE BAD	10%
LACK PASSION	9%
FAILED GEOGRAPHICAL EXPANSION	9%
NO FINANCING / INVESTOR INTEREST	8%
LEGAL CHALLENGES	8%
DIDN'T USE NETWORK	8%
BURN OUT	8%
FAILURE TO PIVOT	7%

From "The Top 20 Reasons Startups Fail" by CB Insights, cbinsights.com/research/startup-failure-reasons-top/

CBINSIGHTS

not going to analyze all twenty, but I will highlight a few reasons on this list you may not have considered before.

No Market Need

That's right, 42 percent failed because they didn't build a product that people would use or pay to use. That's crazy! So, how do you figure out what people want before you get that far down the path? You ask them—a lot of them! Each month you'll be interviewing your target customers to better understand what they want and why they want it. The CB Insights article identifies two companies as examples of solutions looking for problems. In other words, these companies had built products no one wanted. Sadly, these numbers are consistent with my experience working with founders. Many have spent several years working on a "platform," a euphemism for a product that everyone could use, but no one actually does. To be clear, at scale you can be a platform. A platform is defined as a system you can build and deploy while supporting your customers. As an example, Amazon's AWS is a platform. Your MVP isn't a platform (at least not yet). But at the early stage, when you say "platform," your investor hears "no revenue."

Customer development is the process of discovering what the buyer or user wants. By doing customer development, you minimize your risk of becoming a statistic for failure reason number one—building a product the customer doesn't want. And that means getting out and talking to real, live potential customers and asking if they want the product you're thinking of building. You skip this process at your peril.

Three valuable books are worth mentioning here. *The Startup Owner's Manual: The Step-by-Step Guide for Building a Great Company,* by Steve Blank and Bob Dorf, does an excellent job of outlining the need for customer development. So does Eric Ries's book *The Lean Startup,* which details a process to help you build, test, and learn from customer development. Ries's book particularly applies to later-stage products when you have actual customers to test (versus pre-revenue, pre-customer interviews). Both books encourage founders to get away from the keyboard, halt the coding, and conduct real customer interviews. *Talking to Humans,* by Giff Constable, is a fast read and a great resource for customer development interviews. This means both cofounders, not just the nontechnical one. Customer development is an incredibly important part of the process—if indeed customers know what they want! We'll be diving into customer development in detail in Chapter 7.

Ran Out of Cash

Though this may seem obvious in retrospect, it's far from clear at the onset of your new venture. That's because at the early stage, you don't have a realistic view of how long it will take to launch and build a company. "Twice as much and twice as long" is a common theme when you talk to experienced entrepreneurs. It means it will take twice as much money to create and sell the product as you thought and twice as long to build it—and that's if you know what you're building. This is partly because your original product plan isn't perfect, and you don't yet know what you don't know about the product and customer. As you are building, shipping, and testing it, you're going to get customer feedback that requires you to change your product. This is why you should do customer development before you build the product, before you leave your job, and before you blow your savings on the wrong product.

Not the Right Team

One of the biggest challenges for a startup is the failure of cofounders to gel into a team early in their company experience. This can be due to different working styles, or conflicts in values or communications. These are human relationships, with stress accentuating all that's good and bad of our personalities. Since many cofounders haven't spent much time together, or haven't faced the challenges a startup presents, they will have a tough time pushing through and surviving. In his great book *The Founder's Dilemma,* Noam Wasserman outlines common pitfalls that can sink a company and the telltale signs you may not make it. It's a useful resource if you're in the midst of awkward cofounder discussions, which we'll cover later in the book.

Teams are so important that many accelerator programs will filter out companies that don't have teams in the selection process. And they have a preference for teams with a track record or those that have a history together. But people are involved with different motivations. Here are a couple examples of red flags:

- You've never had the conversation with your cofounders about what you want to get out of the business, e.g., big exit or lifestyle improvement.
- You decided that you should be 50/50 partners. This is like kicking the can down the road because you've deferred your first difficult decision. Not a good sign for your relationship or your company. Someone needs to lead. So decide and move on.
- One of you needs to take money out of the company, which requires the other to put money in. This is another indicator of future problems.

Pricing and Cost Issues

When considering your costs, don't stop with a budget for building your product. You also need to cover the costs of marketing, sales, and profit margin for your company. You need to have a plan for profit. We'll cover pricing and business models in Chapter 9.

Yes, These Reasons Do Apply to You

No one goes into a startup saying, "I can't wait to fail." But like every new relationship, it starts with the euphoria of the moment where details just don't matter. Let's face it, getting started is exciting! But the data still applies to you. Kill your bad idea fast and decide to pursue a better one. It might be that the timing of your idea is wrong, either too early or too late. Or, after you look at the numbers, you decide that though you could build the product, the cost of sales will be too high for the price that customers will pay. Again, discovering this early is a good thing.

In that euphoric state you are also likely thinking about the business at scale versus at launch. It will be awesome if you make it to scale and become a global monopoly. But the first challenge you face is actually making it through launch because this is where you have to match the customer requirements with the product that ships.

Another list of startup killers from another study is offered by Harvard Business School's Shikhar Ghosh. His main reasons for failure include:

1. Lack of focus;
2. Lack of motivation, commitment, and passion;
3. Too much pride, resulting in an unwillingness to see and listen;
4. Taking advice from the wrong people;
5. Lack of good mentorship;
6. Lack of general and domain-specific knowledge such as finance, operations, and marketing;
7. Raising too much money too early;
8. Scaling too early—if you try to scale your organization before you have product/market fit, you'll burn cash too quickly.

Nearly all the issues in both the Ghosh and CB Insights lists are business related, not product related. Identifying and addressing the reasons for failure will increase your opportunity for success.

What Makes a Startup Successful?

I like to be positive; I am a founder after all, so the glass is always half full! So, let's look at why startups succeed, rather than fail. And who better to learn from than three legendary thought leaders in the startup community: Bill Gross of Idealab, Andy Rachleff of Benchmark Capital, and David Cohen of Techstars.

Founded in Los Angeles in 1996, Gross's Idealab is probably the original incubator/accelerator program. In 2016, he gave a seven-minute TED talk that outlined a major shift in his thinking after more than twenty years of experience and analyzing the data. In the talk, he ranked five factors that determined the success of more than two hundred companies. In order, these factors are:

1. Timing
2. Team/Execution
3. Idea/Truth Outlier
4. Business Model
5. Funding

Let's take a closer look at each one.

Timing

Timing turned out to have the biggest influence on business success. If the market forces were in your favor, your odds of success went up. Gross used Uber and Airbnb as examples of good timing in that they came along during the Great Recession, when people needed extra income. Are consumers ready for what you have as a product? This idea is consistent with Gartner Hype Cycles analysis, which reveals that when innovation happens, people get excited (blockchain technology is a 2018 example). Expectations first go off the chart, then slide into the Trough of Disillusionment and climb the Slope of Enlightenment before reaching the Plateau of Productivity. A founder's enthusiasm often precedes the market and opportunity. You need to prepare for the long haul as the market matures.

But can you really "time the market"? Venture capitalists would say yes, but that's likely revisionist history. For example, coming out of the COVID-19 pandemic, there are businesses that will flourish. Some can be predicted, like digital transformation or the shift from in-person business to remote work. Others, less so. Education technology (EdTech) is now a hot category that was previously hard to fund. I think the best you can do is to look at headwinds versus tailwinds. Headwinds are when other bigger competitors are spending large amounts of capital in your market. Tailwinds are when customers are spending in your category. Just remember, it's not easy to pick your timing, and external factors like recessions aren't within your control.

Team/Execution

Teams matter, even more so if you think you want to raise outside institutional capital. Venture capitalists prefer teams over solo founders and seldom, if ever, fund solo founders. The team should have a healthy balance of experience and non-overlapping skill sets. Bonus points if you have a history of working together.

Idea

Gross named his company Idealab, so he thought the idea would rank number one. Yet it came in third. Of course, having a big idea still matters.

Business Model

Having a clear path to revenue that creates cash flow is critical and a shared characteristic of the winners versus the others. We'll cover this in detail in the funding section of Part Three including why different business models perform better at early stages than later stages of the company. Being underfunded, or overfunded, for that matter, can dramatically impact your success or failure. If you think overfunding is not possible, look at the results so far of Softbank's Vision Fund with a portfolio of unicorn startups they have had to write down in valuation.

Good and Bad Markets

Rachleff's view is that market always wins. According to his Law of Startup Success, the number one company killer is lack of market. "You can obviously screw up a great market," he writes, "and that has been done, and not infrequently—but assuming the team is baseline competent and the product is fundamentally acceptable, a great market will tend to equal success and a poor market will tend to equal failure." In short, market matters most.

Techstars' Perspective

At Techstars, CEO David Cohen and their team evaluate companies based on five criteria (a video interview by Cohen that includes a great summary of the value of teams is in the resource link):

1. Team
2. Team
3. Team
4. Market
5. Idea

Cohen's point in emphasizing the team is that they are investing in a group of people they believe in regardless of whether the product is a hit or the market has a problem. From their experience, backed by market data, the product or idea that you start with is often not the product or idea you finish with, which is why team is so important. The team is going to have to adjust along the way to find the right path. Investors are betting on the team rather than the CEO/founder alone. A solo founder is likely to follow an idea down a dead end longer (and at greater expense) while a team will likely adjust and pivot sooner. Investors will usually see you once a month or once a quarter. You have to see your team every day.

Market Leaders, First Movers, Last Movers, and the Rest

Which is best: First mover? Last mover? Market leaders? Or is there a best?

> @mfishbein I agree—as Peter Thiel says, the key is to be the "last mover," not the "first mover."
>
> **—Marc Andreessen on Twitter**

In October 2015, Uber was looking at raising another round of funding, with a valuation of $60–$70 billion. At the same time, Lyft announced a plan to raise close to $1 billion. And then there was a company named Sidecar, which raised $35.5 million and sold to General Motors in 2014. That's only one comparison of first mover and last mover. Remember, if a market already has a massive market leader, or multiple companies that have been funded over $100 million, then the odds of a new entrant securing funding in the category, let alone competing, are incredibly low.

I remember when Groupon came out and hyperlocal was the rage. Hundreds or even thousands of "just like Groupon only better" companies followed. And died. LivingSocial raised $928 million and sold to Groupon. The timeline for Groupon is worth looking at:

- 2007: Groupon raises $1 million in angel investment
- 2009: Revenue is $14.5 million
- November 2010: Google offers $6 billion for the company
- 2011: Revenue is $312.9 million
- November 2011: Goes public at $20/share and $10 billion valuation
  - Closes the day at $26.11
- 2012: Revenue is $1.6 billion
- December 2018: ~$3 per share or $1.8B market cap
- May 2020: ~$1.20 a share and $680M in market cap

Why the tumble in price? Well, if you read the media (instead of those that were just envious or jealous), there are a number of reasons. Here are a couple of headlines, blogs, and analysts with their takes:

- Associated Press: "Groupon's Fall to Earth Swifter Than Its Rise"
- *New York Times*: "Is Groupon's Business Model Sustainable?"
- Investing Daily: "Groupon IPO: Worst Internet IPO of the Year"
- GeekWire: "Groupon IPO: Is This the Next Amazon.com or Pets.com?"

Some of Groupon's major competitors include Amazon Local, Woot, and Gilt City, so a lot of investor dollars have flowed into this market already. Plus, it has made thirty acquisitions already in mobile and products like Groupon Now. Like it or not, Andrew Mason created the fastest company to reach sales of a billion dollars ever.

Knowing Your Risk Factors

Every public company has to disclose their "risk factors" in the S1 or Form 10Q. Here's what you can learn from Groupon's filing. By the way, don't let the number of pages of Risk Factors surprise you because it's common for every public company to defend against shareholder lawsuits.

"Subscriber Acquisition Costs": from Groupon S1 Filing

Over time, we believe we will reach the conclusion that the resources presently being devoted to online marketing initiatives are not yielding sufficiently attractive investment returns due to a variety of factors such as changes in subscriber economics, achievement of subscriber saturation levels in various markets or a determination that subscriber growth objectives can be satisfied though alternative means. As a result of such factors, **we anticipate significantly decreasing the amount of such investments**. [Emphasis mine.]

If any market is crowded with large incumbents (with cash), and your business model shares the same challenges with those incumbents, and there aren't likely any investment dollars available for your startup, should you start that company? The answer is, if you're going to need outside capital, you're going to face headwinds.

Stroke of the Pen Risks

Both you and your investors want to avoid markets or opportunities that can be vaporized by a "stroke of the pen." Government regulation can turn for or against you as politicians change. Don't build dependencies on these market factors turning in your favor.

State of Funding in Your Vertical Market

Is your startup going into a market that has been overinvested? Investors are generally pattern matchers—this deal looks like that deal, and that deal was good, so this one might be as well. Some invest in specific vertical markets or investments at certain stages. Most investors tend not to invest in markets where they have lost money before. (Does anyone remember nanotechnology?) One reason for this is that institutional investors, VC and private equity, have limited partners. And it's tough to sell a limited partner on reinvesting in a market in which they have already lost money or where it's difficult to see a return based on the amount of competition.

Zombie Startups: Worse Than Failure

A zombie startup is a company that sits between life and death. This generally means the founders can't raise capital for growth, and yet can't sell the company either. Thus, they are sitting between the hope they had for their growth to go "up and to the right" (life) and really needing to close the company (death). Not where you want to be.

An attorney friend of mine once told me about a deal he was hoping to close by the end of the calendar year. As we discussed the deal, it became obvious that it was a good exit for the founders, but in the form of closure instead of cash. The company was about seven years old, and though they had some initial traction with their idea, they never saw the customer adoption they had hoped for. They had raised some money for growth. But after a while, they saw the original concept wasn't growing as fast as they wanted, so they made a significant pivot by launching a new product within the same customer segment. Regrettably, that pivot didn't really take off either, so they were stuck in zombie land. They had invested a significant number of years in the company, so in order to salvage something for themselves and their outside investors, they decided to sell the business. It didn't provide a meaningful amount of cash return for the time spent on the company.

You're building your business to make money, or you'd create a nonprofit. If your startup can't create cash flow to pay you and it can't sell for a meaningful return, you have to ask if it's worth your time compared to having a job—remember the topic of Opportunity Cost we discussed above. What should you do if you have a zombie startup? Ask yourself three questions:

- Do you have the passion to make another run at it? If it's been seven or eight years, you're likely tired. Tired of the company, maybe tired of your cofounders, or tired of the market.
- Do you have a compelling pivot idea? Or is it really more of a life preserver? If it's the latter, it's time to ask yourself some tough questions.
- Do you think the pivot has a faster path to growth than your current alternatives? If not, you may want to rethink your options. It might be a good time to wind things down and let your investors know you will be confirming what they already know: this one didn't work and it's time to close it down.

Startup
Economics

I enjoy cooking. In fact, I've become a pretty good cook over the years, though not a chef by any means. I've learned there are times when you can fiddle with a recipe with little risk. Baking, however, is different than cooking. You need to be precise and it's best to stick to a recipe, so you don't have to start over if you added the wrong ingredient or wrong amount. I've discovered that many founders tend to lump together a bunch of ingredients and call it a soufflé, or the catchall in this case, a "business model." But a business model is not the same as a financial model, a revenue model, or a sales model. To stick with the analogy, if you follow the recipe, you can do it. Stray from it and you could get into trouble.

Let's break down the ingredients in a recipe for a successful startup:

- You and your team, or those who will become your team, including how your company is organized.
- The product or service you will build that the customer finds valuable and worth buying.
- The distribution process, including marketing and sales, which handles how your product or service gets to market.
- A method for capturing value so your startup can get paid, including pricing and your revenue model choice.

Building a product is great. Just be sure it's worth building first. You'll need to get paid as well. As the first investor in your startup, you need to figure out if the idea is worth your time. After all, time is the only capital you can't replace. To help you decide, let's start with the three big economic components of any business:

1. How you **create** value through your product or service. This includes the cost of building the product and delivering the product.
2. How you **deliver** value through marketing, sales, pricing, and monetization (revenue model), and the corresponding cost of sale.
3. How you **capture** value is the margin after removing those costs from the sales price of the product.

THE VENN OF BUSINESS MODELS

Venn diagrams are a great way to visualize a concept. In this case, the three overlapping circles represent the three components of the business model described above.

Creating Value: Product

Capturing Value: Reasonable to Exceptional Returns

Delivering Value: Price, Marketing & Sales, Revenue Model

Creating Value: The Cost of Building (or Delivering)

There is a cost to creating value. It's either your time to build a product or the people to deliver a service.

"It won't cost me anything to build it" is an oft-heard refrain said by my engineer friends about a software product. Except they aren't calculating their time when they say this. What they mean is that it won't cost them cash for someone else to build the product. If you're building a product, whether software or a physical item, there is a cost associated with the design and development. You also need to consider the cost of supporting the product over time. This includes server time, customer success/support, migrations to new or updated platforms, and other factors. As you look at your development team, how will you divide the duties of core development and customer support (including inbound queries from customers)? And if you're a service business, will you need to hire employees or contractors to deliver the service?

For both products and services, we tend to discount or undervalue our own time. This is the opportunity cost that you give up by not choosing to do other things. I've watched founders wave away this cost as they have worked on developing a product over a three-year span—while at the same time forgoing a big annual salary from a company like Amazon. Opportunity costs are real, and you should consider them as you become the largest early investor in your startup.

Delivering Value: Price, Marketing and Sales, Revenue Model

How you price the product affects everything. And it needs to cover the cost of building as well as the cost of selling.

How you will market or create demand and awareness for your product is a cost center—how you, or your team, will sell the product is also a cost. We'll cover some of the options in greater detail in the marketing and sales section later in Chapter 9. For now, let me highlight some of the basics. The costs of selling include:

- Marketing: How your customers will discover your product.
- Sales: Who will sell the product or service to the customer.
- Distribution: If a channel will be delivering your product or service, you need to know how long it will take to get the product into the channel and what percentage of the sale that channel will require for facilitating that sale.
- Business development: This includes building partnerships with other companies or people who help to sell your product.

These unit economic costs are captured as customer acquisition cost (CAC), lifetime value (LTV), churn, time to close, and others, all of which should be considered early in your process.

Capturing Value: Reasonable to Exceptional Profit

Unsurprisingly, the more exceptional the profit, the more investors will be interested, while the more reasonable the profit, the less likely you are to find funding. Zero profit equals little interest. At the very least, you will need to have a path to profit. The near-term exceptions are companies that have utilized the "new media" model used by WhatsApp or Pinterest, in which customer acquisition is a future proxy for revenue. You'll find a detailed explanation of this model in Part Three on business and revenue models.

What If the Venn Is Out of Balance?

Here are some problems with not addressing the Venn:

- Cost to build: It took more time and engineering to build the product than you anticipated. This will force either the cost of sale or profit to go down.
- Cost to sell: You discover that no one in your target market is looking for your product using search words. This requires you to use a sales team to sell the product, which causes the cost of sales to go up. So, either the profit comes down or the cost of building the product needs to come down.
- Profit range: You've decided you want to use a "forever free" marketing program to acquire customers. However, your product doesn't yet have enough features to have two versions, free and premium. This limits your profit potential and puts the pressure on cost of building or cost of selling.

TWO PERSPECTIVES—FOUNDER AND INVESTOR

Here's another way to think about the Venn diagram above that provides some necessary perspective: You are looking at your product; investors are looking at your returns. Investors know it's easy to get a check into a company, but it's hard to get a check out. For them to get a return, you need more than a product or service. You need a business model that accounts for unit economics. We'll spend time on that in Part Three.

You can earn back money you've lost, but you can't get back the time you've spent. I want to help you prioritize the best things to spend your time (and money) developing and then do those things first. Here are some contrasting ways of thinking about your business idea and how investors will see your idea.

Scalable startup versus a lifestyle business. A scalable startup business is one that can expand beyond your geography and country boundaries and possibly grow exponentially. This is generally the type of company we mean when discussing startups. In contrast, lifestyle businesses generally include franchises or local businesses designed to serve your immediate geography only. A lifestyle business can also be one that employs family or friends.

"Lifestyle business" is not meant as a derogatory phrase. It can be a great goal for many people. For example, my accountant has a lifestyle business. However, when he quits working, the value of his business will decrease rapidly. He does have a list of clients he can sell to another accountant, but the business doesn't make money while he sleeps, as a scalable startup would.

And if one cofounder wants to build a lifestyle business and keep control and the other founder wants to exit, you've failed to address a big issue in your awkward cofounder discussions below.

Product versus service. Except for the business model for "productizing a service" most of the focus of this book will be on product companies, which can

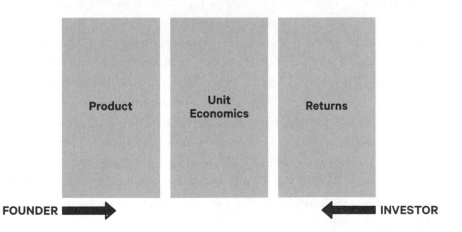

make money while you sleep. Services businesses typically scale with people; for example, a consulting business or law practice that hires additional staff as its customer base grows.

Fundable versus bankable. Most startup businesses building products in the technology sector will look for funding at some point. Fundable businesses will require a path to a return on the investment. However, your need for funding and your ability to raise capital for your company are different things. They are not correlated. Fundability by investor is a bet on market potential, product, team, and traction. A bankable business is usually one that can be funded through banking relationships when the business is at a more mature state or has credit based on the creditworthiness of the founder combined with the bankability of the business itself. It's about cash flow, not potential.

Is Your Startup Fundable?

At the risk of over-indexing on your desire to raise venture capital, let me state the obvious here. Raising venture capital is not a sign of success. However, I do think you should have the same critical eye on your startup idea as any investor. This includes thinking of yourself as not just a founder, but as the first investor. Would you invest in this idea if someone else presented it to you? Most founders or inventors look at their ideas as if they are their children—they are amazing and should never be called ugly. But as those in *Shark Tank Nation* know, few startups get funding; many startups think they are fundable but aren't.

Even if you're putting up your own savings rather than raising capital, I suggest you use the same evaluation criteria that investors would use to vet your own idea. Your need for funding doesn't mean your idea or startup is fundable. Many founders confuse these two topics. The less you need funding, the easier it will be to raise funding. The more you need it, the harder it will be. In the early days, you're nearly always out of cash. As you mature, many venture funds, or institutional investors, won't even seriously talk with you about fundraising if you have less than six months of cash on hand. In startup vernacular, this monthly expense is called "burn rate." It's the amount of cash you have until you run out, or monthly burn rate, that amount you'll spend net of revenue. You'll likely find you can go a lot further than you think you can on that cash, but it often means you and your team won't be getting paid.

On AVC.com, Fred Wilson wrote a blog post entitled "Burn Rates: How Much?" about what are acceptable burn rates given the stage of the company:

- Building product stage: <$50,000 a month
- Building usage stage: <$100,000 a month
- Building the business stage: <$250,000 a month

If you require funding and your idea isn't fundable, you need to know sooner rather than later. Can you research if your idea is fundable or not? Yes, and you'll learn more about investor profiles in Chapter 10, and I'll address research as a method in the Chapter 6. But for now, let's start with what makes a company fundable, and what factors keep companies from being fundable. We'll cover the ten criteria and how you score yourself in Chapter 6.

Are *You* Fundable?

In this case I mean you, personally. Investors are investing in people, so if you're not very likable, it's going to be a significant challenge for you to get funded. There are any number of things that can make you unfundable. If you've taken outside money and failed before—that's a good sign to some investors and a bad sign to others.

Getting funded means you, as the founder and CEO, can sell. If fundraising is required, and you don't like to sell, get over it. You'll need to sell your idea and yourself to get funded.

In general, investors will overindex on self-awareness—your ability to know yourself, your motives, and character. Are you open to feedback from your team? From your investors? Being arrogant works only for those companies that have outrageous growth numbers.

Let me take on a hard topic here for a minute. Some of the folks reading this book have a lack of self-awareness or a blind spot. You know the person; they can see everything that is wrong with someone else's idea or product but don't apply the same discipline to their own idea or startup.

In his book *Creativity Inc.*, Ed Catmull talks about managing "creatives," specifically the directors and producers at Pixar where he was a cofounder. One of the many things that makes these people talented is that they are pursuing their own ideas and stories. That same passion and focus is also the thing that will blind them to the problems they will face. I think entrepreneurs are the same. We fall in love with our ideas. It's what makes us great at doing things that have never been done, but also what keeps us from seeing the forest for the trees.

If that's the case, how do we create a structure that allows passion to flourish while still maintaining healthy checks and balances? Look for a cofounder who can balance out your weaknesses. Build a team of people smarter than you, especially those who fill gaps in your own knowledge. Founders often see the future as if it exists today. That makes them prone to embellishments. They will talk about customers when no one is actually paying them for their product. In reality, those are prospects; they are not customers unless there is a commitment. Founders will also blend the current product as it exists today with the product road map. For the most part, I don't think this is completely delusional—it's part of the vision. However, be aware that constant embellishment will create reasons for investors and others to question the integrity of the founder if the statements are not consistent with reality.

Regrettably, some of these investor heuristics reflect intrinsic biases. On the negative side of the tech/venture world, too often this means funding goes to white guys who went to the "right" schools.

- Only 2.9 percent of venture capital flows to companies with women as CEO/founders
- Less than 1 percent of venture capital flows to Black and Latinx founders

Sadly, one report I remember reading stated around 3 percent flows to guys named Dave. The fact is, the venture industry needs to do better, and though progress is being made, it's slow in coming. You'll need to find allies who believe in you and your vision and can help.

Founder/Market Fit

I've never liked the term "founder/market fit"—it always felt forced. But the idea behind it is relevant. It's a way to answer such critical questions as: Are you the right team to build this product and this company? Are you the right person to lead? Does your team have unique industry or market knowledge that provides a competitive advantage? And do you have unique technical knowledge or connections that will help your marketing? Whenever a new product category emerges, everyone in that market is new to it. Whether it's the internet in the '90s or blockchain in 2017, it's not hard to be an expert in a new market.

Building Your Team

Choosing the right composition of your team is essential. At Startup Weekend events, we break down product companies into three main roles:

1. Technical/Developer
2. Business
3. Designer

In the startup community you'll also hear these roles as hacker and hustler, but I'd still include a designer. Let's look at them one at a time.

Developer/Hacker/Builder: You need at least one person on your team who can build product. So much of the early stage of the process is about prototyping ideas and getting a preliminary product out the door to validate the idea with actual customers, so you'll need someone who is good at those tasks. Ideally, it will be more than one person. But having the first person is the starting point. While you can certainly outsource your development to get prototypes built, you need to recognize that an outsourced team won't help you in the funding process. Because so much of your intellectual property (IP) is based on the ability to create product with speed, an outsourced team will be viewed as having less value than a team you are working with every day.

Business/Hustler: You hope to have a prototype, so you will need someone to sell it. Someone to get out in front of your potential customers and do interviews and research. Then there will be pricing, marketing, and promotions as you get ready to launch. This role also includes building a team to cover finance and legal tasks. Each team will define its duties and titles as you go. You may not need a big team to launch, but you'll need to be focused on the top priorities. Can you use interns for some tasks? The answer is similar to one about the outsourced tech team mentioned above. There are tasks that can be completed by interns, but the fundability of the company is going to be evaluated on the quality and size of your team. Most interns will take a significant amount of time to train and ramp up, so it's not really "free" labor.

Designer/User Interface/User Experience: If you are building a tech product, design matters. Lowering user friction will matter. That ease of use will get your customer to increase frequency or refer a friend. Like many Apple products, you can drive a premium price, not because a product is technically better, but because the design is better. When something is clunky, the user thinks about it. When it's well designed, it blends into the background. This can be a hard topic for back-end developers and architects. They tend to love their own site designs so much they can't really be bothered making them "look pretty." I'd compare this with a plumber who is working on a new house. They are so impressed with the quality of their own work that they can't imagine why a designer would want wallboard, paint, and artwork to cover up their brilliant work. Yes, clean code matters, and you should take pride in that work, but you also have to realize that you aren't your user, and the user is going to care how they interact with the app or site. Today, design is partly about user experience (the user interface—UI) and interaction. It's aligning your product with expected customer interaction.

A final thought here on teams. If you don't yet have a team or a cofounder, you aren't likely to get funded by an institutional investor. This doesn't mean you won't get funding from friends and family, but angels and VC investors aren't likely to write a check to a solo founder. Bringing on a cofounder represents your first major sale—getting another person to believe in the idea so much they are willing to put their name on the incorporation documents. In later chapters I'll discuss early-stage stock allocations, defining roles and duties, and how to unwind these early-stage relationships, but for now, what you need to know is that investors view teams as better bets than solo founders.

Market

Seasoned investors put their capital into markets they know and understand and where they have made money before. You won't see many VCs back both biotech and software, for example, because the factors to consider are too great to be a good investor in both categories. One of the companies that I launched did business in China. As I talked to investors, I found that those who knew the China market immediately understood the business and product. Those who didn't know China, or hadn't invested there before, had to first understand the market before they would invest in the company (the minor exception being people I already knew well). So I started weeding out potential investors by asking qualifying questions in advance of a meeting, such as, "How well do you know the China market?" or "Have you invested in a company doing business in China before?" If the answer was negative to this type of question, I wouldn't have a meeting. You can start this work even before you have direct communications with the investor by researching their investment profile.

Investors will look at your company and compare it to others in the market to see what similar investments have been made. If you don't know what market you are in, that will be a problem from the start. This idea of pattern matching is a consistent theme that individual and institutional investors will use—e.g., "Have I made or lost money in this category?"—so be prepared to address this.

There is a lot of funding data available for startups today. Many of the details included in this book are based on open-source data that was provided by Crunch-Base, a summer intern project from tech blog *TechCrunch*. The company found that it was writing about emerging businesses that lacked data, and so it created a database of companies from past articles. The team then crowdsourced additional funding data from the community about these companies. This crowdsourced model is similar to Wikipedia in that authors build credibility based on contributions. Because CrunchBase has limited free access and inexpensive paid access, I suggest you start your market research there.

Another way to provide context around how to think about your business and fundability is to figure out your category and current stage of development. For example, categories include:

- Software
- Apps
- E-commerce
- Business Service

while the stages are:

- Pre-Product
- Shipping Product
- Pre-Revenue
- Revenue

I'll go into greater detail of categories and stages in the research section of Part Two, but a quick note before we go into evaluating your specific startup. This is a good time to ask yourself whether there is anything that can keep you from being fundable. As investors analyze deals, they are first looking for reasons to not invest, or to screen out investments that don't meet their requirements. In general, I call these reasons "hairballs." I'm talking about cofounder issues, legal issues, a nontraditional corporate structure, IP issues, and anything else that will be discovered in the due-diligence process.

HOW INVESTORS MAKE MONEY

You're looking to get an investment check into your company. The investor is looking to get paid at a future date. You need to convince them your company is worth the long-term investment. Most startups end up selling to bigger companies through a merger and acquisition (M&A). A few will go public. The rest will create profits and distribute them in the form of dividends to shareholders. It takes a long time for an investor to get a return check from early venture deals.

Unlike public equities or mutual funds, venture investments are not liquid. Investors can't come back to you as CEO and say, "Hey, I've had a life change and need to get my cash back at a better value." At the same time, institutional investors have the expectation that venture is a long-term investment. And in exchange for that time value of money, they expect a disproportionate return.

Venture Power Law

The general idea of the "power law" is a statistical model that expresses a functional relationship between two quantities. Compare this to a "bell curve" of even distribution across a range—what would be the "average return" for a venture investment company. A power law distribution assumes that there isn't average, but rather 80 percent of the returns come from 20 percent of the investments.

Within venture capital, the power law is the concentration of performing investments as part of the fund's portfolio. Most venture funds include multiple funds, normally named as simply as Fund 1, Fund 2, or after the type of vertical market that fund is focused on for investment. Each of these funds has different limited partners or LPs. Given these types of returns, fund managers are looking for deals that can "return the fund" multiples. If your company makes money, but not a huge return, they won't have the same interest as a potential blockbuster. Later in the fund's life cycle, when they have deployed the majority of the capital, they might look to fill in with some other types of investment that they believe would

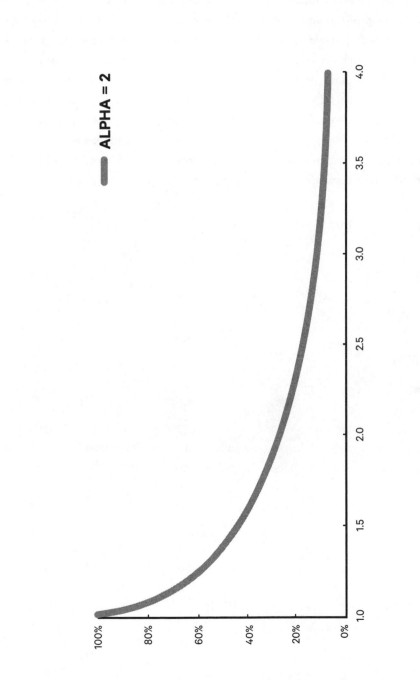

have a good return, but not a blockbuster. However, that also means that they won't likely have "dry powder" to add to a follow-on round of funding.

Your likelihood of success with a startup depends on many variables. Startup economics begins with understanding the cost of building and selling your product or service as well as the level of profit you reasonably expect to produce. Investors want to get a check out of a business in a reasonable timeframe. That means you need to understand the business model and profitability as well as product. Then there are the external factors outlined above that will affect your company including the size of the problem, size of the market, customers' willingness to pay, and timing. The amount of money already invested into your vertical market is also a factor. If you set out to start an Uber-like car service today, investors and friends would shake their heads because that market and its leadership are already set.

PART TWO
Doing the Work

Startup Next was originally designed as the program to follow Startup Weekend. We went through a couple of iterations and settled on building a six-week pre-accelerator program. A pre-accelerator is a program, but lacks the capital investment of an accelerator. Today that program is called Startup Boost and is in several cities worldwide. The participating teams that succeeded included both those that got into an accelerator program following Startup Weekend and those that had enough momentum to go directly to funding.

To run the Next program in six weeks required us to set a higher bar in three areas:

- Team: A solo founder couldn't complete the necessary tasks in six weeks, so teams of people with non-overlapping skills were required.
- Product: At least an MVP version of a product was required because there was no way to complete the work and the product in six weeks.
- Traction: The teams needed to have either preexisting users, a letter of intent, or some level of revenue.

These changes produced teams that were more likely to get into accelerators or get local funding based on their results. With this book and programs, I wanted to start at that earlier stage, before team, product, and traction, and compress that development cycle. You might still be looking for a cofounder, you probably have an idea, or you might have a product. Regardless of where you are on this continuum, you'll have monthly deliverables that will help keep you on track and get to your results. When we run the in-person program, we usually see about half of the participants drop out after month four, the section on how companies make money. That's usually because they discovered that their idea doesn't meet their own personal requirements to create a great product or company. That's OK, it's good to kill bad ideas fast. And the participants still developed skills that are transferable to their next idea.

Though the work isn't hard, it is going to require you to discipline your time. You're going to need to get out of your head, away from your keyboard, and meet your target customer. This will require scheduling and introductions. We'll talk about some tools that will make that process easier as we go through the monthly deliverables. By doing the work outlined in the next section, you'll build conviction and momentum—conviction based on data from customer interviews, and momentum from prioritizing your product features and benefits and value proposition and, ultimately, knowing your customer.

This isn't "homework," it's the deliverables for you to prove your product and company are worth pursuing over the next five or ten years of your life. We found that if we called it "homework" at Startup Next, the founders didn't take it seriously. There are no grades for your deliverables. But discovering what your customers want early could save you months or years in your company's growth. That time could translate into millions of dollars and even the difference between success and failure.

You have an opinion about your idea, product, and company. Investors also have opinions, and they have a checkbook. To get access to a checkbook, you'll need data to back your opinion. The steps over the next few months are designed to help you get that data.

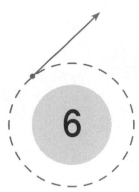

Ideation, Research, Competition, Markets, and Scorecard

There are two things you can't find on the internet—just like two things Robert Hooke couldn't find in the Bible or the decrees of King Charles the First: You can't search for answers to questions that haven't been asked yet. You can't Google a new idea. The internet can only tell us what we already know.

—Brian Grazer, *A Curious Mind*

You may already have a well-honed idea that you're bringing into the process. If so, great, but stay flexible. If you have six ideas, we should be able to help winnow them down to a lead idea. And even if you don't have an idea, but want to be a founder entrepreneur, I've outlined some tools to get you started. But the focus of this section is validating that your idea is worth pursuing and getting you ready to explain that idea for product development and fundraising. If in the process, you decide your idea isn't worth pursuing, don't be discouraged—ideas are all around you when you know what you're looking to find.

IDEATION

Tom and David Kelley are the brothers behind IDEO and the book *Creative Confidence*. IDEO is famous for the first Apple mouse and the notebook computer. Today you would know them for Helix genomics or packaging design for PillPack. They are also known for the Stanford design thinking school. Or as they call it "d.school" (as opposed to "b-school" for business school). The program is based on four steps:

1. Inspiration
2. Synthesis
3. Ideation/Experimentation
4. Implementation

For me, inspiration is not generally a bright light from heaven. There are no angels singing or bolts of lightning. The Kelleys suggest you write down things that bug you, because you'll start being more mindful. I like this idea, only I tend to divide things between two questions: "Why does that not work the way I'd like?" and "Why is this so hard?" The point is, don't just solve the problem for yourself! For some undergraduate university programs, the professors will suggest that students solve a problem they know. No offense to the university, but most undergrads have very few firsthand experiences with meaningful real-world problems. If they do work on problems they know, it's usually within a limited set of problems to solve, often around books, food, or dating. And, yes, some blockbuster companies have come from these three problem areas:

- Chegg: With a focus on textbook rentals, the company raised $289 million in funding and acquired fourteen companies.
- Facebook: I don't think I need to explain this one. If you don't know the details, including how it was started in a Harvard dorm room, watch the movie *The Social Network*.
- Tinder: It introduced us to the process of swiping left or right. They only raised one round of funding and sold to Match.com for around $3 billion.

These B2C companies solved a problem and were obviously well rewarded for their effort. But you don't always have to solve a problem. In the case of gaming companies like *Angry Birds*, the product was all about fun. And fun can pay, too. Rovio, the Finnish company behind *Angry Birds*, has a major movie as part of the brand extension as well as Angry Birds Land theme park. The company was founded in 2003, six years before three university students from a hackathon with Nokia and HP brought them *Angry Birds* success—let's hear it for corporate innovation events! By the way, *Angry Birds* was their fifty-second game. Yup, this may take a while.

If you're still in the ideation stage, the following books are worth your time:

- *Made to Stick*—Chip and Dan Heath
- *Abundance*—Peter Diamandis, Steven Kotler
- *Creativity, Inc.*—Ed Catmull
- *Thinker Toys*—Michael Michalko
- *The Industries of the Future*—Alec Ross
- *The Third Wave*—Steve Case

All these books will inspire you and change the way you look at problems as well as trends in the market. Remember, by breaking down a problem into its parts, you can work toward a solution for the whole. You should also be thinking about where the market is going to be in a few years. If a current technology trend continues, where will it lead?

Tracking Your Ideas

I'm a strong believer in tracking your ideas. There are many ways to do it. Use your notepad on your phone to capture your idea or summarize it in a paragraph you could use to explain it to someone else. Then let the ideas mature over a few weeks. If you come back to the idea and it's still interesting, you can start on the research. Is it a problem you know? Is it in an industry you understand? Are you the target customer? It's good if you deeply understand the customer. For example, when Facebook launched as "TheFacebook," it met a need familiar to college students: finding a date. This process will make you more aware of ideas around you. I read a book in which the author stated that ideas are out there just waiting for you to be a cosmic match. Well, I don't have any insight into your cosmic destiny, but the more you summarize ideas and problems, the more you'll be able to look at them with a well-trained eye.

I wouldn't suggest that you go buy domain names for all your new ideas just yet. At one point, I had more than one hundred domain names. When I went back to look at some of them, I couldn't even remember the idea that sparked the domain name. Save yourself some cash. We'll get to naming and branding in Chapter 9.

Ideas do matter, especially when they are bad ideas. Great execution won't make a bad idea great. However, you can execute a bad idea quickly to failure! Which is a form of success. Truly great ideas (billion-dollar, unicorn-type ideas) are rare. In this chapter, I've taken some of the buzzwords associated with ideas and defined them in the context of ideas. I've also pulled quotes from some top investors to help you understand how they look at ideas. Defining a great idea is a matter of your goals. However, if you're looking for investment, you'll need to consider the investors' goals as well. Does your idea involve a product or service? One idea or many ideas? Ideas come to me at different times. I've found that it can be a latent need that comes as an observation in the moment. It can also manifest itself as a recurring frustration, a "Why isn't this easier" moment when you make an observation.

A recent favorite is Brex, a credit card company for startups. A few years ago, I had a meeting with a large bank. I was educating them on the differences between a small business and a startup business. A small business serves a geography, so a better term is really a local business. A startup has grander visions, maybe even to change the world or serve an entire nation or region. I was talking to the bankers about how I built my first company using personal credit from my American Express card. I carried a platinum card for business expenses and a gold card for personal items. It wasn't that I wanted the charges to be on my personal card, it was that the banks had no path for a young and fast-growing company without a multi-year track record of profitability to build corporate credit that wasn't a complete pain. I was trying to talk the bank into creating a card for startups because I saw the frustration and friction. They didn't. A few years later, Brex hit the scene with a business credit card for companies that have venture backing. Their target market for venture-scale startup isn't millions of potential business customers, but it is a billion-dollar market. Instead of talking the bank into a new product, I should have started a new company. I totally missed that one!

Here's another way to think about your ideas: Are they disruptive or incremental? Paul Graham used to post startup ideas that he'd like to see apply for Y Combinator (YC), the startup accelerator he launched in 2005. It's a practice he began in 2008, with a list of thirty ideas—some have aged well, some have not. In 2012, he posted another seven on his personal blog. Here's a quote from the blog: "The biggest startup ideas are terrifying. Not just because they'd be a lot of work. The biggest ideas seem to threaten your identity: you wonder if you'd have enough ambition to carry them through."

Nearly all venture funds have a thesis. They are looking at future trends in the market. As of this writing, the combined category of machine learning (ML) and artificial intelligence is a current theme. The funds are trying to predict the future, the next internet. Sometimes they are right, sometimes they are wrong.

Framing Your Ideas

Frameworks are useful ways to think about your ideas. Below, I've outlined some of the company examples and frameworks used by other founders to move from an idea to a product. There is no right or wrong way to judge your idea, and no single yardstick to follow. Rather, you should look at your idea within a number of these contexts to consider how your customers and investors will view your idea. I've followed the frameworks with some bad examples as well. To create a successful startup you need to move from idea to product, from abstract to concrete or something you can ship and a product or service your customer can use.

The Value of Ideas

Another thought from the "what I wish I knew then" file. I mentioned earlier that it takes as much time to build a product and launch a company for a small idea as it does for a big idea. While that may be oversimplified (obviously, launching SpaceX will take more time than delivering a mobile app), the principle is important. Even with a small idea, it can take years to validate whether or not customers will accept it. To help you decide, let's look at ways to evaluate if your idea warrants the time required to build a company.

Starting with a Product or Innovation

In his book *Zero to One,* Peter Thiel discusses building around a monopoly. He writes:

> If you're a technologist or innovator at the university level, you likely have some unique insight into a set of technology. This may be in computer science in the form of an algorithm; Google's team at Stanford had developed unique technology around search and the method to display those results through Page Rank. There was obviously more to their success than just those two components. There are universities around the world with academic works that have never seen the light of day.

Firms like Intellectual Ventures have built massive patent portfolios around a core technology, plus additional patents that cover a range of business processes in a given industry segment. Some of these patent portfolios represent audacious long-term bets. For example, TerraPower is striving to "develop sustainable and economic nuclear energy technology." The idea is truly transformational and has attracted large investors including Bill Gates. This patent portfolio model is very expensive to assemble. In some cases, along with having a core patent, firms will hire experts to either identify or create an ecosystem of patent coverage to support the core patent while also creating a high level of defensibility. I'm guessing you don't have those resources. And you're not alone.

Some technology innovations will eventually get to market, but most never escape tech transfer programs. The patent isn't the important thing. Keep your trade secrets confidential in the near term. You can work on your plan to build a moat for your company as you grow. If you have limited cash now, spend it on validating your idea by building an MVP and getting it in front of customers first.

Innovation & Curiosity

Innovation and curiosity by themselves don't make a startup or entrepreneurship. Especially if it's too early to market or if you don't have a go-to-market plan. There are warehouses filled with innovations at universities, research facilities, and government agencies across the world that have never seen the light of day. Innovation matters when it meets an application of that innovation. The steam engine was invented in 1698 and developed slowly over time. It only found its application when James Watt introduced his version of the steam engine in 1776, which powered the Industrial Revolution of 1760–1840. If your product is too early for the market, you can be very enthusiastic about it, and it may be a great idea, but it will never make any money.

Market Trends

Example: Smartphones created the app market.

Market trends are a great way to think of new ideas. The internet created brand new opportunities for companies that build infrastructure, just as the gold rush did for picks, shovels, and, in the case of Nordstrom's, providing shoes for the goldrush.

The launch of 5G will also provide a trend for brand new startup ideas.

Problem/Solutions

Example: 1Password. You don't want to get hacked, and the problem is you need long passwords with alphanumeric and special characters that are too long to remember. The solution is an app you can secure (with a long password) that will create crazy long passwords.

As mentioned, most startups are based on solving a problem. It may be a solution for consumers as noted above, or it may be for business. If it's a big consumer market, the payoff can be huge, as with Uber. If it addresses a big business problem, say office productivity, like Microsoft Office, it can deliver a big payoff in sales, for both businesses first and consumers second.

Many founders start with a solution and then look for a problem. I don't recommend this. Instead, start by identifying a clear problem to solve for an identified customer. You can then pivot the product to fit to the need.

The Ecosystem or Waterline View

Examples: Uber Elevate. I had an opportunity to sit in on the first Uber Elevate conference in LA in 2018. Elevate was about the future of "flying cars." Uber envisioned big drones filling the sky above the highways in major cities. To bring this vision into the future, they included city officials, members of the Federal Aviation Administration, building owners, Bell helicopter, various manufacturers, and other stakeholders.

They had an entire market or ecosystem view of the problem and solution.

Using this as an example, let's apply the problem/solution approach to this idea starting with the customer workflows. This idea requires:

- Mobile app to find a landing spot
- Uber to get me to that parking garage
- Destination, timing info
- Pricing/billing/credit card
- Landing location and infrastructure
- Car to final location

Now consider the other problems to be solved:

- Who will manufacture this fleet of drones?
- Who will service the drones?

- Where will they land?
- How will the drones be powered? If by electricity, how do you get power everywhere it needs to be (such as landing pads on tops of buildings)?
- Who will pilot the drones?
- Who will train the pilots?

Uber designated most of the problems on the second list to partners. It's also where the margins were lower, and product and services were harder. They kept the high-margin, highly scalable problem/solutions and looked for partners to push those problems. You should look at your problem and market the same way. Identify the problems and solutions. But also identify where the cash is and who will pay. Don't stop at the first problem. Identify all of them in all the workflows and start with the problems where people will pay.

Think of it as a waterline. There are problems that are above the waterline and ones that are below the waterline. Even if it's a big problem, if it's below the waterline, you won't make money. You have to focus your launch on revenue, then you can reinvest on the other problems. The bigger problem may not make money at first, though people recognize the size of the problem.

Copycats and Playbooks

I've done work in a lot of international markets. One trend there is that a local company will copy an international or US company that has already raised significant cash, then localize for language and culture. Regions and cultures vary greatly about whether or not "copycats" are OK. But let's look at the data.

Most high-growth VC-scale startups in the West should focus on their home market first before expanding. That's a six- to eight-year process before they are considering launching in a different language or currency. That's a great window of opportunity if you're in an international market.

You also have that company's playbook of their observations of their effort that you can follow as well as validation of PMF from funding. As a founder you'll still need to build the company in your language, currency, and international marketing. But it can be less risky than starting from scratch, and you'll likely find an upmarket buyer when the first mover comes to your region. You'll need to have customers and revenues, however, or instead of a buyer, you'll find a well-funded competitor.

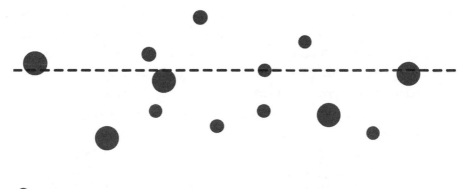

● Problems – – Waterline

However, copycats in the same market as a dominant competitor are really hard. Being the next new food delivery app today is the same as being number 1,000 to copy Groupon in 2012.

GEOGRAPHIC-BASED BUSINESSES

Uber and Lyft are examples of businesses that require geographic expansion, and growth requires adding services and infrastructure in new cities or countries (unlike a software company, which can be used regardless of geography). This creates an interesting challenge: an opportunity for competition. For example, Uber launched in 2009 and went live in San Francisco in 2010. Seeing the same need in Brazil in 2011, Tallis Gomes launched a similar service called EasyTaxi at a Startup Weekend, before Uber reached the country. They've since expanded to thirty countries. The note here is that if you have to do a rollout city by city, you'll face local copycat competition. That's not necessarily a bad thing (Brazil is now Uber's second-largest market after the United States), but know that it will create unique partnership or capital requirements for growth.

What Is Transformational?

Example: AirBnB or Uber.

Occasionally you'll hear a founder say that their startup is "transforming" the industry. Generally, it's an aspirational claim. It's the same as the person who claims to be a philanthropist or visionary on their LinkedIn profile but isn't (yet). The point is, avoid hyperbole in your pitch. If your idea is remarkable, the investor will recognize it, and you can talk about how you're going to get from your launch to your vision. Time will tell if your company is truly transformational.

Precious few genuinely novel ideas come around. Same with those that create a new category or become a category killer. Uber and Airbnb are two of these rare examples. If you're creating a new category product, I'd encourage you to read *Play Bigger* by Al Ramadan, Christopher Lochhead, Dave Peterson, and Kevin Maney. The book covers several examples of companies that created categories, killed existing categories, or were killed along the way.

Incremental improvement is generally not enough to get customers to switch. Think about the last time you switched banks or auto insurance providers. Since these services are commodities, the pain and hassle factors are high. If you're building a technology solution, you generally have to target being ten times better than the next alternative.

Elizabeth Yin wrote a post about the cost of switching that's worth noting. She talks about when it's not enough to have a good product. You'll need to understand how to work with your customers' existing workflows. Ideally, you want your product to be easy to switch to (adoption) and difficult to switch away from (retention).

Pain Pill or Vitamin

Example: All of the apps that are on the first screen of your phone versus the fourth screen.

In that same vein, you'll hear the phrase "pain pill or vitamin" a lot when launching a new product. The implication is that the customer will pay nearly anything for a pain pill because they must have it. A vitamin, on the other hand, is nice to have, but only if it's convenient and reasonably priced.

Stripe is a great example of a pain pill. Before Stripe's swipe device and a smartphone, I couldn't sell tickets at an event or venue. With Stripe, I could monetize. Technically, I could have gone to a big bank and done something with a credit card machine. But their process was expensive and cumbersome—nice to have, but a vitamin.

"Power to the People"

Example: Zillow or Expedia.

I first heard this idea when I interviewed Rich Barton, the founder of Expedia and Zillow and an investor in many other companies. All the companies he has backed have the same theme—making formerly proprietary information easily available to the public. Expedia took the information available only to travel agents through systems like Sabre and put it in the hands of the people. Similarly, Zillow took proprietary data that was then only accessible to Realtors via the Multiple Listing Service and gave consumers access through a simple web and mobile interface. Glassdoor is another example. This service allows job seekers to read what current and former employees have to say about their employers. It takes an opaque data set and data and makes it transparent to anyone. Does your idea bring power to the people?

Information Asymmetry

Example: TrueCar price information on new cars.

Some startups take advantage of information asymmetry, the idea that one party or group has more information than the other. For example, a seller knows the history of the car they are selling, but the buyer doesn't. These ideas will often become marketplace businesses. The same is true when you think about startup ideas. If you know the industry, but the customers don't, you can take advantage of that asymmetry. But don't take advantage of the customer.

Upstream and Downstream to Your Idea

If you launch this product, what happens upstream, before your product? And what happens downstream, after your product? For example, do you have a dependency on a single vendor's data source? Does your product require the customer to change their behavior (which is hard)?

The smartphone was required before Uber was successful. What has to be successful before and after your product is successful?

What Big Ideas Aren't

Big ideas aren't a service. Service companies can be a great lifestyle business, and, in some cases, they can even grow to be very large businesses. Think of Electronic Data Systems (EDS), now a division of HP, or Deloitte Consulting. But every time you add a customer, you need to add more staff to serve that customer. These types of companies generally get sold for 1X of revenue rather than a significantly higher multiple of revenue for a product company.

Big ideas aren't a feature. A feature is something that a larger company will likely build at some point. One of my founder teams was building a great feature to visualize your life's timeline on Facebook. A month after they launched, Facebook released a feature we all know today: the timeline. Facebook didn't release it because of the team, it was just an obvious extension in retrospect.

Big ideas aren't a tool. I have a number of tools that I love to use in my day-to-day work. Skitch is a great one, because it allows me to capture a screenshot and annotate it with notes, arrows, colors, etc. It was an inexpensive tool that was ultimately acquired by Evernote.

In March of 2013, there were more than 500,000 apps in the Apple and Android app stores. As of July 2015, there were 1.6 million in the Android store and 1.5 million in the Apple store. As of November 2018, Android had 2.87 million apps and Apple had 2.2 million, with $155 billion in app sales for Apple. Most are free (or cheap) to download and use, and most use in-app sales as their revenue model. The average revenue a company will make from an app is less than $6,000, which means if you're paying only for your time, it's likely a break-even proposition. You don't have to work on a big idea to make money for yourself.

Don't Be a Tool—Use Them Instead

Should you build a tool that fits into someone else's platform? Tools are niche by definition. Apple has continued to add features into their operating system from tools discovered on the App Store. So if you're small, creating a tool might be a good first step to building a product suite, but recognize your dependency on the bigger player in the market.

Tools are a step up from a feature, but they aren't necessarily a product. Tools can be awesome, and there's nothing wrong with building them—you just need to recognize that's what you're building. It's like creating an app. Building one doesn't mean you have a company or an enterprise ready to raise capital for future growth. There are countless useful tools available to help you reach success, and I suggest you use as many as you can. For example, you can use a tool like SendGrid to deliver transactional email rather than building the function yourself. Sending email is easy. Getting email delivered to the user inbox is hard. So, using a tool that improves those statistics is advisable. Twilio is another example of a tool company that grew up into a platform company. The company has made it easy to integrate communications technology into your site or app.

A Big Cause Isn't Necessarily a Big Idea

I know you have a big cause that you want to serve. I recently had a company that wanted to connect mentors with students around the world. That is an awesome cause but is likely a nonprofit instead of a for-profit idea. Why? Follow the money in this example:

- Students from around the world are the recipients of the benefit, or the customers. Students in the US or other developed countries may have some cash to pay but it would be a very small amount.
- Global mentors are providing the service. They are already contributing their time, so they likely won't contribute their money, too. And they likely won't appreciate a company making money on that contributed time.
- Who will pay? Advertisers? Not likely, because the bulk of the users don't have any money to purchase their items. Besides, you need millions of unique visitors before advertising becomes a viable revenue model.

So how should you look at your market? Here are some contrasting factors to consider.

Are You Standing in a Graveyard?

I meet with a lot of entrepreneurs who are myopic about their idea. They have been convinced by their hunch they are right, and some are just whistling past the graveyard, happy-go-lucky, not aware they are surrounded by dead startups in the category. This will likely lead to a painful outcome, especially if they are in tough market conditions. "Standing in a graveyard" is a phrase I heard used by Adeo Ressi, the CEO of the Founder Institute in reference to a company that was in a market that had seen many failures in the past. A few graveyard categories include:

- Music sales
- Photo sharing
- Communications platforms (like VoIP)

Many of these markets have been overinvested in over the years. So, in addition to being a tough market, you're not likely to find investors in some of these categories because their previous investments have bombed. Fund managers aren't likely to go back to their limited partners to tell them they will be investing in another music company, for example, after they had already lost a few million in that market. The graveyard isn't limited to startups either. Notable companies have their share of flops, too. Google's graveyard includes Picnik, Wave, and Google TV. (I bought a Sony TV that included the feature set. Now it's been replaced by Android TV and as well as Fire TV Stick by Amazon.) Microsoft's list of failed ideas includes WebTV and the first tablet PC, both of which were too early to market. Note: being too early is expensive!

How do you know if you're standing in a graveyard? Let's start with your research. Where are your competitors in their development process and market success? Are all the comparable companies only historic and not current? Here are some resources to help with your idea research:

- Kirill Makharinsky talks about Zombie Startups.
- You may want to look at the TechCrunch Deadpool.

In addition to market research, you need to look at the market timing. As we've seen, some of the failed ideas mentioned above really had to do with timing, so you need to decide if the market is ready for your product or service. *But Dave, you don't understand, my product is innovative!* Yes, innovation matters. And by definition you're creating something that people don't know they need yet. But if your innovation is in the graveyard, you better make sure the timing is better than it was for those companies that were buried there before you. We'll talk more about market timing in a later section of this chapter.

Fatal Flaws

Does your idea have a fatal flaw? Many startup ideas have one primary question to answer, yet it can be obscured among other less important details. I'll give you an example. I was working on a project to create beer-making equipment that split the difference between home-brew kits and commercial brewing tanks. The goal was to improve profits for restaurateurs, and I knew I could build a mobile app to help them receive customer orders or even order the equipment, but I didn't have an answer to the most important question: Could the equipment make good beer? Because if it couldn't, the other stuff didn't matter.

Most fatal flaws can be found early in your entrepreneurial journey. The problem is that most of us as founders don't really want to know about the flaw, especially if we're only working on one idea. Because if the idea is flawed, the dream is dead. If there is a fatal flaw, do you want to know in six weeks, six months, or six years? Personally, I want to know as soon as possible so I can move on to a better idea.

Account for Market Downturns

Market downturns happen, so you need to account for them. Ask yourself the following questions: Does your product or service have durability for a down market? Is there enough margin in your product to sustain downward pressure? Is your product a luxury or a necessity? Answering these questions now can spare you some heartache later.

Innovator's Dilemma

Some founders think big companies are going to swoop in, take their ideas, and kill their companies. But that's seldom the case. Entrepreneurs have ideas but lack customers, business models, and revenue. Big companies have proven business models but lack innovation. Discovering the next billion-dollar idea requires one elusive thing—knowledge of what the customer wants. In writing his 1997 classic book, *The Innovator's Dilemma: When New Technologies Cause Great Firms to Fail*, Clayton Christensen extensively researched why big companies failed to find innovation that was right in front of them and could have been exploited for billion-dollar gains. That book, as well as his many follow-ups including *The Innovator's Solution* and *The Innovator's DNA,* are worth reading.

His basic idea involves disruptive innovation, the type that changes markets—for example, like the way Craigslist virtually vaporized the classified section of the daily print news business. Large companies have established business models, including customers and revenue mentioned above. They are generally looking for new products they can shoehorn into those models. Most startup founders will agree that big companies rarely create disruptive new products because they won't take the level of risk required to fail, and budgets and teams become more important than the product. They become blind to innovation. If you've worked for a large company in the past, or you're working at one right now, you might be violently nodding your head in agreement. Why is the management blind to the opportunities that you may see?

But the inverse is true for founders as well. They are often blind to the business models that have made these companies successful. Keep in mind the business model of the company in a mature state is likely not the same one it started with. For example, multiple revenue streams are often an indication of a more mature company, though it probably started with a primary revenue model at launch.

RESEARCHING YOUR IDEA

What makes a fundable company or, for that matter, a high-growth company? Over the last ten years, the highest-valuation companies have included a mix of five elements in a mature or scaled state, starting with the idea:

- Big and some nascent markets
- Quality team
- Either big ideas or fun
- Scalable business models
- Execution resulting in traction

Every startup founder needs to learn how to do competitive market research and analysis. There is nothing worse than pitching your idea to an investor and having them say something like, "Oh, you're just like X Company that was just funded." Especially if you're standing there frozen with your eyes wide open because you've never heard of that company.

By doing research and comparing your idea to other companies in each category, you'll be able to find parallel strategies for business models and occasionally market launch and marketing ideas. If you're doing a "copycat" style company in a global market, you can actually follow the playbook of the competitor. They have product/market fit already. Uber ended up acquiring several companies as they expanded globally.

Keep in mind, we'll dig more into competitive landscapes and features later in this chapter. For now, the goal of research is to identify the big picture, big markets, and big problems.

There are many research methodologies you can use in this process, so where do you start? Below are some excellent books on in-depth strategy and methodology that I recommend:

- *Blue Ocean Strategy,* by W. Chan Kim and Renée Mauborgne, argues that highly competitive markets create a bloody, red ocean, so you should look for markets and opportunities where there is a blue ocean.
- *Business Model Generation,* by Alexander Osterwalder and Yves Pigneur, uses the business model canvas (BMC) as a structure to review competitors and the nine categories of the BMC.
- *Crossing the Chasm,* by Geoffrey Moore, is the bible of how products grow into new markets.

The consulting firm Gartner created the four-quadrant box analysis when looking at products in specific categories, or what they have trademarked as the Magic Quadrants (MQ). They create the two axes for evaluation and place the competitors onto the chart as a heatmap.

- X-axis—Completeness of vision
- Y-axis—Ability to execute

Gartner doesn't describe its methodology of choosing the companies; however, suffice it to say you only want to be in the top right corner in the analysis. Just be careful with how you define the axis so it doesn't look like straight manipulation to get to the top quadrant. The results are categorized as:

- Leaders—score high on both criteria, e.g., salesforce has a very complete vision and a massive amount of cash to execute on the vision.
- Followers—have a high score on ability to execute and lower on completeness of vision; your product is going to be significantly less mature.
- Visionaries—have both the thought leadership and capacity to scale.
- Niche Players—find vertical markets to own versus the broad market.

You can find an aggregated list of Gartner Magic Quadrants analysis on Wikipedia; here are a few examples of vertical markets that they follow:

- Business Intelligence
- Business Process
- CRM Multichannel Campaign Management
- Data Integration Tools
- Salesforce Automation

Your high-level research should begin to answer the timing questions that we addressed above. As you research, be sure to keep notes with sources. I suggest building a Google doc you can share with a cofounder in the future. This is your primary research, so it's going to look like a random set of data and facts, but that's fine for now. Keep the URL links as well as article summary notes. You may end up putting this information in your investor deck or corporate presentation, and there's nothing worse than having to remember which article had the data in the table or that the graphic file you used isn't searchable. Keeping your research organized will save you time and trouble. Remember, good entrepreneurs connect dots, and you'll need multiple dots to create a line that signals a trend. What trend do you believe is in your favor and worth your time?

Startup Market Research

There are two ways to do research. One is top-down, as outlined above, and the other is bottom-up, which is a more hands-on method. To start, first install the following Chrome browser plug-ins:

- Google Trends will show current trend information based on country and language.
- DataMiner is a tool that allows you to extract tables and lists.
- Open Ahrefs blog of SEO Stats allows you to see how the page ranks for traffic, keywords, and site and page info with one click.
- Keywords Everywhere will show you the volume, price, trending data, and competition of each search listed like the image on the following page shows.

Additionally, get Skitch (or a similar app) which allows you to copy components of a page (like the image below). Then open a Google doc and start taking notes. It will feel a bit circular at first because you'll be bouncing between browser windows and your notes, but the document will take shape as you compile your research.

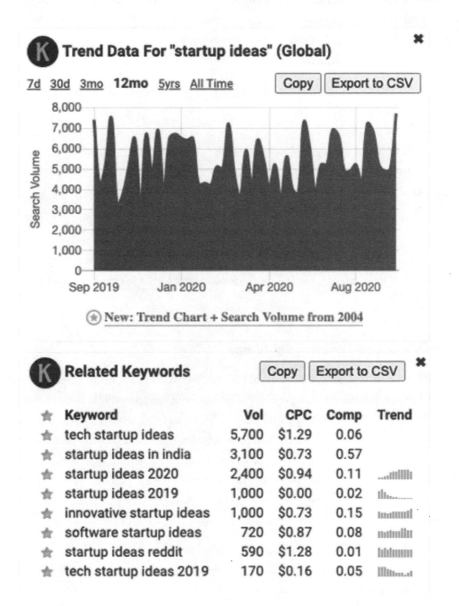

Start with the Theme

Every idea has a theme. To help you get there, think of the theme as the keywords someone would type into Google if they were looking for your product or solution. Maybe it's something like "crowdsourcing real estate down payments." Then go to SEOMonitor Topics explorer and type in the phrase. You'll see which companies have the top rankings and other helpful information such as:

- Competitor list
- Keywords (start building a list of keywords for future use)
- Search volume
- Cost per click (CPC)
- Relevancy
- Annual trends

Now head to Google.com with the start of the competitor list. But instead of typing in the URL, search for the company names. Who is buying those "branded" keywords? Add those companies to your list to research. Repeat this process with the expanded list and build out the list of those companies that are internet savvy enough to be buying keywords. Use those company URLs in Google's Ads keyword tool to gather their keywords.

Add Some Intelligence to Your List

Using the companies list, build another list with URL links for future reference, and start filling out the company profiles with third-party resources. Use CrunchBase to learn more about the company including the amount of money they have raised, how many employees, check out their press releases, etc. There is both a free and paid version of CrunchBase, so some data will be limited. None of this data in isolation is enough to make a go or no-go decision about your startup. What you're doing is putting together a market profile, so keep pushing ahead with collecting data. Make sub-bullets under the company names for products lists with details such as:

- Features—How do they position their product?
- Pricing information—What are they charging monthly or annually? Are prices hidden behind a modal box that requires you to provide contact information? How they position their price indicates the sales model:

- High or hidden prices indicate that a salesperson needs to be involved in selling the product, likely due to complexity as well as expense.
- Low prices indicate a self-service or inbound sales model where customers can do a thirty-day free trial and convert to paid with a credit card.

Look at the TechCrunch Deadpool list. If companies or products like yours have failed, consider the reasons and what you would do differently. Use the Wayback Machine at archive.org to look at how companies positioned their products over time.

Also think about your indirect competitors in adjacent markets or services and make lists of these companies and products. For example, could someone configure Salesforce.com to do the same thing you are doing with your product? Some other useful research ideas include:

- Following key executives on LinkedIn;
- Creating Google Alerts for each of your newfound competitors;
- Reading blogs, journals, and other sources focused on your industry.

Thought Leader List

The next tab on your spreadsheet is your list of thought leaders for your industry. This list includes corporate executives, journalists, and bloggers. List them by:

- Name
- Social profile links
  - LinkedIn
  - Twitter
  - Other
- Blog/publication URL

Once you have a thought leader list, create Google Alerts for each name and subscribe to their feeds and articles. Go out of your way to find opportunities to comment on stories or blog posts. Be thoughtful, refer them to additional resources, start a dialog that's publicly interesting, and don't pimp your product. Writers of all types track their readership, and this kind of engagement can pay off. I've even gotten meetings based on comments I've made, so don't miss an opportunity to build a relationship.

COMPETITIVE LANDSCAPE

You need to know what's going on in your industry and with your competitors, so you're not surprised by a press release or change in pricing. To do that, you're going to build out your competitive landscape. Create an additional tab on your Google spreadsheet for competitors. Start dropping in the info on that sheet as you go. Your list should include:

- Company
- Web URL
- CrunchBase URL—This allows you to see how much capital has been raised, from whom, and the date of the last round of funding.
- CEO
- Key executives
- Employee count—Determine whether it's going up or down so you know how many people are competing with you. You can also track employee count on LinkedIn
- Product names
- Direct or indirect competitor
- Notes
- Recent media—Include date, news source, and author. Then add author to thought leader list (see below).
- Google Alerts—Use alerts to monitor the web traffic of the company as well as the key executives.

MARKETS

Please note, determining the size of your market will take a long time, and yet it will manifest itself as just a single slide in your pitch deck. But it's important to get this right. If you do it well, the best you'll get from the investor is a head nod of agreement. However, if you get it wrong, it will call into question nearly all the other assumptions in your pitch. You will be tempted to spend way too much time explaining your analysis to investors, mostly because you put so much work into it. Don't. Get a head nod and move along.

Market sizing can be a difficult challenge for startup founders, yet it's important in helping you establish the potential market share your product could attain within the total market. I know you want to prove you're going after a multibillion-dollar market, but be wary of delusional thinking during this market-scoping exercise. My goal here is to help you to avoid the "1 percent of China" market-analysis trap—the one where a person with an awesome product claims that if they just sell it to 1 percent of the consumer market in China, they will make billions! Of course, the other example is that you just need to sell one customer for $1 billion. The numbers may be impressive, but the analysis is worthless.

To help understand market sizing, let's use a software example. Say you want to build a better CRM product to compete with Salesforce.com. (Though I'm a Salesforce fan, I recognize it may not be the best option for every company.) You'll first need to figure out the target customer and market for your product. Your target customer is a person with a profile, sometimes called a "persona." When it comes to marketing, you need to remember that someone is actually making a decision to buy your product or service. Your target market represents that group of people or companies that fit that persona. You will often see this diagrammed as a series of nested circles like the following figure.

Total Addressable Market

Total Addressable (Available) Market (TAM) is the entirety of the market for your product, or everyone worldwide that could buy your product. So, in the competitive scenario above, your total market would be any person that interacts with customers or potential customers across all industries, geographies, and sales models. If these markets are covered by analyst firms like Gartner or Forrester, these resources can give you the total market and forecast the future market growth.

Example: I'm a cyclist and I use the Strava App to track my rides. Strava could have looked at the market size for their app before it launched and said, "Everyone with a bicycle globally." But that wouldn't have been correct. Their TAM would have been everyone with a bike (or runner or swimmer) *who cares about tracking their performance.*

Service Addressable Market

Service (or Serviceable) Addressable Market (SAM) is the market you can acquire with your product. An example of a limitation: if your product is only in English, you would only be able to target a subset of the TAM that would be willing to buy your product in English. The next filter might be the vertical market that you are

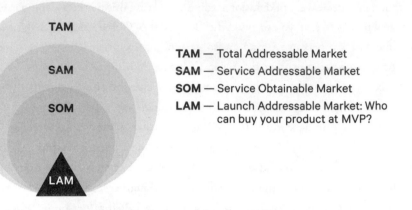

targeting, such as technology companies with sales teams versus drug companies with sales teams. In the CRM market, your SAM would now be the people in sales and customer service worldwide who use English as their primary language for business.

Example: Back to Strava again. Their SAM would be everyone with a bike who cares about performance, owns a smartphone, speaks English, and has a credit card. That's a much smaller circle from their TAM.

Service Obtainable Market

Service Obtainable Market (SOM) is the portion of the market that you can garner or get to use your product. What is the realistic market share that your company can garner at six months and one, two, and three years after launch? This is where the analysis gets harder to calculate. It now has to do with the features you have at launch and the needs of your customers. And since you can't sell to everyone, who is the most realistic target customer? Continuing with our example, if you've decided to target your CRM product at the technology sales market, you'll need to narrow your market again by:

- Small sales teams
- Medium sales teams
- Large sales teams
- Complex selling cycles
- Educational sales cycles
- Transactional sales cycles

Example: In this case, Strava's SOM would be the subset of the SAM that could use your product with the limited launch feature set and are willing to pay the price for the subscription.

Launch Addressable Market

I'd like to add my own concept to this: Launch Addressable Market or LAM. It doesn't go in your pitch deck directly. But it does connect your market slide with your go-to-market slide. Today's startup market is very familiar with the concept of Minimum Viable Product and lean startup methodology, which emphasizes "getting out of the building" to validate your idea with real customers (well, technically, prospects, because they haven't purchased anything yet). The LAM concept addresses where your market-sizing exercise meets your MVP and product road map.

LAM also connects with your customer acquisition model I'll talk about later, in getting your first ten, one hundred, and one thousand customers.

If that LAM customer falls into the "meh" category, they are underwhelmed by your offering, and you're never going to get to your SAM market. Remember, there is a difference between your launch product/market and your scale product/market. If you don't find customers for your launch, you'll never get to scale! You'll need to convince investors that the market is big and that you can find the path leading to that market. That's your go-to-market plan.

Think of that triangle on the wheel like the dial on a compass: it can move with your evolving customer focus. You are likely going to have to move your launch customer around until you find the right idea customer who can buy with the features you have today.

Example: Final Strava reference. The LAM would be the first ten influencers who could help bring one hundred users to the application. Recognize the type or influencers and groups that can help you get to one thousand users.

The Vertical Market View

How does the venture community see markets? Here are some sample categories and subcategories. You'll need to know where your company fits in the category as well.

- Energy and Utilities
- Business and Financial Services

- Consumer Services
- Information Technology
  - o Semiconductor
  - o Electronics and Computer Hardware
  - o Communications and Networking
  - o Software
- Healthcare

See CrunchBase for a more complete list.

In general, investors like billion-dollar-plus markets. They also stick to categories they know, or where they have invested before.

Market Trends

Can you build a case that your market is trending in a favorable way? Will you face headwinds or tailwinds? When the COVID-19 virus hit, some vertical markets and businesses faced headwinds overnight. Others, like work-from-home solutions, were instantly hot. What are the current market conditions that allow you to tell your story? Keep in mind that Gartner and Forrester data, though interesting, imply more mature market research. That means that if Gartner has written about an enterprise trend and you are a nonfunded startup, the market leaders are already funded and in front of you.

What to Do When There Isn't Data

If you're building a product or service in a new category, you may not be able to find any clean references to the market data. What do you do then? Look for a market proxy using a logic problem. One example is an interview question used at some tech companies in which they ask candidates to guess the number of piano tuners in Chicago (or New York or wherever). The actual answer is that no one knows, but that's not the point. The question is supposed to gauge logic skills. First, you make an educated guess about the number of households with pianos and how many times a year they would have their pianos tuned. Then you guess how many appointments a day a tuner can make, including travel, etc. You get the idea. Now apply this method to your product or service. And when you do, make sure you're on the low end of the range and don't inflate your first number. Then refine your logic as you gather more data. You can also triangulate your adjacent markets. One founder I met with used a mix of three different markets to create their Venn diagram to capture their TAM. That's fine, too, as long as you have data for the Venn.

SCORING YOURSELF

What's the difference between a good startup idea and a bad one? That depends on how you define success. For the purpose of this book, let's define it as returning capital to you or your investors in the form of enterprise value, or selling through a merger and acquisition (M&A) in seven years. Or, getting to a profitable company in three to five years and returning dividends. If you're a social enterprise, it means that you need to break even or better (turn a profit) so that you're not a nonprofit and you're raising capital in the form of donations to keep the doors open and staff paid.

To be clear, your startup needs to last longer than six months to be successful. But you should also know within six months if the idea is worth pursuing. It's time to get out of your head and actually get started so that you can test your hypothesis.

I've met with hundreds of founders over the years who have been working on their ideas for three or four years, or longer, without ever getting the product into customers' hands or earning any revenue. This is too long. If you're going to do a startup, get it launched. Remember, an entrepreneur without drive is just unemployed!

For the next six months, think of me as your personal trainer for your startup. We'll be working in regularly scheduled time slots to keep you focused on the task at hand and putting the first things first. Your training includes a monthly checklist of action items. If you aren't doing the work, it will be difficult to proceed to the next step. For example, there is no substitute for customer development interviews. If you don't do enough, proceed at your own risk because you won't really know if the real customer wants your product or not.

Let me frame this in a positive way: Customer development interviews will accelerate your product launch and your go-to-market strategy. Looking back, many founders would tell you they spent three years on a set of tasks and deliverables that they could have completed in a year. Learn from their lessons. If you become an expert at doing customer development interviews, it will accelerate your growth and save years in the process to profitability.

Here is your current goal, and repeat after me: *Six months from today, I will know if I have a good idea and how it will make money or not. If I can't prove the idea,*

I will be able to park it for now and work on a different idea or know what I will need to continue working on this idea. You'll notice the headline for each month includes customer development. Once you've done fifty interviews, you will have a great idea if your product will be used by your target customer and what they will pay for it.

Venture-Ready Scorecard

How do investors evaluate your startup company? Let me take some of the mystery out of the process and reveal one approach. It's not the only approach, and some investors will weigh certain parts of your company differently. But the goal is to help you be self-aware enough to know if now is the right time to pitch your idea to investors for funding. (And note this is a different process than pitching your idea for validation.) Please remember that your personal or business need for investment is not at all correlated to your ability to actually raise money. Your business may require money. But the stage and traction of the business will determine whether you get it or not.

I developed these scoring criteria for venture funds and accelerators as a way for applicants to do a self-assessment prior to our meeting. Then we could compare their score with our score and provide feedback. This scoring applies to venture-scale companies, not all companies. Venture scale is where an institutional investor (one investing other people's money) can get a 10X–100X return on their investment. Other investors may look for smaller returns, but in general, VCs are looking for the potential for outsized returns.

Scoring

All scores are ranked on a 1–4 basis. This is by no means based on quantitative factors. There are areas that can be measured for investment. However, this process is simply assigning numbers to predominantly qualitative criteria. Even so, it's a critical qualitative measure. This is how to interpret the scale:

1. We strongly dislike your idea.
2. We don't like it. This is not as negative as a 1, but it likely means your pitch lacked something important or you missed a major milestone.
3. We like it. It's not a 4, but it's a good place to start. You're on to something.
4. We love it!

This is the scoring form we use for the venture fund, pitch contests, and feedback for accelerator programs.

Judging Criteria

Event Name: _____

Event Location: _____

Event Date: _____

Company Name: Presenter(s): Event Name:	Evaluator Name
Notes/Comments	
Team Domain experts; Serially successful founders from great companies; Functionally competent (a builder, a marketer or designer, and a seller or hustler); Bonus points for diversity	1–4
Idea/Problem Big "category" idea; Early/late continuum; Technically achievable "pain pill or vitamin" in the investor's thesis	1–4
Product Customer-first focus; Clear value proposition; Design/Ease of use; Clear launch and scale offering	1–4
Market/Customer How big is the market—TAM/SOM; Unmet customer need; How many incumbents or nascent? Go-to-market plan?	1–4
Competition Barriers to entry; Differentiation; Well-funded competitors in CrunchBase	1–4
Business Model/Finance High transactional value; Clear profit model; Capital efficient—anything about previous financing/cap table? Scalable; No "bad" things on cap table	1–4

Traction Customer adoption; Customer engagement; Early revenue; Know the unit economics	1–4
Timing Emerging trends; "Meta" factors are favorable; Established vs. dynamic demand	1–4
Intellectual Property IP; Required IP in process	1–4
Clear Ask Do you have a clear ask? Are you looking for customers, employees, or investment? Don't leave us guessing.	1–4
Total	10–40

Notes on Scoring Examples

The examples below are just that, examples. Each investor is going to look at your startup company through his or her own lens. This scoring is designed so you can do a self-evaluation as well as understand how you will likely be judged. Scoring high does not mean they will invest in your company. Investors tend to fund markets they know. For example, if your business is a B2C game and the investor does enterprise software, it's unlikely they will invest. I've also found that people seldom invest in markets that are new to them, even if it's a huge market like China.

Let's look closer at the scoring for each criterion. As mentioned, they range from 1 to 4; 4 is what you'd aspire to.

Team

The investor will look at who is on your team and judge on the following criteria.

Domain experts: Are you specialists or authorities in this area?

Serially successful founders from great companies: Have you launched a startup (or startups) before? How successful were they? If you're serially successful, you likely don't need an unknown VC to invest.

Functionally competent: Does someone on your team have the savvy it takes to actually execute it (do you have a builder, a marketer or designer, and a seller or hustler)?

Here's how you might understand your scores:

1. You're a solo founder or part-time founder. As explained earlier, teams are preferred to solo founders.
2. You have an incomplete or unbalanced team (such as lacking a tech or marketing role) or offshore development with no plan to bring on employees.
3. You're a balanced team with complementary skill sets, market experience, startup experience, and some track record together.
4. You're an experienced startup team with industry knowledge.

Bonus points: For teams well balanced in gender and diversity. The data show that diverse teams produce better results. Also, an early-stage investor is going to be with you for seven to ten years, so likability matters.

Negative points: Are the cofounders a married couple? Sorry, though I'm a fan of marriage, investors view it as a compounding risk. A relationship ending poorly is the fear, whether the risk is real or not.

Idea/Problem

A potential investor will assess your idea based on these criteria. Is it . . .

A big and disruptive idea? Or is your product incremental and a feature for someone else's product?

Technically achievable? Is this easy to build or do you need a new technology to find a real breakthrough? (For example, the smartphone was required for Uber to be successful.)

You might be scored as follows.

1. You're doing the next Groupon or entering any other crowded, competitive market (food delivery, home repair, travel rankings, etc.). You're solving a problem that isn't really a problem and there are too many competitors there already.
2. You're a feature of someone else's product or a tool. It doesn't mean you are a bad tool, but it likely won't be venture scale. Think plug-ins for WordPress or Shopify instead of Shopify itself.
3. A good market, though not huge, with potential to change that market but not the world. Think about a product that has a limited geography; for example, one only in Brazil or in the Portuguese language.

4. Disruptive, billion-dollar ideas are rare. Big market with the right timing
    solving a genuinely big problem.

Bonus points: It's a unique, truly remarkable idea, and every idea is crazy
right before it works. Excitement is valuable, too, as people like to rally around
a great idea.

Negative points: Your nondisclosure agreement (NDA). No real investor is
going to sign an NDA unless you have a cure for cancer or a breakthrough scientific
discovery. Investors see hundreds, even thousands of startup ideas, and the liability
and cost to track NDAs for each is simply impractical. Ideas are a dime a dozen,
and what really matters is execution. Don't worry about someone stealing your idea,
worry instead that you'll waste three years of your life not discovering that your idea
had a fatal flaw that other people could have shown you early on.

Product

Next, they'll assess the product.

> **Pre-product or launched with revenue:** Do you have users that are using the
> product every day? Do you have a product roadmap that aligns with your
> customer's confirmed needs?
>
> **Customer first:** Does it solve a real pain point for the customer or is it sim-
> ply "nice to have"? Do you have an acute focus on the problem versus
> the product?
>
> **Clear value proposition:** Can the customer repeat your message or are you
> still a concept?
>
> **Ease of use:** Is the product easy to use and a complete solution—so it works
> within your customers' workflow?

Understanding your scores:

1. You have a concept on a napkin. Granted, the idea might be interesting,
    but it's still just a concept without a working prototype. There are a number
    of ways you can get a prototype showing for cheap, so there's no real excuse
    for not having one.
2. You have a working prototype, but it's ugly. And functional yet ugly seldom
    gets a second chance. This is usually where the developer is the designer.

Minimum Viable Product shows what's possible. At the very least you should have a PowerPoint demo that includes your design.

3. All the pieces are there and you're gaining valuable customer feedback from people. Basic functionality should be illustrated, not just a landing page.

4. The prototype works and the design is beautiful. MVP moves to KAP. You'll know it's a kick-ass product when people download it after your demo.

Bonus Points: You've taken customer feedback and built an email list of prospects to get even more feedback. Plus, you have a regular schedule or cadence of product releases (two weeks). That email list should be growing every week as you get feedback.

Negative Points: Your live demo doesn't work. Or it's a platform. And as I've mentioned, platforms happen when you have scale, not at your launch. Though that may be your aspiration, you don't have it today, and that usually means you don't know what customer you are going to serve.

Market/Customer

Both you and the investors need to know the size of the market and the customer profile. Is it a large and growing market or a small and niche market? Is your buyer a corporate manager or a 24-year-old gamer? Not everyone can be your customer and you'll need to connect the customer to your launch strategy given your limited budget.

Market size: How big is the market? How many customers could you conceivably get? The market and customer are two sides of the same coin but warrant some explanation.

TAM/SAM/SOM/LAM: are terms that address the market components (see pages 99–102).

Customer profile: reflect the micro market and user profiles and ICP.

Understanding your scores:

1. Small markets suck. Selling to customers that don't have money means you are doing a nonprofit. Sorry to be the bearer of bad news here, but an app for the homeless needs to be funded by grants and donations, not by investors that expect a return on investment. Customers that don't have money to spend on your product can also be a problem.

2. You have a great launch feature, but the market and customer need a complete solution to use it. This means you're going to need to raise more capital before getting funding.
3. It's a good market, but no longer growing.
4. You know both your market (large and growing) and your customer (persona). Nascent or new markets like Uber or Airbnb are exceptional.

Bonus Points: If you have experience in this industry or unique knowledge of a complex market.

Negative Points: You calculate your TAM wrong because you want it to be HUGE! Hypothetically, you make headrests for front passenger seats for trucks. In the bad example of your TAM, you'd say the market was the entire automotive market. But you only do trucks, and only do interiors, and only do headrests, and only do passenger-side headrests. It's a ridiculous example, but you'd be surprised how often founders routinely overblow their TAM. Be realistic about the actual TAM.

Competition

Next, they'll look at:

Barriers to entry: Do your competitors have a strong defensive position? Can you build a path to defense through speed to market or knowledge of your customers? Is there any intellectual property or "secret sauce" that you've created?

Differentiation: This could be product features, pricing models, or your go-to-market strategy. What are you doing differently than your competitors that is novel from the customer perspective?

Funded competitors: Look at CrunchBase to analyze who's raised capital in your market, how much, and whom they have raised that capital from. If your competitors have raised $25 million from a brand name VC, it will be hard for you to get a smaller VC, to write a check.

1. There's no competition, which likely means there's no market. The positive version is that you are too early to market and it will take a long time for the market to catch up to your visionary status.
2. Busy market with a lot of competition that has already been funded. This equals late to market. You know you are late to market if there are

already multiple companies that have raised more than $10 million in the market. Even if your product is better, your ability to raise cash will be severely limited.

3. A little late to market but the competitors in your category are lethargic. Entrenched incumbents have yet to be disrupted, but conditions may be right for them to fall.

4. Early, but not too early, is a great place to be. Keep in mind this rarely happens.

Bonus Points: You know the gaps in the market that current competitors are not offering. These gaps have been discovered because of your knowledge of the market and customer interviews (say fifty to one hundred).

Negative Points: Being cavalier about the competition. One challenge I see often is people waving off the competition instead of taking the Andy Grove approach he wrote about in his book *Only the Paranoid Survive*: give them credit and be a little paranoid.

Business Model/Finance

I admit I'm super geeky about revenue models (hey, someone needs to be). There are plenty of products that can be made with technology but shouldn't be because the founder hasn't thought about the cost of selling the product and how to make a reasonable to exceptional profit. Knowing how you are going to make money is critical to the investor. If you can't explain the economics of how you're going to make money, don't expect a check. They'll assess:

High transaction value: Will your customer give you a small amount of cash, but a lot of transactions, or a few transactions at a very high price point? Small transaction volume at low price point is bad.

Clear profit model: Are there similar companies where they have made money before? Pick your top two revenue models from the list (see pages 212–229).

Scalability: Does the company scale so that you can make money when you sleep? Or are you going to need to hire more people for every customer you sell?

Capitalization Table: Is there anything bad on the cap table, such as a founder who has left the company or a nonparticipating member that didn't put money into the company?

Understanding your scores:

1. You don't know how you're going to make money yet and you've only thought about the cost of building the product, not the cost of selling the product and reaping a reasonable margin.

2. Product is in a low transaction-value market. If you make less than only 10 percent margins or your margins are in basis points (one hundredth of a percent) there isn't a lot of room for error on execution. You've created value for your product, but you haven't captured payment for the value created. Services businesses also fall into low rankings in this category because they don't scale without adding additional staff. If you productize a service (we'll talk more about that in Chapter 9) it will help, but they don't scale like other models.

3. Starting with high transaction or high margin (or ideally both) shows you can capture value for the product.

4. Recurring revenue subscriptions and combination business models (such as transaction fee and subscription) win the day for best score. Monthly recurring revenue is the truest gauge of churn. Annual Contract Value (ACV) is a good measure, but if you have a large price point, you'll likely have higher churn as you develop the product. Note: you don't have to accomplish all these things yet, you just need to know where you are going and have some early traction.

Bonus Points: Your model is prepared by an experienced model builder.

Negative Points: You lead with the comment, "These financials are conservative," which at the early stage is still a guess. Or, "We'll be cash-flow positive in eighteen months"—this implies you don't know how expensive it is to run the business.

Traction

Revenue is the obvious starting point here, but it's not the only measure. Depending on the customer profile (think consumer versus enterprise), you may need to offer a whole solution before you can charge the customer.

Customer adoption: Your launch feature may be popular and become an "on-ramp" product that acquires customers for future revenue.

Customer engagement: Time spent using the app or on the site may also be a measure of success, especially in the B2C category.

Early revenue: Do your customers show a willingness to pay for your solution, even in early pilots or proof of concepts?

Unit economics: Do you know your early numbers? What does it cost to acquire a customer, and how long will the customer stay with you (LTV)? What's your churn?

Understanding your scores:

1. No users. This may seem obvious, but if no one is using your product, you have a problem. You may need money to fix it, but you're not likely to get it from an investor.
2. No payment from users. Again, not the only measure.
3. Proof of concept (POC) or letters of intent (LOIs), as well as early revenue, will get a score on the board. It shows a level of commitment from customers.
4. Strong customer usage or strong initial revenue. Some rare B2C companies can move past word of mouth and into network effect or viral marketing, but if you've figured out how to get strong initial customer growth, or for people to pay you early, you're going to score well in this category.

Timing

I mentioned earlier that Bill Gross from Idealab called timing the most important factor of success. (And if you still haven't watched his TED talk, do yourself a favor. It's the best seven minutes of video on the internet for startups.) There are many outside factors that should influence your decision to start a company, but you don't ultimately control timing. Know, however, that your belief in why it's the right time may not sway your investors to that same belief.

Emerging trends: An upcoming trend will be 5G network deployment and how big bandwidth will affect mobile apps. What are your trends?

Meta factors: Covid has created big headwinds and tailwinds for companies, but there are always some form of those winds. Where are you in the big picture trend?

Established versus dynamic demand: If you're launching into an existing market, you need to move your customer to your product where there is static versus dynamic demand—5G, referenced above, will create new dynamic demand for some products.

Understanding your scores:

1. Too early or too late. You might be a visionary, but the market still needs to catch up to your idea. The other extreme is that you're late (see discussion about "big ideas" above).
2. Unclear timing. You and the investor may not know enough about the market to make a judgment. If you don't have any data about the market timing, your score is going to fall into the "don't like it" category. Think of this timing as "headwinds" that will make it more difficult to grow.
3. A little early or a little late. In this case, the investment capital is still available since it hasn't been pulled out of the market by two or three large players (think valuations of $100 million and up with more than $25 million raised).
4. You're still in front of what could be a nascent market. You can think of timing here as "tailwinds." You may also be in the current "hot space."

Intellectual Property

There are market segments where intellectual property (IP) is critical, like pharma or medical devices. And if you're in one of them, you need your IP to be defensible. This may include patent, trademarks, and trade secrets. However, I avoid the investor question "What's your sustainable competitive advantage?" In most modern tech-related companies, your advantage will be speed to be nimble and compassionate knowledge of the customer (through customer development). Regardless of IP portfolio, you need to have an answer to the question of how to build a competitive moat over time.

Required IP: Do you need to license an existing patent or technology; is there any infringement risk?

Understanding your scores:

1. No barriers to entry or defense. This might be because you're selling someone else's product (as a reseller) or you're operating with technology that's in the public domain or commodity product.
2. There is already a great deal of IP created in your market. You have a unique idea and product, but the margins will make it difficult to build a defensive position or moat around your business.

3. You have a path to defensibility. Building IP requires legal budget and time. People with patents tend to overvalue them. People without them tend to dismiss their value. They both have a place depending on the industry or vertical market.
4. You have speed, IP, and knowledge of the customer. You also have the budget to defend your IP.

You don't need to spend a ton of cash on IP at this early stage. Validate what product the customer wants first. As of this writing a patent could take five to seven years to perfect.

Clear Ask

Investors know you have an agenda. You want or need something, that's why you asked for the meeting. Your ask might be that you're looking for introductions to potential customers or potential employees. You might be asking for capital and investment—just don't expect to walk away that day with a check. You'll need to build a relationship first. But whatever your ask is, be clear. People want to be helpful, but if I have to guess what you need, I will be wrong. Don't make an implicated ask, make your needs known.

Total Score

What's your score? _____

Note the areas that are weak because we'll be working on them as we take on the monthly deliverables. For example, team is a discussion in month two. Product is month three, etc. In the in-person cohort, I show a picture of a pyramid. Fundraising is at the top, ideation and market are at the bottom. You can't build the top of the pyramid until you build the piece underneath.

An Early Note on Fundraising

Over the next four to six months, you'll put together your story backed by research. You'll bring data to the table to show that your market is strong. Doing the work is no guarantee that you'll find an investor. However, not doing the work will ensure that if you do find the right investor, they will be convinced you have work to do before they would ever write you a check.

Venture capital firms tend to overindex on trends. Smart capital will lead in that market based on their investment thesis. Others will follow. Then the category will move toward being overfunded. Once that happens, "buzzword bingo" begins and startups begin to inject trendy terms into their pitches that came from the categories that are getting funded.

Deliverables

1. Ideation—List the ideas you want to consider. Write a one-paragraph summary of the value proposition for each idea. Use this to test your idea with people that could inform your decision.
2. Markets—Did you find data about your target market? Is this data free or did you pay to access it? How big is the market? A venture-scale market needs to be in the hundreds of millions or billions. What were the most reliable and interesting data sources? How is it spread across geography? What's the TAM/SAM/SOM?
3. Research—On a Google sheet, build out a tab for articles, blog posts, and thought leaders. Capture the URLs and write a brief summary of the relevant articles.
4. Competitive Landscape—On another tab of the same Google sheet, list all the competitors and various stages: company name, URL, CEO name, team size, city, etc.
   a. Using CrunchBase, research how much capital they have raised. Add the URL to CrunchBase for each competitor.
   b. Use AngelList to look for investors in key companies.
   c. Use the Wayback Machine.
   d. Set up Google alerts on each company.
5. Key Words/Phrases—On another tab, add key words and phrases currently used by your competitors.
6. Complete your venture-ready scorecard and total your score.
   a. Look for your low scores and think about how to systematically improve these weaknesses.
   Resources for each chapter are listed in the link to my website that is in the Addendum/Resources section at the end of the book.

NEXT STEPS

OK, time to take a break and think about how all these pieces fit together. Don't forget it's better that you ask the hard questions in advance of the investor's questions. If your product idea is going to fail, when do you want to know, in three weeks or three years?

- If you had to rank the competitors based on what you know today, who would be first and why?
- What are common features between companies? These become a minimum feature set required to launch.
- What is the average price? What are the high and low prices? Do you think you can build, sell, and make reasonable returns (35–70 percent) on your product for that price?
- Who has raised capital? From whom did they raise the capital and when?
- If you have no competitors, why do you think that is?

In conclusion, research is an ongoing process and is seldom conclusive or inconclusive. But it will make you more educated and knowledgeable about your market.

Customer Development, Pivoting, Awkward Cofounder Discussions, and Telling Your Story

There are three steps to creating a truly valuable tech company. First, you want to find, create, or discover a new market. Second, you monopolize that market. Then you figure out how to expand that monopoly over time.

—Peter Thiel

In this chapter, you'll be creating your customer development questions and a process to capture the data. If you have a blind spot in your idea, you should learn about it in the shortest possible time. Silicon Valley is a proponent of failing fast, but I'm not. I think you should kill bad ideas quickly before failing. I didn't grow up in an affluent community, quite the opposite. I was raised by a single mom who worked an entry-level job, and I remember being on food stamps for a time when I was a kid. If you're like me, you came from a background where failure wasn't an option. There are no rich uncles or grandparents to act as a safety net. So, it's essential that you reject bad ideas quickly. Customer development helps you do that by testing your thesis, developing a point of view, and iterating and pivoting around your market.

Today, as the founder, or founding team, you're responsible for this customer data. You will likely always be close to this data. Keep in mind that knowledge of the customer is a competitive advantage. You can't outsource this process. Similarly, focus groups and interns are no substitutes for sitting down with a customer yourself. When you do, ask great questions, including the "five whys," to better understand the customer. The five whys aren't literally asking the same five questions over and over. It's the concept of not taking the first answer at face value, especially if it confirms your question. Dig deeper.

CUSTOMER DEVELOPMENT

Customer development is a core learning of the Lean Startup movement. Though it was first presented by Steve Blank, it was popularized by Eric Ries with *The Lean Startup*. The basic premise of customer development is to get out of the building and ask your potential customers what they actually want in the product that you are building.

But let's back up and start earlier in the process, before you have a thousand people visiting your site every day. You're at the ideation stage or pre-revenue. You want to do a startup, but before you start building and testing you can (and I would argue should) ask yourself a set of questions.

Customer development is the scientific and systematic process of discovering if your target customer actually cares about the product you are thinking of building. There has been some great work done in customer development in the past; I want to recap some of those resources here and draw some further distinctions of areas where you can find answers before you actually spend any money on a prototype.

Steve Blank's article and follow-up book "The Four Steps of an Epiphany," and the definitive startup work with Bob Dorf in 2012's *The Startup Owner's Manual*, captures Blank's early work on customer development that he began in the 1990s. Lean LaunchPad is a class that he started at Stanford and UC Berkeley in 2011. The Four Steps to the Epiphany are:

1. Customer discovery
2. Customer validation
3. Customer creation
4. Company building

The first two have been practically combined and become customer development. Blank's idea is that customer interactions drive the behavior of the product-development model. This is the opposite of what often happens, which is the product team proceeds as if it knows what the customer wants and can't be bothered with interviewing the customers to validate the idea. This view is sometimes expressed when a very "smart" founder quotes Henry Ford's famous quip, "If I asked the customer what they wanted, they would have said a faster horse." This is usually the same founder who has "Visionary Entrepreneur" on their LinkedIn profile. If that is you, please go change your profile right now. You don't get to call yourself a visionary entrepreneur until you do something amazing.

Alexander Osterwalder's book *Business Model Generation* and business model canvas is a great way to outline and test your hypothesis because of the interrelated parts. The components of the canvas are:

- Key partners
- Key activities
- Key resources
- Value propositions
- Customer relationships
- Channels
- Customer segments
- Cost structure
- Revenue streams

We used the business model canvas extensively as a tool when we launched the first version of Startup Next in 2011/2012. The BMC works well in larger organizations that have existing resources and are considering how to validate or create new innovations for an existing customer base.

Customer development never stops for your business. You always have a hypothesis that you want to test.

Customer Development Mechanics

What we learned in the Startup Next process was that founders generally wanted to ask customer development questions that validated their conclusions. This confirmation bias can cost you years of time and millions of dollars. That's why it's so important to learn the right things from your customer interviews. And that starts with asking the right questions. There are copious resources online for B2B and B2C companies based on the target customer as well as product and services. I recommend these three: Neil Patel's customer interview resources, Justin Wilcox's video at Customer Development Labs, and Mike Fishbein's "Ultimate List of Customer Development Questions." Fishbein's questions are used with permission below.

First, a few general interviewing tips.

- During your interviews, start with generic, high-level questions before moving to specific ones.
- Always capture contact information because you'll be asking participants to provide future feedback on your process via email updates.
- Include questions that can be asked throughout the product development life cycle, from identifying problems and generating ideas to improving a live product.
- Follow up most questions by asking why or why not. People will usually elaborate without being prompted when you're interviewing them live, but if not, ask them.
- In addition to the questions below, many products seem to require specific ones that aren't "template-able," especially in the product discovery and validation phases.

Let's move on to Fishbein's ultimate list of customer development questions. Note that a lot of these will yield similar responses, so pick one or more from each group below that best fit your situation.

Customer Segmentation

Depending on how you obtained the interview, and how much background you have on the person, you may need to make sure they are within your customer segment, and/or understand more about their demographic. I usually try to keep it to a max of three questions per category. Set expectations in advance of how long the interview will be.

- What do you do professionally?
- Who handles [process you're improving] at your home/office?
- Tell me about your role at [company]?

- How much time do you spend on [process you're improving]?
- Specific questions related to your product/customer, for example, *Do you have kids?*

Problem Discovery

These questions are designed to validate your hypothesis about a problem, or to learn about problems your customers face.

- What's the hardest part of your day?
- What are some unmet needs you have?
- What product do you wish you had that doesn't exist yet?
- What tasks take up the most time in your day?
- What could be done to improve your experience with [process/role]?
- What's the hardest part about being a [demographic]?
- What are your biggest/most important professional responsibilities/goals?
- What are your biggest/most important personal responsibilities/goals?

Problem Validation

If your customer did not talk about the problem you wanted to address, use the questions below to begin validating/invalidating that your customer has the problem you think they have. In addition, it's often not enough to just solve a problem, sometimes it also needs to be one that people are highly motivated to solve. Some of the below questions can help with that, too.

- Do you find it hard to [process/problem]?
- How important is [value you're delivering] to you?
- Tell me about the last time you [process you're improving]. *Pay attention to complaints here.*
- How motivated are you to solve/improve [problem/process]?
- If you had a solution to this problem, what would it mean to you/how would it affect you?

Product Discovery

These questions will help generate ideas or validate your idea. They are intentionally open-ended. By asking yes or no questions specifically related to your product, customers may feel inclined to agree with you or not be critical. Asking more open-ended questions helps avoid this and gives you more confidence that they're providing honest input. If your customers' responses tell you they're looking for similar to what you have in mind, you might be on to something.

- What do you think could be done to help you with [problem]?
- What would your ideal solution to this problem look like?
- If you could wave a magic wand and instantly have any imaginable solution to this problem, what would it look like? *I've found that about 80 percent of the answers I get to this question are not very informative—solutions that aren't feasible or most certainly wouldn't be profitable. But the other 20 percent of the responses are really informative—that makes the other 80 percent acceptable.*
- What's the hardest part about [process you're improving]?
- What are you currently doing to solve this problem/get this value?
- What do you like and dislike about [competing product or solution]?

Product Validation

These questions with help to validate/invalidate your idea.

- What do you think of this product? *This question is intentionally vague. Listen to whether they talk about wanting to use the product or how it could be improved. Given how vague the question is, the former is positive, while the latter may be a sign that improvement is needed.*
- Would this product solve your problem?
- How likely are you/would you be to tell your friends about this product?
- Would you ever use this product?
- Would you be willing to start using this right away?
- What might prevent you from using this product? *This might reveal ways that you could improve the product. Potential hurdles might be budget, time, perceptions of the product's value, a competing product, etc.*
- Will you pay $X for this product? *See if they will put their proverbial money where their mouth is. Often when you ask this question, no matter how small the price, you will start hearing key insights that you wouldn't have thought of otherwise.*

Product Optimization

These questions help improve your idea or product.

- What could be done to improve this product?
- What would make you want to tell your friends about this product?
- What's most appealing to you about this product?
- What might improve your experience using the product?
- What motivates you to continue using this product?
- What's the hardest part about using this product?
- What features do you wish the product had?

Ending Interviews

Be sure to ask for contact information at the end of the interview if you don't already have it.

- Summarize some of their key takeaways and ask: "Is that accurate?" I usually do this throughout the interview as well.
- So based on the conversation, it sounds like x is really hard for you, but y is not. How accurate is that?
- It sounds like x is very important to you, while y is not. How accurate is that?
- Is there anything else you think I should know about that I didn't ask?
- Do you know anyone else who might also have this problem that I could talk to? *If they're willing to give you referrals, that's a small sign of validation.* Can I keep you in the loop on how the product develops?
- Can I follow up with you if I have more questions?

Create a Google Form

Once you have your questions outlined, create a Google form to capture the data. Your survey questions will populate a Google sheet for a simple database to start tracking your data. Google Forms will allow you to capture the data in a systematic way as well as posting it on your website in the future. Trust me on this: After you do your first fifty interviews, you will have forgotten which person gave you that specific feedback or which one wanted to make a purchase after you released that specific feature. Using this method will allow you to track those potential customers.

Email Updates

This process of creating an email list and sending regular updates is copied with permission from my friend T.A. McCann, a managing director at Pioneer Square Labs (PSL), a startup lab in Seattle. By training, T.A. is a mechanical engineer. He's also a six-time startup founder with an interim step as product manager for Microsoft Exchange. I've known him for many years and personally have had the chance to use two of his methodologies to help you in your customer development process. The first is building your email list for following up, and the second is the in-person interview process of working the room.

Building Your Email List

Imagine how valuable a list of hundreds or thousands of prequalified potential customers would be to your startup. And since you don't have such a list yet, you're going to build one. To do that, start with building a landing page. (Ideally, the landing page will be on your branded URL website that you will be using going forward.) You can use Instapage, Launchrock, or a similar tool to build your landing page. You'll then drop your Google form onto that landing page. In addition to your value proposition summary, you should also capture:

- First name
- Last name
- Email
- Company (if B2B)

Landing pages should capture the least amount of customer data necessary. The goal for now is compiling your email list. You can build profiles of those emails over time. You're going to connect this landing page with a free Mailchimp account and then map these fields to your account (don't worry, it's easy to do). This will allow you to send personalized emails that include "Dear Dave" (for instance) where <FName> is inserted automatically.

Provide a "forward to a friend" option in your email as well, so if they really love your idea and want to suggest it to others, they can easily do so. You can also use Mailchimp to create A/B testing on campaigns. This allows you to vary the headline, value proposition, pricing, or offers to see what resonates with your list.

It will also sharpen your call to action because it will be based on data and not just your personal opinion.

The more the site looks like a real company, the better your responses will be to these early marketing efforts. However, you will likely disappoint some of the people who sign up because they will think you already have a product to sell. That's OK if you disappoint some people. When you do, at least you'll know they actually want your product. We'll explore this topic more later in Chapter 9 when we talk about advertising testing to drive traffic and hone your messaging.

In the future, this list will begin to evolve into cohort analysis. A cohort analysis is when you start looking at your customer based on the timing of when they become a customer. For example, if a customer joined shortly after you launched a new feature, that would be a clue to what attracted them. You will also be tracking lead attribution, which is your ability to trace the lead to a specific source or channel, such as a referral from Dave via email, a trade show, paid search, or a blog post, to name a few. Mailchimp allows you to track these attributes using tags, so don't feel like you need a more complex CRM product like HubSpot or Salesforce at this point.

Before you start doing regular product releases, you'll be sending out monthly email updates that include:

- What you did this month (product, testing, features, etc.)
- What we're going to do next month
- How recipients can help

You won't have a lot of people respond to your "how they can help" request, but the ones that do will provide valuable feedback. If you don't have progress to report this month, you're likely not working on the right things. And if you don't have progress two months in a row, you might want to rethink the idea. Maybe it's not a good product or you're not as excited about it as you once were.

Working the Room

The following process works well if you have a consumer product and you're going to trade shows with a high density of likely customer-profile attendees. To be successful here, you need to know your target customer and focus on them. Don't waste time and energy pitching everyone at the event on your idea. Narrowing down your prospects is essential. Before you get to the event, you need to ask yourself which questions you want answered. Here are a few examples in a B2B context:

- What job do your customers do?
- What role do they have?
- Do they have the problem you are trying to solve?
- How have they solved the problem so far?

You have three goals at the event:

1. Talk to as many people as possible and quickly qualify them.
2. Score the top 10 percent of your interactions.
3. Get contact info for these 10 percent, not everyone you talk with.

To accomplish this, you'll need to quickly determine which people are most likely to buy your product. If there is a list of attendees you can review in advance, that's great. If not, you can look at name tags for recognizable company names. If those aren't options, well, just go meet some people! When you realize you're talking to someone who's not interested, you need to graciously move on. When you find a potential customer, you're going to learn by listening, not talking. You'll want to spend 90 percent of your time listening to them talk about your product or solution.

You also want to determine if they are an early adopter or not, both as a person and a company. You want to find out if they have ideas for additional features or how they would rank the features that you are thinking about. When they start talking about their ideas for the product, you likely have an early adopter. These people will be evangelists for your product and provide valuable early feedback, so cultivate the relationships.

Jobs to Be Done Framework

Another helpful way to think about your product and customer is to use the Jobs to Be Done framework created by Clayton Christensen, the HBS professor and author of *The Innovator's Dilemma* I mentioned earlier. It answers the question of why the customer uses your product. Christensen describes this as a process of "hiring your product" for a job to be done. What job is your customer trying to get done? Regardless of business or consumer, most users have a struggle (rather than a need), and the existing solutions may be inadequate for that job. For example, people used Microsoft Excel for years for things that required no calculation like task lists, moving lists, and Gantt charts. Smartsheet came along years later with a tool designed to replace the spreadsheet. The same can be said for Lightboard.

Within the framework, there is both a main job to be done and a related job to be done. And within both there are functional jobs, emotional jobs, personal and social implications, and other details on how the customer is perceived by others.

Customer Segmentation

Customer segmentation involves dividing a large customer list into logical groups such as existing customers, potential customers, and their shared characteristics. For B2B, these shared characteristics could include job title, company type, company size, and industry type. For B2C, it could include age, gender, demographics, and geography. This brings us back to the idea of creating a customer persona or ideal customer profile (ICP).

PIVOTING

Pivots are a change in strategy to accommodate the customer, the market, or external factors (pandemic?). Iterations are course corrections based on customer feedback. You'll be making iterations with nearly every build and customer interaction. Taking feedback is part of the early process. There are some exceptions—enterprise software is hard and takes time. New media is about growth, not about cash.

Pivots are disruptive. For proof, check out Mike Maples's video about "thunder lizards" in which he talks about Twitter's pivot from Odeo, its original idea and company name. Since the company was switching markets and products, not to mention name and brand, the Odeo team offered to give the remaining money back to the investors. Maples declined the offer and ended up as one of the early investors in Twitter.

Early on, you're trying to find a viable market and a solution to a problem in that market. There is a risk of pivoting too soon and never discovering the real opportunity. There is also a risk of not pivoting and then crashing as a result. You're going to make a lot of iterations as you move from the base camp to the summit. Once you discover why the customer will buy, you may have to change your

go-to-market plan, for instance. The most successful founders have strong opinions, lightly held. The market is going to confirm or reject your product. If you're
like Jack Dorsey at Odeo, you'll have enough cash to pivot to Twitter. Oh, and then
go on to launch Square. Slack was a gaming company that built a great communications platform between gamers. Before their pivot to enterprise.

When should you pivot? If you're 90 to 180 days of effort into customer development and no one understands what you're building, that is an indication. If you
can't find positive signal in the first one hundred customer interviews, consider
pivoting. Pivot before you run out of cash.

When you pivot, make sure you're positioned where your customers' pain level
is high, and they have a willingness to pay.

AWKWARD COFOUNDER DISCUSSIONS

While you're doing your customer development efforts, this is also a great time to
start the awkward discussion of how to split equity before you incorporate. This will
not get any easier, and talking about it after you incorporate is a bad idea. Regardless of the timing, it will be awkward because you'll be negotiating and resetting
expectations. And I recommend you get it done while it's cheap! In this section,
I will outline the discussions you need to have, including a framework for those
discussions. I'll also suggest some tools to help you define equity splits at both the
early stage as well as the operating stages of your startup.

Let's start with why a 50/50 split is the only wrong decision. Someone should
be the lead. When I see a 50/50 split, I think about the first hard conversation the

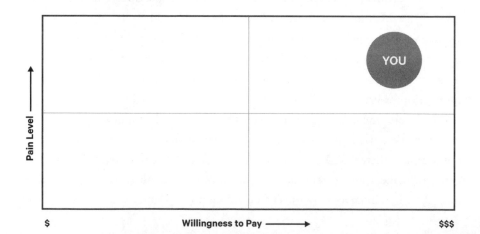

cofounders had to face and notice they put off a decision to avoid the conflict. Even 50.1 percent and 49.9 percent is better.

Pre-incorporation Discussions

This conversation will require two meetings, so get the first one on the calendar now because it should be a priority. Plan it off-site, not at the office. No whiteboards are necessary; it's just a discussion.

Grab a beverage of choice and settle in for an extended conversation. It's not so important that you get to the answers at this point, but you'll need to start discussing the questions. First, recognize this moment is likely as good as it gets for your relationship. It's still the honeymoon period, everything is potential and rainbows and butterflies. I don't mean that to be negative, just realistic. Right now, the world is laid out in front of you. You're in love with your idea, the product is brilliant, and you're either going to change the world, get rich, or both!

However, you haven't been tested yet. You haven't done the eighty hours a week while your partner works at their day job and brings home a paycheck when you don't. You haven't yet talked to fifty investors and had them tell you to come back when you get "traction," whatever the hell that is. Tough days are ahead, which is why you need to figure out your split now.

Here are the discussion topics:

- What do you want to achieve with the company?
  - Grow and sell? How much is enough?
  - Build a great company over the long haul? Is this your forever company?
- What type of company culture will you build?
  - How do you value people?
  - What type of culture will your company be known for?
- Capital in versus capital out.
  - How much cash are each of you putting into the company?
  - Do you need to take cash out?
  - How long a "runway" do you have until you need to go get a paycheck?
- What's your passion for the idea?
  - Who's leaving their day job? Or who doesn't have a job?
  - How passionate are you? Do you want to stay when it's tough and you're not getting paid?

- Do you share the same work ethic and how it manifests?
  - Do you work early or late?
  - Are you more of a nine-to-five or do you stay until the task is done?
- How well do you talk about awkward topics?

Homework

Following your first meeting, each cofounder needs to go to the Startup Equity Calculator using foundrs.com to input your individual views on the amount each founder will contribute. Print out your results and bring them to the next meeting for discussion. If you feel awkward about the results—for example, you've overstated your contributions—you can recalculate and see the differences. But each of the partners has expectations, even if they are unstated. This tool just forces the discussion. A few things to note here: The value of the idea is always higher to the person with the idea. Quality and viability of the idea matters, bad ideas matter, and big ideas are truly rare. It is true that execution is more important. However, if you execute a flawed idea, you'll just fail faster. Now, take a week to process what you've learned and set a date for the second meeting.

Meeting Two

With printouts of your completed homework in hand, meet for your second appointment to cover the following questions and topics:

- What did you learn about each other and yourself from the last meeting?
  - Any surprises?
  - Did everyone have time to talk and listen?
- *Share the printout from the equity calculator.*
  - How close are you?
  - Who over- or underestimated their contribution?
  - Why did they evaluate themselves that way? *Listen.*
- How will you be dividing up the responsibilities?
  - Are roles and deliverables clear? How about deadlines?
- Who has put in cash at this point, and how much?
  - Will you each bring it to pro rata amount? This will determine your basis at time of incorporation.

If necessary, set a third meeting to have more time to discuss the outcomes.

Time to Incorporate

Now that you've had the discussions and presented some market-relevant math, you should be ready to incorporate. Have you agreed on the splits? If not, now's the time to address them head-on. No passive-aggressive behavior and no taking care of it later—the time to take care of it is now!

One of the things you'll want to include in your documents is a "Reverse Vesting Schedule," which grants you stock for a minuscule price at the time of incorporation. The stock is granted, but it works like a vesting schedule, so if you leave early you don't get to keep all your stock. That way the clock can start on your 83b election and (hopefully) when you sell the company, you can be taxed at the capital gains rate instead of the regular income rate. (This is a slight digression, but if you're based in the US, be sure to select an attorney with experience with 83b election forms to put together your paperwork. The 83b election is an IRS provision that allows you to be taxed on your equity when it was granted to you rather than when it vests.) Reverse vesting is important because if one of the cofounders departs the company, say, at the twelve-month mark, you'll need to get the remaining three years of unvested stock returned to the pool as compensation to recruit and backfill their role in the company. If they were the lead developer, you'll need another lead developer. This is a topic about company health and improving your chance for success, not about you personally.

After Incorporation

People, circumstances, and enthusiasm will change as your startup grows. You need to address those changes as you build out your product and ultimately a company. For this, you'll find a good resource in the book *Slicing Pie* and the SlicingPie .com website, both by Mike Moyer. The book is designed for bootstrapped startups where your equity is based on contribution. It's a very clean way to think about contribution over time. When you add your profile, you input your market rates less what you are currently being paid by the startup. So, if you were a developer and market rate was $100,000 annually, and you were getting paid $4,166 per month, you'd be getting 50 percent of market rate (I like simple math when I can get it). You don't get to inflate your math, and you should agree on what market is before you start the exercise; that is, agree on your previous salary. Moyer has also built the app to track over time so that you have a "cap table" that can be calculated at the time someone exits, which will determine the value.

TELLING YOUR STORY

As we move into the next chapter about value propositions, a brief word on telling your startup's story. This positioning helps you better explain your concept, product, or idea to your potential customers. This is for more than just customers. You also need to tell your story to potential cofounders and investors. I joke with founders that the message is always clear when it's inside our own heads but getting it out can be a challenge. To help structure the pieces of your story, here's a modified Mad Libs structure. Original credit for this idea goes to Adeo Ressi at Founder Institute. I've added to Ressi's original one-sentence version the parts about how you make money and where you need help.

> Hi, I'm *<your name here>*, and my company is *<insert Company Name here>*. The problem I'm solving is *<insert problem here>*. Our product *<insert product info here>* is designed for our target customer of *<insert target customer here>*. We make money by *<insert method here>* and our team is the right team because *<insert why you're awesome here>*. I need help with *<insert help needed here>*.

Let me break down each of the bracketed components of the story here.

- **Your name here.** In the rush/passion/enthusiasm to pitch, people sometimes forget to say their name.
- **Insert company name here.** Say it slowly, especially if it's a domain that's hard to spell.
- **Insert problem here.** Is the problem to solve really a problem?
- **Insert product info here.** Do you have a product, service, or a concept?
- **Insert target customer here.** Do you know who your target customers are?
- **Insert method here.** Do you have a hypothesis for how you will make money? Do you have traction?
- **Insert why you're awesome here.** Teams matter, and if you're a solo founder you're not likely to get funded. If you're going to brag, make it about the team.
- **Insert help needed here.** Where do you need help? We know you have an agenda for the meeting; it's best to get the agenda out there early and be clear about how they can help.

You'll get better at telling your story over time. Many of us founders can talk for hours about the idea, product, problem, and market. But if no one remembers what you said, that's a problem. Make it simple, then explain more based on the questions you get asked.

DELIVERABLES

Here are the tasks you need to complete for this month. It will take time to get through the customer development interviews.

Customer Development

- Write your customer development questions.
  - What are the top few questions you want answered?
- Create your form in Google Forms, and embed it into your website if you have one.
- Get your first twenty interviews completed in the next month.

Competitive Landscape

- Build your competitive landscape as a Google sheet.
  - Subscribe to Google Alerts for all your competitors.
- Resources and plug-ins:
  - Open SEO Stats—Chrome toolbars show traffic, page info, speed, and keywords.
  - SEMrush—Chrome plug-in opens a new window and shows traffic on topics.

Awkward Cofounder Discussions

- Schedule both cofounder meetings.
- Complete the Foundrs survey, print out the results, and bring it to your second meeting. Decide who's responsible for which tasks and equity splits.

- Get the discussion out there before incorporation, or if it's after you've incorporated, address any outstanding issues.
- Document the results.
- Set up the Slicing Pie tool. And set a regular schedule to track your progress.

Get Your Story Together

- Write out your Mad Libs pitch.

Please see the full list of resources, blogs, tools, and books at www.dkparker .com/books/trajectory-startup/.

Value Propositions, MVP, Features, and Costs

If you address a market that really wants your product—if the dogs are eating the dog food—then you can screw up almost everything in the company and you will succeed. Conversely, if you're really good at execution but the dogs don't want to eat the dog food, you have no chance of winning.

—Andy Rachleff

Congratulations! You've spent the last few weeks interviewing potential customers and building your email list. With those interviews under your belt you can now make more intelligent assumptions about the value of your product to the customer, not just as technology.

In this section, you will be working on framing up your MVP, understanding and prioritizing your features as it relates to a product road map, and beginning to understand your costs associated with building the product. We'll also cover some initial assumptions about driving traffic to your site to sell your product. This work will require you to roll up your sleeves and possibly learn some new tools. Though some of the tool sets will change over time, and the specific step-by-step options may vary, I've outlined a process that nontechnical founders can follow. And even if you're not building a tech product, you can still use the marketing content in this section to acquire customers for your local business or franchise.

Is Anyone Looking for What You Are Building or Selling?

If you haven't yet created a customer persona, go back to your research and conduct more customer development interviews. Before you build a value proposition you need to have a customer in mind. At this point, the concrete is still wet and you're testing your customer profiles, which is totally OK. When in doubt, pick a customer and pick a set of features and benefits and test, test, test. Continue down that path until you prove it to be false, then change. If your approach is too broad, your value propositions will be off or too abstract to land with your target audience.

This is the virtual version of the process I outlined with T.A. McCann above in the "Working the Room" section. Remember, you're not interested in all of the attendees, just the one or two most receptive to your messaging and offering.

This is your ICP. If you're selling B2C, you're defining the age, demographic, and buyer profile of an individual. If you're selling B2B, it's the company type, the user profile, and the buyer profile. In B2B, someone will have the budget to make the purchase, but your actual user may be another person in the organization. Your target is the person most likely to become a customer combined with the highest revenue potential.

VALUE PROPOSITIONS

Your value proposition is a concise explanation of your product benefits to the customer or user. If your messaging is wrong, all your marketing will be wrong, so start with your customer and your value proposition. Value propositions help you make your product attractive to your customer by addressing their wants, needs, or fears. It's a promise of value to be delivered. Your value proposition should cover:

Features—List all your features and prioritize them based on your customer development. Focus only on these for now. More features on the list aren't necessarily a good thing if no one cares about them.

Benefits—Customers don't look for features without benefits. So, every time you create a feature, ask the question: Does it make the customer money or save them time? If it doesn't, then it's not really a benefit.

Experience—What will your customer experience when using your product? To answer that question, ask yourself:

- What does your product do for the customer?
- What overt or latent needs does it address?
- What are customers currently using?
- No purchase is a rational purchase—how will your product make them feel?
- What wants, aspirations, or fears does it address?

Two tools to help with this part are the Value Proposition Canvas, by Peter J. Thomson, and Wordstream: "7 of the Best Value Propositions," which includes examples of corporate value propositions.

The customers should always be the center of your story, so start with them, not with you. If you're new to marketing, I'd suggest you pick up Don Miller's book *Building a StoryBrand*. We used Miller as a consultant at Startup Weekend because we had a complex audience, multiple products, and sponsors. We thought our message was simple, yet it wasn't landing with our audience, so we needed to sharpen our value proposition. He helped us do just that.

Using Startup Weekend as a product example, let's look at an effective way to do this based on Miller's suggestions. First, consider the customer. In this case, Startup Weekend had several customer types:

- Event attendees
- Sponsors ranging from global giants like Google to local law firms
- Event organizers, the people on the ground putting together and running the events
- Event facilitators, the people that motivate the crowd and "herd the cats" through the weekend's activities.

All our customers are important because the event doesn't work unless people show up. But we had to prioritize the customers and refine the message to each group, since creating one message for all customer types proved to be confusing. Here's what that looked like.

We started with the local event organizers because nothing happens without them. So, they became our first customers, and we needed to direct our value proposition to them. We knew that a desire to see their community grow was what motivated organizers to volunteer their time to Startup Weekend. Personally, the influence they gained by running our programs motivated them. Because they didn't get paid and we had no "power" to give, we focused on showing them how they can influence their community.

To do this, we had to eliminate a number of legacy points of friction for organizers. Originally, we had them fill out an online form (good) but set their expectation that we would get back to them in a couple of weeks (bad). That expectation had been established when our team consisted of just a very few people and the demand was crazy. So, we were trying to manage expectations appropriately, but what we missed was that they were the center of our story. To fix this, we required that an organizer first attend an event before being able to bring a Startup Weekend to their own community. That meant we needed to promote that message at the end of each event.

Next came attendees. Messaging to this customer group was easier because it was more aligned with what we had on the website at the time. Also, most of these customers found us through Eventbrite rather than our home page. This messaging was a straight call to action to buy a ticket and attend an event. However, it lacked the reason for buying the ticket. We learned we needed to align the messaging to the first-time attendee since the repeat attendee was already our evangelist. This is what we addressed:

- Wants—they want to meet new people that are like them;
- Needs—we provided help to move their startup vision ahead;
- Fears—generally speaking, people don't like the unknown, so you need to ease their fear and let them know it's going to be OK.

Sponsors were next, with a focus on local event sponsors. The HQ team was working with global sponsors, but we needed to separate the messaging to address both, allowing the local team to get a larger budget for food and T-shirts. Here we had to focus on marketing resources (like one-pagers) and streamline the process of onboarding sponsors and getting that cash back to the organizing team to spend on the event.

For global sponsors, we focused on storytelling and impact, which required getting feedback from teams in the field. This wasn't easy because we had more than 1,200 events in 120 countries in 2014. Though we had regional managers that covered the markets, they were already busy. We had to keep asking for stories from events around the world to post on our blog. We also put out an annual "Impact Report" as well as a thought-leadership piece with Google on the "5 Ingredients of a Startup Community." These documents served as the tools for global sponsors.

The last group consisted of the facilitators. This was a group of about three hundred experienced attendees who had been trained to run the event. They loved to travel and meet their tribe in different cities and countries. But they had a "season" until many of them turned their attention to their own startup, so we always needed to add to that pool of facilitators. We keyed in our recruitment around repeat organizers and emphasized the travel opportunities. The call to action was to take the online training and apply to be a facilitator.

Remember, if you don't pick the right customer first, and follow up with a clear value proposition, your marketing effort and expenditure will be wasted.

Saving Money or Making Money?

Does your product help your customer make money or save money? Will they use it to have fun or improve the quality of their life? Your value proposition should position your product as a benefit. Don't be implicit or subtle in how you communicate the value, be explicit. If you're selling into the enterprise, products that make money will nearly always find budget. I'm thinking of sales or marketing departments that have budget to drive revenue. If your benefit is savings, whose department wins if they buy your product, and do they have budget?

Testing Your Value Proposition

In the following step-by-step guide, you'll be using your value proposition to test keyword campaigns. Make sure you continue to track your key phrases and keywords in a spreadsheet because you'll need them for your next stage of research. It's important here that you don't just pick the words or phrases that you like, but the ones that resonate with your customer.

MINIMUM VIABLE PRODUCT (MVP)

Your minimum viable product can take many different forms. It can start with a PowerPoint or keynote presentation version. You can use a landing page or a simple website. In the last year or so, a number of no-code options have been released so you can build a solution with products like XMind, Airtable, and Bubble. Or, if you are a developer or have software developers on your team, you can build on a variety of technology stacks, the type of services and coding language your product is built on. Regardless of the platform you use to build your product, there are some common factors you'll need to have outlined in advance.

Another way to look at your MVP is that you are testing your riskiest assumptions—Rik Higham called it a *RAT*, the riskiest assumptions test. The product requires you to test your most unknown assumption—not a perfect design or a perfect product. The focus of your effort here is to learn what the customer wants. Tom Chi, cofounder of Google X, called it "maximizing the rate of learning by minimizing the time to try new things."

Wireframing Process

Wireframing is a simple process of outlining the function and workflows of the app or website before you build anything. It's a slideware/PowerPoint version of what you're trying to build. I use a tool called Wireframeapp.io and Balsamiq is also popular. These apps are easy to use via a browser, with the ability to collaborate (invite others). You can actually demo functionality without writing Swift (Apple) or Android code.

Wireframes don't look great, but they communicate the idea. Design is important; however, at this point, design follows function. Start with a site or an app that you like or even a competitive site to replicate its design. Give the wireframes to a designer to make it look good at a low initial cost. If you don't have a designer, you can use Fiverr to find one. Give them the wireframes, direct them to a site design you like, and ask them to give you a similar design.

To create a wireframe, start with each screen used in the process flow of the app or website. You'll be able to move the screens around later. Stay big picture and crank out the basics of each pages, including form data or order page information. You can make a copy of any of the pages to add features later. Export this wireframe to a PDF or PNG and load it on your phone or tablet to give the demo. Again, you can do this without writing code.

This will give you a mock-up version of the MVP your potential customers can use to provide feedback before you take the next step of building it. You want to be able to dig into how people react, or don't react, to your hypothesis and ask the *why* questions that need to follow. The best methods for customer development are, in descending order:

1. In person because you can watch how people react to the demo.
2. On Zoom/Hangouts so you can see their face and watch their reaction.
3. Phone is tougher because you can't see body language.
4. A survey is the least valuable because it's impersonal and you can't gauge a person's reaction.

Step 2: Problem First, Then Features, Then an App

Let me note here that many people approach an idea like this as an app with features that, hopefully, map back to find a problem. The better approach is to start with an acute focus on the problem, not the solution. Then after you get feedback, you can define the features and finally answer the question of what the final product will be, for example, a mobile or web app.

This is important because, as you talk to potential customers, you're going to dig into the problems you're really solving (setting aside gaming and entertainment for now). And is it really a problem? In other words, is it a big enough problem to warrant their time and, ultimately, are they willing to pay for said solution? Taking these steps may involve making changes to your MVP, so the first version you ship isn't likely to be the version they will pay for. Remember, the problem first, please!

I no longer fall in love with my own ideas. I treat them like disloyal friends that will just as easily tease me onto a long road of misery as they might be a partner in a great adventure. Here's why. Your ideas will lie to you (well, technically they allow you to believe what you want to believe) because they are the ultimate form of confirmation bias, one of nine bias types. Confirmation bias is when you give weight only to a favorable response to your hypothesis and dismiss evidence contrary to it. And if you only have one idea, you are definitely going to dismiss that contrary evidence. Founders tend to dismiss this feedback and blame people for not getting it or being too dumb to understand the idea. This externalizing of the problem is very bad for the customer development process. It's just another form of confirming what you want to hear.

Writing a Specification for a Software Product

If you've never written a specification document before, don't freak. (For my technical friends, this outline is overly simplistic.) Start with your page-by-page wireframes and write out the functionality per page and the actions required. For example, what happens when you click on a specific button? Does it record information in a database, does it query a third-party application programming interface (API) like Google Maps to return directions? I suggest using Google Docs as the tool to capture these requirements because it makes for easy collaboration and clear revision history. Begin with naming that doc and assigning Version 1.0. Every significant document will then include a 1.1 or 1.2 reference change. Also, when you invite comments, make those notes in Suggestion mode rather than having multiple primary editors. Be sure to capture your initial required features, not all features.

Future Features

Add a section to your document for future features. This is a bulleted list of ideas, ranked in no particular order, that you might add to the application in the future. Push all non-MVP features to this list. You aren't going to launch a product with all these features included, so ruthlessly move nonessential features to this list. If you don't, you can quickly move from "Scope Creep" to "Scope Leap." Even if you're a repeat entrepreneur, you still need to limit scope so you can ship a product on a reasonable timeline. The other option, the historical "pre-lean" option, is to spend two months (or years) building a product. Don't pursue this option. The risk of shipping the wrong product is very high.

You've drafted the specification. Pages, bullets, and versions are numbered. You've ruthlessly moved future features into its own section of the document (give it another hard look before you continue, and resist the urge to jam all features into the first version). Finally, you think you have the features outlined to make the MVP a worthwhile first step to show your potential customers. Great! Now you have a decision to make: Should you hire a developer or development company to do the work? Or should you find a technical cofounder to work for free?

Finding a Technical Resource

People don't work for free. Get over it. Really, I've seen this approach go bad so many times—please don't go down this road. You have three and only three choices if you want to build and ship a software product:

1. Become a developer. This is a faster process than you may think. Great coding schools can crank out a developer in about twenty weeks. You can also take a super cheap online class and learn the basics in about the same amount of time. You'll just need to be insanely focused and motivated during that period.
2. Hire a developer or development firm to do the work. We'll walk through the hiring mechanics later in the chapter.
3. Incent a developer to do the work by offering a significant percentage of equity in your company. Developer skill sets are in high demand, especially in markets like Seattle. Depending on your market and demand for developers, you may need to find someone that will work on your project as a side hustle.

"But you don't understand Dave, I don't have any money!" Great, recognize that you are never going to ship a product. You have two choices: start training yourself or start saving some cash to hire someone. That's it. Sorry to break it to you. I've seen people "work for free" and then ask for 60 percent of the company. I've also seen developers hold the code base hostage until they get paid.

Think about it for a minute. If you decided to learn to code back when you started thinking about this idea, you'd have skills by now. I'm not saying everyone should pursue a career in coding, but if you have no budget, you don't have many choices either. I taught myself with an online course to MVP the crap out of stuff. Am I fast? Absolutely not. But I can hack stuff together if I have to.

Choosing a Technology (Stack)

A decade-plus ago, the technology stack of choice for startups was Ruby on Rails. Then the trend was toward JavaScript. Python is also popular for back-end development. Swift 3.0 replaced Swift 2.0 for iOS, and Android has its own version. I don't have a strong preference about the technology you choose. I tend to think about it in the broadest context: Where can I find talent? That's with the most current technology. You have to assume that someone will inherit the project you are building, so make sure it's using a skill set that allows you to find talent to maintain and improve it.

A more recent trend is to use no-code platforms like Airtable and Bubble. You'll still need to train yourself on these tools and become an expert or hire one. But it's not as expensive as writing code.

Choosing a Single Technical Resource or Company

You have your draft spec in a Google Doc. Your summary and hypothesis are written. Now you're ready to post that job on a site like Upwork or Fiverr where you can find freelancers and companies looking to do technical projects. Create an account but recognize you are an unproven client on the site. That means that you can't post lowball prices on fixed-bid projects and hope to get people to respond.

At this point, you may want to consider breaking your MVP into pieces. For example, can you separate the mobile functionality from the website functionality? Is there a way you can do a staged build or engage a developer to work on just a part of the functionality? A side note here on going "off network" with developers or vendors: If you have a public profile and WhatsApp or Skype address, you will get solicited by developers outside of Upwork. Don't go off network. The system is set up to protect both parties. Outside vendors will ask that you pay them in advance. Don't do it. The rated and vetted programmers that Upwork gives you access to are worth the 20 percent fee it charges to the developers as a commission.

Posting a Job on Upwork or Fiverr

When you post to Upwork, you select whether you're looking for part-time, flexible workers. The site allows you to put money into escrow and pay the vendors when they deliver the milestones of the project. That way the vendors know they are getting paid, and you know they have to deliver code before they get paid. You don't need to pay up front for services, but you will need to commit your budget based on milestones. Don't expect developers to start until you fund the next milestone.

Also, don't let your grandiosity get the best of you here. Start with a part-time option and test your project and developers. Recognize that, like all MVPs, you may end up throwing away your first build when it comes time to produce your final solution. This one just needs to work or mostly work. Also, you may need to hire more than one developer to test their skills. If they both deliver, you'll pay twice. But if you pick one and he or she doesn't deliver, you could be weeks behind.

After putting out the summary of the job post, I like to add a review process as the first step to evaluate the short-listed candidates. I call it something like "Project 1: Review My Scope Document for a Fixed-Price Project." Then do the following:

- Create a fifty- or one-hundred-dollar job, depending on scope. This fee will be paid to each of the three finalists.
- Hire three vendors to:
  - Review the specification document in advance;
  - Ask them to bring questions to a conference call;
  - Lead a sixty-minute Q&A conference call:
    - Have them write up the meeting notes and next steps.
    - Who asked great questions?
    - Who provided great feedback on the document?
  - Review the three developers for their feedback:
    - Who took good notes (a sign of project-management skills)?
    - Who provided follow-up and feedback?
  - Ask them to provide feedback on your spec (you should have at least two developers or teams in the process).
  - Use the Suggestion feature on Google to create two different specs (e.g., 1.1a and 1.1b).
  - Ask them to help you break down the milestones into two-week sprints. This is the amount of time that they work on a section of the project with a deliverable in mind.
  - As a nontechnical person, don't mess with the sprint cycle between sprints because it will take more time. Don't change features or priorities until the next sprint.
  - Ask them for an updated budget for the project to see if you are still within the original scope and cost, and whether or not you can cut any features.

This should give you a pretty good idea of who you can work with and if they are realistic about the project scope. For example, if one says two weeks and another says six, dig into the reasons for the disparity. After this initial vetting process, post the larger project and let your short list know that you will invite them to bid on the work. At this point, you're going to have to commit to an amount to spend. But you'll have some data to bid it out. A fixed-price project could be $1,000 to $20,000 (or more). This is why you need to mitigate risk at the early stage to get the price and project scope down to a reasonable amount.

Whether to hire a team or an individual is a budget-driven question. Ideally, having a team that can do design, mobile (iOS and Android), front-end, and back-end technology is ideal. However, that will be more expensive. And don't expect your developer to be a designer or vice versa. That's not who you're hiring. Finally, a note about managing this process. You'll either do it yourself or pay a firm to include project management in their services. Either way, someone needs to act as project manager.

Creating a Two-Week and Monthly Checklist

Now that you have defined the milestones and sprints for the project, you should have a general budget in mind and know how to break up the payments. You also need to decide whether to spend the money and whether you or an outside contractor or company will manage the project. The calendar and reporting are based on the sprint schedule. To help you decide, answer the following questions:

- Do you have the budget to see this through?
- Do you need to do more customer development to make sure your target ICP is willing to pay for the product before you commit to the escrow?
- Have you completed the draft of your MVP scope document?
- Have you submitted the project for bids on various sites?
  - Can you break the project down into smaller chunks for initial delivery?
  - Will customers pay for this "skinny" version of your MVP?
- What is the budget you will need to deliver the product that customers will pay for?
- How long will the product take to develop?
- How will you fund the work?
  - How will you fund you and your team during that time?

Choosing a Vendor

We already covered your milestones and sprints, so you should have a pretty good idea of the scope of the project. For example, is it four two-week sprints for a total of eight weeks? If you have one developer declare they can whip it out in a week while another says twelve weeks, keep looking to find some middle ground in project scope. If it sounds too good to be true, it likely is!

Contracts

I highly recommend a contractor agreement on this type of project. The typical contract agreement is a two-part document—a master services agreement (MSA) and a statement of work (SOW)—and it can be generated by either party. I've included a sample version at www.GetTrajectory.com/startup-docs. Please note, I'm not an attorney. I've only hired a lot of them. Also, you don't want to get into the process of paying a developer and then having them ask for more money while they hold your code hostage. *Never* pay in advance, unless you want to be parted with your cash.

An MSA is a single contract for what could be multiple projects, so you will only have to change the SOW for future work. The MSA should:

- Outline the parties, contacts, and invoicing.
- Outline ownership of the work. In a traditional work-for-hire situation, the developer doesn't own the rights to the work, you do as the buyer.
- Detail your warranty. For example, code to be delivered via GitHub in working order, with no bugs.
- Lay out contractor and employee status and include a non-solicitation clause.

Components of the SOW should cover:

- Services
- Schedule, including sprints
- Deliverables
- Fees, which usually correspond to the sprints
- Payment terms

Signature pages exist for both the MSA and the SOW. Make sure they get signed before you proceed. If there is anything that isn't clear in the SOW, fix it now. If you need to add a second phase or more scope, you can add an updated SOW. Fuzzy contracts and fuzzy scope documents will produce fuzzy products (that don't ship) and create conflict. Get clear on what you're going to have delivered and allow adequate time to negotiate the contract.

Code Review/Bug Fixes

Before the final payout, you'll need to find someone to do a code review. Let your developer know that you'll be having a third party handle this. That will help them produce better-quality code. Bug tracking and bug fixes need to be actively managed by you and the developer. You can use a simple tool like Google Sheets or a more complex tool for bug tracking.

Communications

Set up a regular schedule with the team for check-ins. Email, Slack, or Zoom calls will work. Set expectations on what will be accomplished in the next period of time, and make sure the person responsible for keeping meeting notes captures next steps and action items. Inspect what you expect. A regular cadence will be important in the relationship going forward.

Deliverables

1. Draft your value proposition.
2. Write out your product features and benefits.
    a. Write a draft of the specification.
3. Determine your cost to build.
    a. Scope your MVP and budget.
4. Add another twenty-five to fifty customer development interviews this month.

Marketing, Sales, Revenue Models, and Pricing

Where there is mystery, there is margin.

—Dave Berkus

One of my mentors coined the above phrase a number of years ago. The idea was that there's money to be made by offering unique products or solutions. When products are commodities, there isn't. In other words, look to solve a mystery and you can make money.

Congratulations—we are more than midway through this process. You've completed fifty to one hundred customer development interviews. You have a competitive analysis, and your product positioning continues to improve as you gather more data from the market. Great work! You've also addressed your cofounder issues. After this month, you'll likely be ready to incorporate. It's worth spending the money if you prove to yourself that the idea is worth pursuing. Incorporating is busywork such as buying office supplies at Staples, if you haven't first proven out the idea.

In this section, we'll be diving into the revenue side of company development. In addition to the material in this chapter, there are additional resources in Part Three where I dig into the fourteen business and revenue models.

I want to take a moment to define the difference between models and methods. I never thought the topic was that interesting until I gave a presentation in 2015 that had seventeen thousand views on SlideShare. Since then, I have expanded the original nine B2B models to include B2C and services to give us fourteen models today. The original presentation was done for a B2B Accelerator.

After the original presentation, I added a new revenue model called "productize a service." This was based on a professional services company that was delivering custom software at the same time they were building a product to eventually sell. I bring this up for two reasons. First, I'm not set on fourteen models. If you have an example of additional models, please send them to me. Second, I've been on the board of directors for a "productize a service" model for more than sixteen years and didn't think of it as a specific revenue model, only as a service.

"Productize a service" uses tech and tools in addition to people. The idea is to offer a packaged service with a package price, and to use tools in the back end of the process to take costs out of the delivery of that service. This is in contrast to a law firm or consulting company that works on a billable hours model. Some of the largest global consulting companies are in the business of creating complexity so they can perpetuate the need for consulting hours, but that's a different story.

Models

The *Oxford English Dictionary* defines the word "model" as

> **mod·el**
> /ˈmädl/
> *noun*
> *1. a three-dimensional representation of a person or thing or of a proposed structure, typically on a smaller scale than the original.*
> *2. a system or thing used as an example to follow or imitate.*

We're sticking with the second definition here—a model as an example to follow. In the case of revenue, there are the fourteen basic models, you just need to choose primary and secondary models that represent your best guess. There are also four sales models that I'll outline below. You'll need to pick one of these models as well. If you don't come from a sales background, congratulations, the mystery and secret "will be revealed!"

Methods

The *Oxford English Dictionary* defines the word "method" as

meth·od
/ˈmeTHəd/
noun
1. a particular form of procedure for accomplishing or approaching something, esp. a systematic or established one.

In the case of marketing, a lot of creativity and many methods will go into your efforts; they're not limited to a specific number on a list. You'll get used to testing and looking for novel approaches to marketing.

MARKETING

Marketing is a great example of a method you can use to test procedures and results. Though there are best practices, there isn't one single formula (or fifteen for that matter). If you're not a marketer, you'll need to find a person who loves this discipline or commit a lot of time to learning these mechanics.

Sales and marketing go hand in hand. The goal of a sales process is to create a scalable and predictable way to drive revenue for your new startup. But it will begin with you, quite literally. You will be the first marketer and salesperson. Think of this as the logical extension of customer development. The difference is that you are asking the prospect to pay for your product or service.

Pricing is also a method. It's a process that is more art than science, especially at this early stage of your company. If you're a corporate innovator, you'll have the cash to pay a large consulting firm like Bain & Company to look at your pricing.

Because marketing and sales are deeply entwined, I've tried to break out the components as well as create a draft plan for how you validate your revenue efforts over the next month and going forward. Right now, the tracking for this process is going to be a Google sheet that you can share with your cofounder(s) or salesperson. Choosing a customer relationship management software platform is like the office product reference above: it's busywork until you prove the customer wants your product.

A Brief Note on Naming and Branding

You're likely to change and modify your name and brand over time. Don't overthink it. Spend twelve to twenty bucks at domains.google.com—don't drop a few thousand dollars on a domain name in the secondary market. You have more important things to spend money on.

Find a name that works for now that is either a description of what you do or is brand neutral, just something that doesn't box you in. You can use a .co or other less popular domain suffix at this point. Use LeanDomainSearch.com to search for an available domain based on theme. Or use namechk.com to check for available social media extensions. Also, do a quick search on the USPTO.gov TESS database for trademarks. You don't want to start your business and immediately have trademark issues. At this stage, you don't need a separate name for the product and the company. One name is enough, so build from there.

Being clever isn't your friend when it comes to marketing. Your customer doesn't actually want to think about the deeper meaning of your company's name. Use a name that you can say easily, one that can be spelled phonetically. Avoid double letters and intentional misspellings. If you're wildly successful, you'll be able to spend a crazy number on the .com extension, but that comes later.

Ten, One Hundred, One Thousand Customers

There are many ways to think about marketing, but for now, envision it as a funnel process. As seen in the graphic on page 156, you have channels of marketing activities that sit above the funnel, within the funnel you have stages, and to the left you have a calculation of time called "time to close." The following is a look at several different marketing methods.

Your goal in this chapter is to figure out how you get to your first ten, one hundred, and one thousand customers. Each step will look a little different. At the early stage, it's all hand-to-hand combat. To get to revenue in six months, you need to find customers that receive value for what you have built, and then capture some of that value in return in the form of revenue, beta users, or proof-of-concept (POC) users.

You've done the basic research and the competitive analysis. Now you need to start testing some of the value proposition messaging and some of the channels. Before you get started, you'll need to have a website to push your traffic to or at least a landing page. You don't need an MVP or product to test your marketing messaging.

If you want to start building out marketing content, you can launch a simple website with Wix or WordPress, with hosting by a company like Cloudways. You don't need to be technical to build a site. Content management systems (CMS) like WordPress have a lot of plug-ins to automate much of the process. I would not suggest a WordPress.com website for $99 a year since you're likely to change your URL/name and domain in the first year, so better to use WordPress.org as a hosted option.

LaunchRock was a company that was founded over a Startup Weekend a number of years ago, now owned by Startups.com. They have a simple product idea and landing/conversion page. You can follow their step-by-step guide to pointing a new domain name to their application, adding your content, and monitoring site traffic and the number of people that register (or traffic-to-conversion ratio). Even a good landing page product won't fix a bad value proposition, website copy, or bad offers.

Your home or landing page will host your tagline and value proposition. You will also need to set up a call to action (CTA) with a form to capture customer contact info. You can use a Google form for free. If you have a little bit of cash to throw at it, design matters, and Google Forms isn't beautiful. For a step-by-step guide to building a website on WordPress, go to www.dkparker.com/books/trajectory-startup/.

Building Your Marketing Funnel

You're going to drive traffic to your website or the app store using all of the marketing methods you can afford or find reasonable to test. How should you monitor that traffic so you can move them through a process to convert traffic to leads, and those same leads to customers (and ultimately revenue)?

If I were your VP of marketing, I'd create a marketing funnel. Above the funnel would be the activities and methods we want to track. This marketing expenditure will determine where you put your budget dollars, for example Facebook ads, Google Ads, or trade shows. We should be able to attribute that traffic to that activity by creating unique landing pages.

A marketing qualified lead (MQL) is where we capture basic data about customer interest in our product or service using a call to action (CTA) or offer. Without a CTA, it's just information on your site but not effective marketing. These basic leads are qualified into sales qualified leads (SQL) after someone has actually interacted with the prospect. I've outlined a basic funnel and its components below.

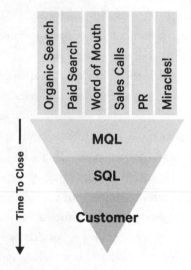

Above the Funnel

Let's look closer at some of the activities that sit above the funnel—not all are in the illustration or apply to every business:

- Organic, nonpaid search, backed by search engine optimization (SEO) fundamentals, is the long process of having Google and other search engines index your site and rank your results in the top listings on the web based on quality content. Please see resource links for more details.
- Paid search is using tools like Google Ads to buy traffic to your site based on the keyword effort you performed in the previous month.
- Social media is a great way to build audience for B2C and some B2B companies. This can be both paid, in ads, as well as organic, by building an audience based on content (video, images, etc.).
- Advertising can include other paid options like LinkedIn or Facebook ads. These ads don't reflect a search inquiry where you are mapping your keywords to the words searched; rather, you are mapping a profile of a person

to your persona. In the case of Facebook, it could be demographic or group members. In the case of LinkedIn, it could be a title or a company that is in your target persona.

- Word of mouth is the effort to track referrals.
- Public relations (PR) is using media to get customers to read a story and then come to your site to buy your product.
- Lists include email marketing, proprietary directories, membership bases, or the Apple App Store or Google Play Store listings. You can use these types of lists to reach out to potential customers with offers and information.
- Sales calls imply that you have a list of people to contact that meet your persona or ICP.
- Trade shows allow you to buy a booth to directly reach a target market of attendees. The guerilla marketing version of this is when you don't pay for a booth but try to do sales anyway. Use the latter method with discretion if you don't want to get thrown out of the event.

There are many other examples you can use at the top of the funnel, but this list is a good place to start. You'll note that I listed "Miracles" as an option in the graphic. Hate to break it to you, but it's not really an option. If you don't list and rank your top options, you're operating from a point of delusion and might as well be counting on miracles as your marketing method.

Inbound Marketing

There has been a lot of buzz over the last few years about inbound marketing. Part of the buzz was created by HubSpot, a great company based in Cambridge, Massachusetts, that popularized the idea. Inbound marketing is useful when you have a product that people are searching for online since it attracts people using content creation, social media posts, and SEO. The downside is that if no one is searching for your product, you'll have a problem. To really use inbound marketing, you'll need to be known and show up prominently in search queries.

Inbound marketing requires content that can be indexed through Google's search engine and a deliberate effort to write content for search or SEO. It will take time to do that. Should you start now? Yes, but do some research first. Go back to the keywords tab in your competitive analysis where you researched the volume and cost of competitive keywords. Go back to Chapter 6 to refine these keywords that will represent the blog posts and page content on your website or app page. They should also represent what the customer is searching for when looking for your product. When you write a blog post, the headline should include the keywords or phrases. Again, think of your customer: When faced with a blank Google search bar, what would they type in to find your solution?

The post you'll create should be at least six hundred words long. You should have a summary of the topic in the first paragraph, again featuring keywords, but written for a human not for a machine. Google wants to show quality results to their customers, so if it's too short, it will push the ranking down. If you're committed to this product and market, you should block out two to three mornings a week to start writing content. Post that content on your blog page of your site, then repost a few days later on Medium.com, LinkedIn, and other sites, with a note that it was originally published on your domain. If you don't have your own domain and site yet, start with Medium to build your audience.

On the consumer side, videos, infographics, Instagram images, as well as both short- and long-form content can generate inbound interest. Each format generates its own SEO "juice" calibration—the data to compare sources. Unique content and linkbacks matter as well; see Addendum/Resources for more information.

One growth hack I have found useful is to find a subject matter expert on a topic that's relevant to my area of interest. I'll ask them if I can interview them and record the call (using Zoom or something similar) on their area of expertise. I'll send over the questions in advance, being sure to include keyword topics. Then I record the call and transcribe it using Fiverr (it costs about twenty dollars) and post that content as a printed interview, not an audio file. The interview process will take about thirty minutes and creates great content for Google. Set up the interviews a few weeks in advance and just keep knocking them out for your content schedule.

Finally, there are some inbound marketing things you shouldn't screw up. Find the "Beginners Guide to SEO" on Moz.com. SEO isn't free, and it takes your time, but it is something as a founder you can do for little cash expenditure.

Outbound Marketing

Outbound marketing requires you to spend cash. It takes on the forms of advertising, email, direct mail, events, trade shows, or other methods initiated by the company. Because you have limited cash, outbound marketing will force you to narrow down your target customers to a specific group or channel. For B2C, your target may be a specific demographic that you find through advertisers like Instagram and Facebook.

My friend Dan Kihanya is a great B2C marketer who uses what he calls "borrowed credibility," where a brand influencer or other entity that has a trusted relationship with its audience/customer base can be a good source to get a halo effect, or positive association from their brand. Influencers on social media use their brand in product placement advertising. The key is that you must get that brand or influencer to introduce you to their audience. That introduction can be as a guest blogger or to be included in their podcast. Sometimes it can be as a recommended partner or as a listed resource. Other times it's via an ad on their property(ies), where the implicit understanding with the audience is that they allow things that are relevant and/or valuable to their customers.

Both Instagram and Facebook allow you to do rapid tests with very small budgets.

Search Terms

We've already covered the idea of having an innovative product in a new market. In that case, it's not likely that anyone is searching for the terms you would use to describe your business. So, what are they searching for? Is anyone searching for your product?

Who Has the List You Want?

I'm a big fan of partner marketing, also known as business development. It doesn't always work, but it's worth the exercise to help your focus on your target customer. Influencer marketing is an area in B2C you can test, but start on a smaller scale, an influencer with 100,000 followers to see if this is a good fit for you. If you could buy a list, find a list, or partner with a list, what would that list be? Some options include:

- Magazines
- Associations
- Reseller lists
- Small businesses in a neighborhood
- Trade show attendees
- Competitors

Building a List

Let's face it, building a list can be as difficult as building a product if you've never done it. Especially since you need to start building a list before you actually need it. My advice is to start with content. Think about what content your prospect would be looking for on the web and match that content to the search words that you've researched above. Go back to the value propositions if you need help. You can use Google Forms for free or a site like wufoo.com to capture data from your website. It makes simple web forms that you can connect to your email service provider account.

For B2C you can consider building a wait-list for paid and soon-to-be-released product. This is the equivalent of a letter of intent for B2B.

Email Marketing

There are a lot of email service providers (ESPs) that can handle your email marketing. If you have a favorite, great. If not, just go to MailChimp and create a new account. Whichever provider you choose, be sure to take advantage of autoresponders. One of the best functions of ESPs is the ability to program a series of messages to engage your prospects and customers. Here's a good example of how to use autoresponders. Hittail, a keyword research tool, offered a seven-part email course that I signed up for. In addition to giving me useful information (which is always critical), it reminded me every morning for seven days that I had subscribed to their service. Plus, all these messages were written in advance and scheduled to go out on a daily schedule, which saves time.

Surveys

Crafting a survey is still more art than science, but running surveys is simple with tools like Typeform or SurveyMonkey. Though you can make surveys quite complex with these tools, I would encourage you to start simple and get some of the data you really need.

Google Ads

Using Google Ads is an effective way to test if you can drive traffic to your site. Google's ads are designed around users' search intentions. You can purchase the key words or phrase. They range from general (puppies) to specific (specific breed, location, price). The more words in the ad, the cheaper the price and the greater the intention is shown by the searcher.

Google's keyword tool allows you to search competitors and see what keywords they are currently purchasing, but it won't show you the price they pay. Using your "competitive research" Google sheet, you can track keywords purchased for each of your competitors. You can also narrow down users by geography to focus your advertising dollars down to a zip code. This will allow you to test a relatively small budget on keywords to see if you can compete against bigger budgets.

You can also buy keywords and phrases and push that traffic to a landing page. To do this, you will need:

- A headline to test
- Body copy
- Offer/Call to action (CTA)
- Landing page URL
- Credit card for charges

This will create visitors, and based on your offer and traffic, you can calculate a basic model for cost of sale.

One final thought on Google Ads: Google always wins. If you don't take some time to understand Ads and how to use keywords, you can blow through a lot of cash quickly. Neil Patel has done a great job creating a Google Ad Made Simple article and he's an awesome marketer in general, so I suggest seeking out his blog posts.

Facebook Ads

Like Google Ads, Facebook ads allow you to test your value proposition and messaging. But unlike Google Ads, it's intent-based advertising. Such banner ads target a group of people on different platforms. Banners also have a headline, body copy, offer/CTA, and landing page, and require a credit card for charges. But you can narrow your ads to specific demographics, geography, or groups based on known affinity.

Keep in mind, for any advertising test, you can purchase the ads and drive traffic to a landing page. You don't actually need a completed product to test the advertising. You could spend $100 or $1,000 to test traffic, value proposition, and conversion data before you ever build a product. Just stop short of taking the credit card info. You can capture email interest for a future release. While this may frustrate the people who think you have a product to sell, if you do it right, you'll learn a lot in the process and capture their email addresses for the future product releases.

Return on Advertising Spend (ROAS)

Return on advertising spend is a way to calculate the return on investment for your marketing spend. You find it by dividing revenue generated by your advertising spend by the dollar amount spent on ads. You can use this formula to compare your marketing expenditure by channel, e.g., Facebook versus Instagram, and then track over time. There are a number of free calculators online to help with this.

Public Relations

PR is a great tool to help grow your business, especially if you have money to spend, and that means in the later stage. PR works only if you have a newsworthy story to share. Wanting to be in the media is not a story. Neither is the launch of your new product. However, showcasing how your customer uses your product might be a story. Getting into *TechCrunch* won't create a revenue miracle.

To find the most relevant publications to pitch your story to, start by researching the writers covering your industry and making a list of those contacts. Subscribe to Google Alerts for this reporter. Then comment on her stories and pitch her on worthwhile ideas (and not about your company at first) to get her attention. Journalists have daily, weekly, and monthly deadlines and are always looking for good stories to tell. Make it as easy as possible for them to tell your story by framing your pitch from the customers' perspective. Explain how your product helps customers and what the newsworthy benefits are and, hopefully, they will follow up with you.

While you're at it, be sure to think about the visual aspect of your story, too, and provide images to the journalists and bloggers you pitch. As a former photojournalist, I always think about attaching a compelling photo to a story. Here's a hint: pictures of people sitting at keyboards are not visually interesting.

Dan Price, the CEO of Gravity Payments in Seattle, created a PR buzz when he announced he was cutting his salary and paying all his employees a minimum wage of $70,000. Despite creating some controversy, the story made the cover of magazines like *Inc.* and *Bloomberg Businessweek* as well as the *New York Times* and many local publications. And the story has created buzz for five years. Whether you agree with Price's philosophy or not, there are lessons to learn from how he leveraged the momentum of that story into the news cycle. I'm not suggesting you pay your staff $70,000, but that's what I mean by having a story to tell. If you don't have a story, think about how to create one.

I will also say that hiring a PR firm before you find product/market fit and get customers is likely a useless expense. If you can't find a story to sell, they won't be able to either. Besides, in the early stage, reporters want to hear from founders, not from someone paid to promote the story. Don't get me wrong, there is a time and a place for paid PR. However, early stages are not the time. You have better places to spend cash.

Marketing Hacks

Marketing hacks are creative concepts that can get confused with core revenue models. Some examples of marketing hacks and tools include:

- **Freemium**—As mentioned earlier, this is the method of giving a free version of a product with the goal of getting customers to upgrade to a paid version. Freemium doesn't work in B2B because the products can't usually be "defeatured" enough at this early stage and still be useful.
- **Freemium with bundling**—Add your product's intro level to someone else's product or service offering.
- **Razor and razor blade**—This is where you give one piece of your product (for instance, a razor blade handle) away for cheap or free in exchange for selling a premium product. Wait, Dollar Shave Club killed the model with a subscription . . .
- **Free forever**—The idea is interesting, but at this stage you don't know what your product is really going to be when it grows up, so keep forever off the price list. In a mature product like HubSpot, the forever free version has a known conversion rate to paid customers.
- **Hard to migrate**—Many companies make it difficult to migrate away from their platform. Again, not a problem at your stage, you need customers first.
- **Pay what you want**—This was hip for a while several years ago but seems to have disappeared. Or at least the companies offering it disappeared.

- **Buy one, get one (BOGO)**—In the case of Toms (shoes), it was buy one, give one. Their model has evolved as a social purpose company, but it's a great example of this marketing strategy. The underlying model is commerce with enough margin to pay for the second pair of shoes.
- **Shortcuts**—These are an example of in-app purchases used in the gaming model. Games are now intentionally designed to frustrate users so they will shell out some cash to upgrade.
- **Limited availability**—Also known as marketing to scarcity, this can be a great tool. I had one company tell their prospects that they were only going to bring on three new customers in Q1—and this limitation made more prospects want to convert.
- **Pre-sale programs**—Concepts like Kickstarter are amazing because it finds customers who will pay in advance for a product that hasn't been manufactured yet. The underlying model is commerce with implied gross margins.
- **Vanity or exclusivity**—This is an age-old marketing method. Yes, I have a Mac. It's more expensive than a Microsoft Surface and the Surface is technically better. But still. Then there is my iPhone . . .
- **Upselling**—Red Hat provided open-source software and sold support. IBM purchased them in November 2018 for $33 billion.

For a great list of marketing ideas and hacks read *Traction* by Gino Wickman.

Marketing Qualified Leads (MQL)

Marketing qualified leads will have a specific definition that you build over time. For now, let's pick the working definition of a potential customer that has visited your site or landing page and has provided at least a name and an email address. As you mature as a business, you may add a survey to further qualify the lead. If you're B2B, you'll likely add company information. If you're using direct sales as your model, you'll want to include a phone number. For B2C, you can get them to subscribe to a newsletter, follow you on social media, or qualify them in some other way as a prospect (wait-list, ready-to-buy survey). Could you offer some info or content for free but in exchange for email addresses (with appropriate opt-ins thereafter)?

To capture useful information from prospects, you'll likely have to offer more than just a value proposition, especially if your price point is toward the high side and there is a level of risk to the buyer. Companies like HubSpot have mastered the e-book, with the Startup Growth Playbook as an example. The idea is that you give a customer something of value in exchange for their contact information. The emphasis here is on actual value (a free demo doesn't count as valuable).

Depending on your customer profile, you could give away an Amazon gift card, a Harley-Davidson, a white paper, or a trip to the Bahamas. Separate out the traffic sources from the offer, however, and make sure the offer is aligned with your product in at least some theme that makes sense. The prize should be proportionate to your lifetime value you receive from your customer. I did give away a Harley for one promotion, but that was not a smart idea in retrospect. We had to make a lot of sales to pay for that promotion—that's what I mean by proportionate!

These leads will either continue in a marketing funnel if you have a low price point and the customer requires a level of education, or the leads will be passed to sales as sales qualified leads (SQLs). If you're building out a marketing campaign, I would recommend going back to your Mailchimp account that we created a couple of months ago and creating a drip campaign (see just below). You're looking to escalate consumers' commitment along the way. Make your product easy to try or experience with full sign-up. Getting them to come back again is hard—hook them while they are there the first time.

Drip campaigns automatically send a sequence of emails on a regular schedule. Each mail should contain some education to further your marketing effort, highlight a feature, or provide a customer testimonial. Each mailing should also have a clear call to action. Once you set this up, it will run automatically. You should continue to test and track the offers and the timing, including email-open rates and click-through rates back to landing pages on your site.

Sales Qualified Leads (SQL)

This effort is about monetizing the list you've created in your marketing effort or one created by your team or agency. Sales qualified leads are a list of prospects that you, your cofounder team, or your salesperson/sales force can call and ask for the order. The emphasis here is on "qualified." The better the leads are qualified in advance, the faster the time to close and the more effective the salespeople will be with their time and effort.

I've only shown this as one step in the funnel, but sales are generally a process. I've seen a few examples of sales being a "one call close" but at the current maturity of your company and product, it's likely to have multiple steps in the process. You'll need to send additional marketing resources, schedule a demo, and involve other people if it's B2B. You'll begin to optimize around:

- Number of emails
- Number of calls
- Time between steps
- Demos
- Customer testimonials/referrals

A trial user is a qualified lead, but not a customer. A user on a freemium account is an SQL, but not a customer. Some percentage of this profile will convert to paid customers. It's OK to have an ever-growing list of free users or trial users. But employ the right term—they are "users." If you don't capture value for the value created, you don't have a business. If the user is the product, for instance, Facebook and Instagram, you'll need to have a process for tracking your advertising sales cycle.

Customers

A person becomes a customer when they pay for the product. In the early days, you'll likely know all your customers and why they purchased. This starts the clock on the lifetime value (LTV) of your customer and introduces the concept of churn. During early days, your LTV may vary greatly compared with a more mature company.

Time to Close

Closing is the part of the process when you or your rep will ask for the order, send a contract (DocuSign), and receive payment. Tracking the time from the top of the funnel to payment is more than an exercise. As your business matures, you will use time as a measure of profitability to choose your best marketing channels. This will allow you to put more capital behind each channel and begin to predict the returns based on expenditure, time, and products purchased.

When you have a VP of marketing for your company, that person will begin to expand this tracking to cohort analysis, which allows you to segment your customers into profiles and profitability. Again, this is a process that matters at scale, not at launch. At launch, revenue creates cash and cash pays the bills.

In the case of the advertising revenue model, the user is not the customer. The actual customer is the advertiser since it's the one paying. You'll need a salesperson to sell that advertiser on a cost per thousand (CPM, originally cost per mille), cost per action (CPA), or a cost per click (CPC), so you'll create a rate card to establish pricing for those ads.

SALES

In many cases, someone will need to sell your product and ask for the order. And the first person to do that will be you. The basics of the process are prospect, qualify, sell, repeat. There are basically four sales models that you can use:

- **Web direct**—Like Amazon or Angie's List, you can go to the web and buy a product or service. It requires the product be known and the price point be below a threshold the consumer would expect to pay on the web via a credit card. If the price is too high, such as a $10,000 cruise, customers won't buy web direct. Customers can get your product directly from your website or through a distributor. If Amazon is that distributor, it sells your product, owns the customer relationship, and sets the retail markup.
- **Direct sales**—This is where a person, either inside sales or outside sales, interacts with the customer to sell a product. The transaction may be completed on the web, but it requires a salesperson to manage a process.
- **Indirect or channel sales**—This is like a reseller selling product. In the case of a complex IT project, it might be a system integrator. Generally, channels fulfill the demand that you have created. They do not generally create demand. This is slightly different from business development as outlined below.
- **Retail sales**—This refers to the storefront where a product is sold. Retail channels will generally require a product to have demand before they will stock it on a shelf. If it doesn't have demand you will likely need to pay for the placement of the product. Physical products that require distribution can still be considered retail.

Take a moment to fill in your sales model choices below.

	Known Market	Unknown Market	Low Price Point	High Price Point	Known Search Words	Unknown Search Words
Web Direct						
Direct						
Indirect						
Retail						

Here's a completed chart using best practices.

	Known Market	Unknown Market	Low Price Point	High Price Point	Known Search Words	Unknown Search Words
Web Direct	✓		✓		✓	
Direct	✓	✓		✓	✓	✓
Indirect	✓		✓	✓	✓	
Retail	✓		✓	✓		

How does it compare to your startup's chart?

- Web direct works in known markets, at low price points, and with known keywords.
- Direct sales have the broadest market. It doesn't work in low-price-point sales because the transaction value of the sale is too low to support a scalable sales team.
- Indirect works in known markets, where demand is already established, at both low and high price points.
- Retail is similar to indirect. The real differences are between B2B (channel) and B2C (retail); other than that they have similar profiles.

Is the result good news or bad news for your product? You have to have a sales strategy; hope isn't an option. This should move you closer to the right strategy for your product. Now that you've narrowed your options to a primary choice, we can start to map out your sales plan for this month.

A NOTE ON YOUR FIRST SALES HIRE

One thing about salespeople: They are always good at selling themselves! They are occasionally good at selling your product or service. Your first sales hire needs to be flexible and good with selling concepts versus a tangible, priced product. In the early stages, pre-product/market fit, they are going to be adjusting pricing and product features all the time. It's a bit of an educational sales process as opposed to a transactional sales process. By transactional, I mean that they aren't selling a specific product based on price and availability. They are going to educate the customer—sell a concept first and a solution second. That's going to take a salesperson with flexibility.

Business Development

Business development (BD) isn't a euphemism for sales. These are two distinct functions. If you're asking a customer for an order, you're in sales. If you're working with partners to sell to their customers, you're in business development. Because the market has shifted away from calling sales what it really is, you need to provide clarity to your team members about their roles and what they need to deliver. Those with quota numbers to hit are in sales. Those with partner relationship goals to hit are in business development.

Business development is identifying potential partners who benefit when you sell your product to their customers or to your mutual new customers. Business development messaging isn't easy because you need a value proposition to the partner as well as the buyer/user. Partnerships also take time to develop, which is why it's best to start thinking about them now. A note of caution: Just like fundraising, don't count on these deals until a) the agreement is executed, and b) clear execution plans are agreed to. On the BD sales process, you, the founder, don't control the deal velocity. Partners can be fickle and hard to navigate. Your champion can get fired or reassigned any time; you can end up starting from scratch or, even worse, be no longer relevant in the partner's perception.

Think about which companies have a list of customers you would like to sell to and what you would have to give that company to cross-promote to that list. Since there is no way a company will give you its list—selling your product is not part of their corporate objective this or any other year—you have to make it worth their while. A few good ways to do this are:

- Use your product to shorten their sales cycle.
- Remove friction from their process.
- Decrease their churn.
- Upsell a more lucrative product.

Simply put, find a benefit to the partner or find a new partner.

Business development is also the activity you'll use as the founder and CEO to help you find your upmarket buyer. If you're selling through a merger and acquisition, you'll get your initial bid and interest from a partner that knows you.

PRICING

Oh, pricing! Is it an art or a science? The answer is yes, it's both, especially at the early stage. If you work for a big company, you can pay consultants to study your competitive market and make recommendations on pricing. Since you're not a big company, you're going to have to figure it out for yourself.

Your starting price is always wrong. Price it anyway.

When I talk about pricing, many founders don't want to commit to a number, and they get a little hand-wavy because they are hedging between the product they currently have and their aspiration. Remember, price is a number that has to fill a cell in a spreadsheet. Your price is likely wrong, but your customer won't be able to say yes until you give them a price. Then you can react given market feedback and move forward with pricing updates.

Here are a few guidelines to help you with your pricing.

- Industry pricing benchmarks are useful because they set the current acceptable rate. But they don't allow for much flexibility. You likely won't be able to move substantially above them, and at this point, I would recommend you don't move very far below them either.
- Don't start your pricing too low. Some founders connect their value proposition and pricing with a goal to deeply undercut the market, and you

may not need to do that. Start at close to market price and look for early promotional discounts rather than offering long-term pricing discounts. I had a friend who branded his company as "half price," and that was a very limiting brand and price proposition.

- Whether you offer customers a one-time, recurring, or pay-in-advance discount is driven by the revenue models that follow. The positioning has a lot to do with how the customer is conditioned to buy from existing competitors.
- There are few topics founders hold as dear as their pricing hypothesis. I prefer testing (and more testing) and data.

Some common forms of pricing are outlined below.

Cost-Based Pricing

Cost-based pricing is taking an average markup over the cost of goods or services provided. Some companies will use markup or markdown models. In retail, pricing is cost plus keystone (or as one of my former bosses used to say, "gallstone"), which is a 100 percent markup over cost when you are the only one with the product. This is the easiest, and, like services or physical commerce, you take your cost of services and mark up the cost to the desired gross margin percentage. Keep in mind that you need to base that on the fully burdened cost of the product or service. For example, if you are doing a setup or service for a customer, the cost isn't just the hourly rate of the employee doing the work, it also includes the cost of their benefits, office space, technology, communications, etc. And for a product, you also need to include shipping or delivery.

Value-Based Pricing

Value-based pricing is the ability to charge whatever the market will bear for the product or service. You'll have to consider direct and indirect competition in the calculation. If you are a monopoly, congrats! If you're in technology, you likely won't be a monopoly for long. You'll want to figure out the most you can charge for your product, but DON'T START BY PRICING TOO LOW. You can always lower your price, but it's incredibly difficult to raise your prices later. Finding the sweet spot will require some testing. There is also explicit value created for customers: savings (time, money, steps) or increased revenue (customers, pricing premium, new markets).

Revenue Share Pricing

The "lead generation revenue model" is based on a marketing company's ability to generate leads better than a company that is actually selling a product. An example is a lead generation company that captures web leads for life insurance and then sells those leads to a life insurance company. The insurance company simply views this partner as a marketing alternative to their other forms of advertising like television. The life insurance companies know their marketing costs well enough to know the value of a lead. I've seen companies that want to do a revenue share with the company providing the core product or service. Over time this model is nearly unsupportable because the larger company will look for alternate vendors.

Customer-Based Pricing

Understanding your customer is key to knowing what you can charge for your product. This involves understanding the value that they are getting from its use. Does your product help them save time, save money, or acquire more customers? Answering these questions will give you data for the value pricing. Pricing can also migrate into a high/low strategy. For example, DocuSign created a product that could be sold as a self-service to real estate agents in the early days and also sold as an enterprise solution for $100,000 to $1 million a year. This high/low strategy shows that you need to continue to test pricing.

Quantity Pricing

You should tier your pricing based on the number of users you have, how much they use your product, and the features you offer. Tiered pricing allows per-unit pricing to come down as volume increases. Align your incentive with customers' goals if you can. At the same time, don't leave money on the table just to get market share. You don't have to be the low-price leader. Look for natural break points in the pricing.

Metered or Usage-Based Pricing

Amazon Web Service (AWS) uses metered pricing based on usage. Other services include video storage or how the wireless carriers used to charge for text messaging.

Note that pricing that is unpredictable for customers is generally a bad idea unless they have few other choices.

Market Comps

This involves basing your price on what your competitors are charging for a similar product. Some of this data is easy to find by using:

- Quora: a helpful Q&A site for asking about business models and seeking pricing data;
- Edgar: provides data on public companies via quarterly and annual reports;
- Competitor websites, which for the most part offer fairly transparent pricing information.

Other ways to use comps include:

- Look for adjacent market competitors or proxies for your product.
- Use surveys to ask customers what they will pay and then use the results as one of your data points.
- Figure out your average revenue per user to calculate the number and frequency of transactions. Hopefully, you aren't selling a customer for a single transaction, but building a lifetime value that will help you establish what you are willing to pay for customer acquisition expense plus profit.

Pricing Methods

Your pricing should become more science than art over time, but for our purposes at the early stage of a startup, it's really a series of market-informed guesses. Keep in mind, anyone can sell a product for nothing, but this concept doesn't make sense outside of the new media model. This is the WhatsApp or SnapChat revenue model where user growth is growing so fast you can defer to a later stage to monetize your users. There is a breakdown of all the revenue models in Chapter 12.

I'm generally astounded by the lack of data and time many startups put into their product pricing. I know, I know, you're busy building a product and can't be bothered by such triviality. But, when it's time to prepare a venture-ready financial model, you're going to need to input your pricing hypothesis into your pro forma document. To do that, pick some numbers. (We'll get to the expense side of your model in Chapter 11.) Remember, to have a $1 million business you need 10,000 customers at $100 or one customer at $1 million.

Cheap is hard to beat and fun is hard to beat. But you need a path to monetize your product.

Using Financial Models for Pricing

I'm pretty geeky on financial modeling. It's how this project started in the first place. There is no doubt that having a great financial model you can use for both pro forma (forward-looking) and monthly forecasting (versus actual reporting) will help you model your pricing. But it will only inform your decision on cost-based pricing and will do little to inform your decisions on value-based pricing, or what the market will bear.

Pricing Committee

Create a pricing committee that meets quarterly. You won't necessarily update pricing at each meeting, but you should plan on looking at competition, new internal feature releases, sales cycle, and churn, and then adjust as needed. The team should include key customer-facing team members.

Deliverables

1. Marketing methods: What methods will you be testing to drive traffic to your site? Should you do trade shows? How will you build your email list?
   a. Marketing hypothesis: Do you think your ads will cost one dollar or one hundred dollars? How many leads can you drive to your site?
      i. Spend one hundred dollars to do an A/B landing page test on this hypothesis
2. Sales models
   a. Sales model choice: This will be based on how you filled out the grid above. Is your product known or unknown? Is the price point expensive?
3. Business development methods: Who has the customers you want?

4. Build out your basic marketing funnel, fill in some basic assumptions, number of leads per month and conversion ratio (guess). See the Addendum/ Resources page for a copy of the table, www.dkparker.com/books/trajectory -startup/.

5. Customer development:

   a. Continue to build your email list

   b. Do another twenty-five customer interviews

   c. Never stop interviewing customers

Preparing to Pitch,
Fundraising 101

When you take money from a venture capitalist, your business model is now their business model.

—Steve Blank

This chapter is not on a time schedule, more of a progress schedule. There are still deliverables due this month, though, so it could feel like Groundhog Day for a while, because you need to be ready before you pitch to investors. By this point you should have completed between one hundred and two hundred customer development interviews. You've tested out some initial marketing expenditures, and you know if you will be using a direct or web-direct sales model. If you're not a technically inclined founder and you're building a tech-related product, you should have your MVP budget. All this knowledge of business models isn't worth much if you don't get off your couch and do something!

Before we continue, I'll apologize in advance for this chapter being heavy on industry jargon. This chapter includes the terms you'll need to understand, but don't get bogged down in the lingo. You can come back to it as future reference.

This is where stuff gets real and many participants drop their original idea. It's time to make a go/no-go decision. Are you going to keep pursuing this idea? Or are you going back to the ideation and research chapter to find an idea that you think can take you all the way through the process? There's no shame in killing a bad idea. But failing is hard—and expensive. Different cultures place at least some level of shame in failing, whether that is right or wrong.

If your idea is an enterprise or complex solution that is going to require a significant build of six months or more, you should break down the process to further decrease your risk before committing to the budget. If you don't have the cash to get started, you should park the idea until you have some savings. You're not likely to find an investor based on a back-of-the-napkin idea.

Capital Requirements/Use of Proceeds

At this point, you must decide how much capital you need to raise and how you will use it. Keep in mind that investors want to fund your future and not clean up your past. That means you won't be raising capital for accrued and unpaid hours for founders or personal debt incurred while you built your business to date. That may not be what you want to hear, but it's reality.

"Use of proceeds" details how much money you need, when you need it, and what you'll use it for. Be specific here. For example, if the money is for hiring, then include how many people you need, their titles, and when you plan to get them on staff. If it's for marketing, tell investors the budget and what channels you plan to use (trade shows, advertising, lead generation, etc.).

Your budget for expenses should be thoughtful—don't simply fill in numbers without a reason. Your goal should be to raise capital for eighteen months. That way, you'll have twelve months to deploy the capital, grow, and validate your assumptions, and another six months to raise the next round of funding. You should be able to double your enterprise value in eighteen months. So, if you raised $1 million on $3 million pre-money ($4 million post-money), you would want to target an $8 million pre-money on the next round of funding.

Some founders raise small amounts at a time, keeping just enough cash trickling in to remain open. I don't recommend this approach because it means you'll always be raising capital. And raising money is a full-time job when you're in that process. You already have other full-time jobs you need to complete.

Types of Funding Rounds

There are several ways to fund your company's growth. Bootstrapping, or funding from cash flow, is always a great option because you don't have to sell equity in your company. But if you are going to raise outside capital, here are the most common forms.

Bank note or debt is used by companies that have regular cash flow and operating history. Banks won't provide lending (unless it is based solely on your personal guarantee) without a track record of cash to pay back the note. If you're a more traditional business, with a history, this might be an option.

Convertible debt is an easy method to fund an early-stage company. It is inexpensive to create and easy for investors to fund. If your lawyer wants to charge you too much for this type of instrument, find a new lawyer or use the Series Seed Notes docs from the Cooley law firm online or find a free open-source version on GitHub. Capped convertible debt has been the standard Techstars document since 2009. A cap simply means that the top price per share the early investor will pay will be "capped" on the future round or won't exceed a specific price. This is fair to the investor as they are taking the risk along with you at the earliest stage.

A Simple Agreement for Future Equity (SAFE), which is the form used by Y Combinator, is the right to purchase future equity. Though not as common as convertible debt, it's a great alternative to a priced round of funding.

There are tradeoffs between a SAFE and a capped note. A SAFE is warrant to purchase stock at a future priced round. A note is debt that will convert at a specific milestone and incurs interest until that time. Do some research to understand the implications before choosing.

Priced round is when an investor buys private and priced stock in a company. Historically, every round of funding was designated with a subsequent letter A, B, C, etc. That's different today.

Seed funding is when an investor commits capital in exchange for an equity stake. Be sure to use a lawyer who knows the Series Seed Docs. Again, the price of customizing your documents should be reasonable—think under $5,000.

Seed *N* is where *N* equals the round number. Today we're seeing a lot of Seed1, Seed2, and all the way through Seed10. Most are institutional, a fund investing other people's money versus an Angel investor, rounds of funding but can be angel rounds.

A round or series A is the following institutional round of funding and is typically used for growth capital (versus risk capital). The average A round in 2018 was $8–$10 million in the entire US and $12–$15 million in Silicon Valley. They have become huge funding rounds, thus the reason to call a small round a Seed3.

B round and above are the follow-on rounds of financial investors that help stage a company for an IPO or a merger and acquisition transaction. These later-stage rounds are usually easier to raise though they are sometimes massive amounts, because the company has more transparent growth measures.

For a deeper dive into funding rounds and funding mechanics, please pick up two books: Brad Feld's *Venture Deals* and Scott Kupor's *Secrets of Sand Hill Road*. Both books will save you thousands of dollars in legal fees and as Brad's subtitle says, you'll "Be Smarter Than Your Lawyer and Venture Capitalist." Though, just to be clear, there aren't any real secrets in Kupor's book, just a great breakdown of funding.

I'll talk about exit and exit-deal structures in a later section. For now, let me make two statements that will be obvious if you've done this before. If you haven't, you might be tempted to wave me off. First, corporate hygiene matters. Get all your docs into a Dropbox or OneHub solution from day one; later this will become a formal "data room" where you can refer investors for due diligence. Data rooms include features like watermarking and tracking that will show what the users actually looked at in the folders. Keep the file structure clean and easy to navigate. Keep your corporate records in the same folders. Share them with your accountant. Instruct your law firm to keep a copy of your corporate minutes off site. All corporate minutes should be signed at every board meeting. Second, use DocuSign to get all the documents signed, including offer letter and option agreements. Both you and your accountant will thank me later.

Finally, once you have more than five investors, you can work with your lawyer to set up the inexpensive version of cap table management software company CARTA.com to manage your share certificates.

Investor Profiles

Introductions between you and investors will be a combination of LinkedIn, email, and personal interactions. Build a Google sheet to track the contacts. Fields will include: firm, contact, email, phone, last contact date, a column for information sent (executive summary, deck, due-diligence package, etc.), as well as a place for you to take notes.

At the end of each meeting, ask your prospective investors if they would like additional information about your company. Or ask if they would consider introducing you to a few potential customers so you can refine your customer profile. You might be able to ask for other investors that like your type (B2B, B2C) or vertical (healthcare, enterprise, gaming) market. But read the room and don't over-ask. It's like a strange dating relationship, and you don't want to be pushy. An example is when I, in the role as an investor, reject a cold InMail/email on LinkedIn—I don't know the person and have no relationship. I try to be courteous and let them know it's not in my vertical market or geography. But without a relationship, I'm not going to spend much time providing feedback. Sometimes the person will ask for other investors' names. I've curated a list of other investors over the years, but I'm not going to refer another investor to a person I don't know. Look for buying signs and interest. Ask if the prospective investor might be open to next steps, for example, a demo or meeting with your team. Most investors fall into the following categories and profiles. Understanding these profiles will help you target the right investor type.

- **Friends and family**—These folks believe in you more than the idea or the market. Some of the early F&F investors (sometimes there is a third F for "fools") may not even understand what you are working on (grandparents, aunts, and uncles are great examples). You should give these folks the best terms because they are taking the greatest risk.
- **Angel investors**—Angels are investing their own money usually because they find the market or idea interesting. Sometimes they invest in markets they know, or where they think they can add value. A big check for most angels is $25,000–$50,000 or more.
- **Angel groups**—Most angel groups are a loose association of people who look at deals together, sometimes pooling their investments. Avoid (like the plague) groups that charge founders to pitch. (Though a small processing fee is totally fine and a way for the groups to filter out founders who want something for nothing.) Angel groups are good at closing out a round of funding if you have a lead investor or you have 50 percent raised. It's rare to find an angel group that will lead a round of funding.

- **Lead investors**—A lead is the person (angel) or team (VC) who will set the price and terms of the funding round. The inverse of a lead is a tire kicker. They will look, but never lead and seldom invest. Angel groups tend to have a disproportionate amount of tire kickers. Sometimes they are service providers looking to sell stuff to the startups. They may be "accredited," but they don't write checks.

- **Early-stage venture investors**—Early-stage VCs invest from a fund of other people's money. That means they usually have a charter and a thesis that drive their investment decision. They have to raise capital before they invest and are paid a fee and carried interest, or "carry" on the capital. The fee ranges between 2 and 2.5 percent of committed capital of the fund. They also receive 20 percent of the carry, after the investment is paid back. In the case of a $50 million fund, the $50 million (or the amount of invested capital) is paid back and they keep 20 percent of the return. Check out the investor profile on CrunchBase to look at recent investments. They will include:

  1. Stage—pre-revenue/revenue or growth
  2. Size—small or large check size
  3. Type—lead or follow, some funds only follow "brand" VCs
  4. Vertical market—what type of investments do they like: consumer packaged goods (CPG), software, marketplaces, etc.

- **Later-stage venture investors**—Stage infers bigger checks, so later-stage VCs tend to write bigger checks. Most have a formula; for example, they want 20 percent of a deal and write a $5 million check. Again, look at their profile and past investments.

- **Private equity investors**—Private equity funds are large funds that generally like to have a controlling interest of more than 50 percent, or all of a company. Private equity funds are better at spreadsheet and financial engineering than any VC. They typically design half of their returns into the purchase price and look for cash on cash returns.

- **Strategic investors**—These are the big companies that will likely be a partner or a future buyer of your company. They typically don't innovate because it's easier to buy a company than invest in innovation. For more on that topic, read Clayton Christensen's *The Innovator's Dilemma*. The entire book is dedicated to how large companies spend big dollars and yet fail to innovate.

Investors from different categories will take meetings with companies that are not in their stage or vertical as a way for them to stay on top of trends. But let's face it: investors, especially associates in a large fund, get paid to take meetings.

All Money Is Green; Not All Money is Good

All investor money will spend the same. But not all investors are great investors. Watch out for someone who is looking to invest so they can get a job. Make sure to do due diligence on your investors with other portfolio companies. You should know their reputation before you take their money. Individuals will act differently than institutional investors. At one point, selling my first company, I needed a bridge loan to get to closing. I had an investor who asked me to sign a note of personal guarantee for my house if we didn't close. Again, not all money is good. And, yes, I did keep my house.

Efficient Capital

Investors have different target investments, but one category is capital-efficient versus non-capital-efficient. Software investments are generally capital-efficient investments. You don't have to build a factory, a warehouse, or inventory. Subscription software has a cost to build and maintain (and grow new features) plus the cost of hosting monthly for usage.

Non-capital-efficient businesses are companies like Tesla. It's a long development cycle to go from an idea to a vehicle, including safety approvals. These businesses have a longer timeframe to returns.

From an investment perspective, early investors in non-capital-efficient businesses will face greater dilution as more capital comes into the company in subsequent rounds. That is one reason that some investors don't do hardware or physical goods.

Venture-Scale Deals

I opened the chapter with Steve Blank's quote, that taking venture capital also means taking on the venture capital business model of the VC. The implication is that the VC wants the return, not to be in the subscription business. Venture capitalists have ten-year timelines, because the average fund agreement is ten years with two one-year extensions. VCs are looking to make investments early in a fund's life, usually years two through four, and then watch these investments mature on their timeline. This works great if you have the same timelines. If you don't, it can be a problem.

It's important to understand that not all deals qualify for venture capital. But keep in mind, raising venture capital isn't a definition of success, either. There are a lot of great businesses that don't fit the target. For example:

- Lifestyle businesses. If you have a business that can create jobs, a lifestyle, and an income that works for you, you don't need venture. After all, when you take on venture, you take on its business model and exit expectations, too. And that might not be what you want.
- Services companies. Your business scales with people, not a product. That's totally OK, it's still a great business, but it doesn't fit the definition of venture scale.
- You can't be a 10X+ return. Venture returns are based on the "venture power law," in which a portfolio is broken into four quartiles of investment.
  - First quartile—Returns the fund, and the strongest companies don't need much help and will likely not take more cash. From the fund's perspective, they can't get enough capital into the company.
  - Second quartile—Provides a solid return and in small funds creates a great internal rate of return (IRR) for the fund, especially when the fund has twenty-five investments versus one hundred investments.
  - Third quartile—These companies take the most time to support and have the greatest need for capital from existing investors. Sometimes, they become the zombie startups or the companies that never quite hit their stride.
  - Fourth quartile—The companies that fail.

In that process, we see some great "second quartile" companies. They are good, but it's hard to see how they return 10X+ to the fund. You're not bad in that category, but you're not exciting to the fund either.

The other category of investments, especially for funds that are at the end of their fund life, are companies that can offer a fast return. When a fund is at end of life, it has limited capital to invest and is looking to fill out its "dance card." The other option is to find a company with a clear exit path that will likely be sold before the need for additional capital. These investments lean to markets that have known buyers with a track record of transactions.

Here's an inside peek at the messy world of early-stage venture funding: When founders are raising capital, we tend to over-index on getting the meetings and honing the pitch. Both are critical to the process. But there are many other factors you need to take into consideration during the process, especially in a venture or priced round of funding. Remember, fundraising is a process, not an event.

Remember, you are in control of the business when you have venture capital investors if you are meeting your numbers and hitting your plan. If you miss those numbers, or worse yet, whiff and miss your plan completely, you can be replaced. The more equity of your company you sell through fundraising, the more control you give to the investors.

Dilution

When you sell stock in your company as part of an investment round, you are selling newly created stock. For example, if you wanted to raise $1 million and your stock was worth $0.25/share, you'd create four million new shares of stock to sell as part of that offering. On average, each investment round will create dilution (increasing the total number of shares in the company) by 20–33 percent. So, to be near the midpoint, you'd likely offer $1 million in shares for 25 percent of the company, or a $3 million pre-money value, $4 million post-money value. The existing shareholders have incurred a 25 percent dilution to the existing shares, and the company now has $1 million in capital that it didn't previously have.

When you incorporated the company as founders, your basis was likely fractions of a penny, or something like $0.0004/share. So, congratulations, your price per share has gone up astronomically! However, your overall percentage stake in the company has gone down. That's the cost of capital.

Remember, in subsequent rounds you, the founding team, and the new investors in this round will incur additional dilution. If all the rounds are "up" rounds, which means the value of the company continues to increase, that's great and your dilution will be in the normal range. However, if you have a flat or down round it will mean heavy dilution.

What will impact the founding team's dilution is the size of the founding team, how long you've bootstrapped the company before venture-funding the amount of capital raised, and valuation at each round.

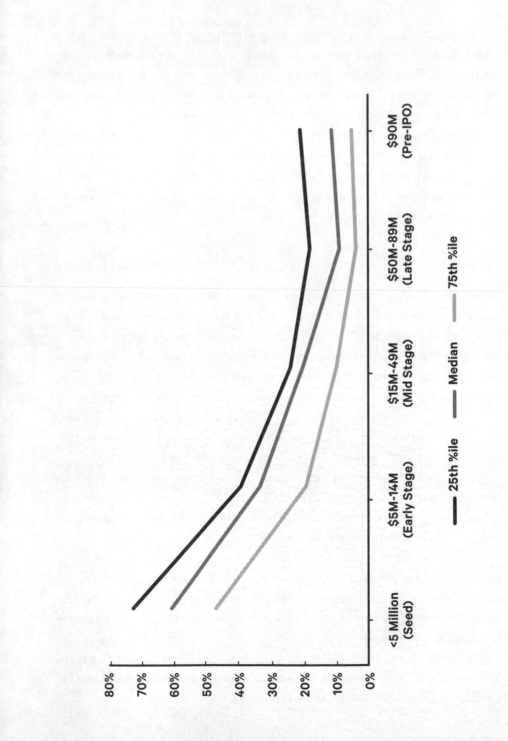

PREPARING TO PITCH

Where you are pitching will determine which variation of your deck you will be using. Startup pitch contests or accelerator final pitches have constraints, and slides will usually be prescriptive. Because of the limited time, you'll likely use an eleven-slide format. When you're pitching to an individual investor or VC, you'll add a couple of slides that will help frame the dialog of the meeting. These meetings are a discussion, and the deck is used to guide the conversation and keep you on track.

Your investor deck—or presentation—is usually ten to thirteen slides (not including build slides that have multiple copies of the same slide) that help you to summarize your business. The executive summary is the one- or two-page description of the business. While you want to be as brief as possible, don't leave out important details either. Just make sure you get to the point. Being brief is hard, I know, but you need to do it anyway. As I stated earlier, no one is going to write you a check from the first meeting. Use the deck and the executive summary to get the next meeting and into the due-diligence process.

For your initial fundraising, the basics of the pitch deck follow the scoring rubric you used in Chapter 6 (and you may want to go back to the Chapter 6 "Scoring Yourself" section for a refresher on the factors). As you get to later-stage rounds of funding, you will be more focused on revenue and spreadsheets. It doesn't always have to be in that order, but when in doubt, it's a good place to start. Also think about creating a story arc that weaves your idea together over several slides instead of having all the parts on their own slides. This approach is usually more interesting to follow and can help investors better understand your idea. For example, tell your founder story in the narrative of the problem you are solving and product rather than having a single slide that talks about the founding team. The components to include in your deck are:

1. Title Slide—This will be on the screen the longest time of any slide, so include your tagline and use the time well.
2. Overview—This is basically your Mad Libs–style pitch. You'll also hear it called an elevator pitch. In the VC meeting you'll be able to ask if there is anything else they want you to cover in the pitch.
3. Problem/Solution—From the customer's perspective, what problem are you solving? What are the product features and benefits?
4. Market/Customer—This includes details on the size of the market and the customer you're targeting. Remember, though you spent a huge amount of time doing the research, the best result for this slide is a head nod.

5. Traction/Timing—If you don't have customers, users, or revenue yet, you'll need to talk about your customer development and validation. Early angels know that traction will be minimal, and later-stage VCs will want revenue. Why is market timing in your favor? Do you have headwinds or tailwinds? Are there any external factors that will create a reason for investors to wait?

6. Product Road Map/Demo—What is the product today, compared to the near-term milestones and at scale or vision stage?

7. Secret Sauce/Moat/IP—You may not have a company to defend yet, but you should be thinking about how you will protect against competition. Speed and knowledge of the customer are two great places to start.

8. Competition—Having no competition is a bad thing. So is competition that has raised $100 million out of the market.

9. How Will You Make Money/Key Metrics—Pick a primary and secondary revenue model from the list as well as addressing your basic pricing and tiers.

10. Go-to-Market—This will summarize your market, sales, and scaling activities, currently, in the near term, and at scale.

11. Financials—Have you done a financial model? You'll need revenues and expenses for three years (maybe five), as well as the use of proceeds—what the investment will be spent on. This slide will have a classic hockey-stick chart, showing revenue moving up and to the right with bullet points to explain revenue drivers. This chart will come from your financial model.

12. Team—Outline why your team has the subject matter experience and skills to be successful.

13. Clear Ask—Clearly and briefly state what you need.

There's an old saying in startups: "If you want advice, ask for money; if you want money ask for advice." Investors have opinions about everything. Use the data from your work to show them where your opinion is backed up by facts.

Executive Summary

You need to tell a story and put the slide components listed above into a brief narrative. If you're struggling with the process, tell the story from a customer's perspective. Introduce your customer, tell their problem, then explain how their life is better with your solution. Tell the investors why there are millions of customers that have shown they are willing to pay for your product.

Again, the goal of the executive summary is just to get the meeting. It's a pass-along document for a VC to forward to a partner or an angel to provide to other investors. If you don't want it passed along without permission, put that into the footer of the document. The summary needs to stand alone, so one page, front and back, should be adequate. If it takes more than that, pay someone to help you summarize.

Design

Ugly is bad. And bad design is both ugly and a distraction. There are so many inexpensive design options these days with Fiverr or 99designs, there's no excuse to have your developer doing design. That's like having a plumber choose your artwork (no disrespect to plumbers). Do what you do well. If your design looks like you did it in crayon or clip art, don't expect to raise a big round.

The better option is to find a designer who does good work and has a great design aesthetic that you like (look at their website or previous work). Choose one and have them mock up a page for your website as well as a slide layout for Keynote or PowerPoint and your executive summary. It will be money well spent!

Due Diligence

No one is going to write you a check the day they see your deck (well, maybe some angels, but not a VC). VC firms represent "other people's money," or a limited partnership (LP). Given that the due-diligence process will likely take thirty to ninety days to complete, they follow an investment thesis or charter that they have provided the LP as part of their fundraising process. This charter can limit the types of vertical markets or geographies where they can invest the fund's capital. There is a method for decision-making in the firm that may or may not be known to you. It may require 100 percent consensus, a majority, or may be decided by a single managing partner. There is a due-diligence process they will go through, usually using a data room on a service like Dropbox or a more secure version with better features like OneHub. In this data room, you'll set up folders and files for the following:

- Organizational matters:
  - Articles of incorporation
  - Bylaws
  - Minutes
- Founder matters:
  - Stock purchase agreements
  - Vesting schedules
  - IP assignment agreement
- Financials:
  - Budget and forecast
  - Balance sheet
  - Income statement
- Security issuances:
  - Prior funding docs
- Employee/service provider agreements:
  - List of all persons providing services
  - Current and past employees
- IP:
  - Patents, trademarks, copyrights
  - Domain names
- Material agreements:
  - Standard form agreements
  - Insurance
  - Indebtedness
- Leases:
  - Real estate
- Disputes/litigation:
  - Any correspondence or documents threatening action
- Regulatory matters:
  - Inquiries or applications
- Taxes:
  - CPA firm
  - Tax returns

For a detailed downloadable version of a financing due-diligence checklist, go to www.dkparker.com/books/trajectory-startup/.

Fundraising 101

The following pages outline an introduction to the fundraising process. Many founders view outside investment as validation of their idea or company. But fundraising isn't a sign of success, it's just a milestone that may or may not be required for your business. Having a "big A round" of funding only guarantees that your investors are going to have a new expectation of a 10X return on the most recent valuation. Make no mistake, when you take outside capital from investors you now have two business models—your primary way of making money and their business model of creating a return for themselves and for their limited partners.

One quick note on the process: You can't outsource this work. We have an old-school email listserv for Seattle Startup founders to ask questions. Though it has grown inactive over time with other technologies, one of the most active topics was paying a fee to someone to help raise capital. A huge number of the seasoned founders jumped into the discussion to explain all the reasons that fundraising for a fee was bad. It happened to me on my first startup. There are legitimate bankers that help companies raise capital, just not at this early stage. The people that want 3–8 percent in cash or equity for raising money for you are the leeches of the startup ecosystem. Run away—don't pay a fee. You will end up doing the work anyway because investors want to meet the founder/CEO.

How to Prepare for an Investment

The most common form of investment as of this writing is a convertible note with a cap. The other option is to price the value of the equity and sell actual shares of the company. A convertible note is a debt that allows a company to take investment with a commitment to price the round at a future date. Most early-stage companies don't know how to price the investment because they don't have enough of the traditional methods (discounted cash flow, assets like inventory or real estate, comparable companies, etc.) to price a round of funding.

This presents a problem that's easily addressed with this type of financial instrument. Debt rounds like this are easy and cheap to document because you can point your lawyer to Series Seed documents as mentioned previously. This is an open-source set of legal documents created by Cooley Goddard and Wilson Sonsini Goodrich & Rosati for early-stage companies. Thanks to these free open-source documents, your attorney should never have to charge you to write this paperwork from scratch. They will still need to review and comment, but these charges are minor expenses. Ask in advance how much your attorney will charge. If the fees are significant, find a new lawyer.

What makes this debt instrument unique is the cap feature. Keep in mind, at this stage, without the traditional measures there is significant risk for the investor to put money into your company. You may not feel that way, but the earliest investor is taking significant risk compared with later capital after you've proven your hypothesis can scale. The mechanics work like this: Debt comes into the company and the debt holders are in "first position" should the company fail. That means the debt holders would get paid at an asset sale before the founders. Of course, if it fails, there is likely nothing to sell, or the sale will require the founder to agree to the transaction. Again, more risk to investors than founders.

The debt carries a nominal interest rate, usually 7–8 percent, that accrues annually. The note will then price at the next round of funding or when equity is taken in at a price to be determined. Let me explain it this way. You take $300,000 in convertible debt with a cap of $3 million. You do well, and at a future date you go to market to sell equity in your company, raising $2 million on an $8 million pre-money value. This equals a post-money value of $10 million.

However, the debt converted at the "cap" or maximum price of $3 million or 10 percent, not at the $8 million pre-money. They were early investors, and that risk paid off in upside to their investment. Note, they aren't selling or liquidating, so it's only a paper gain versus a realized gain.

So, what happens to your debt holders?

There are a few other concepts to understand here:

- Common versus preferred stock—Founders own common shares and investors typically own preferred shares, which means they get paid first when the company sells.
- Participating preferred—Gets a priority payout before it converts to common shares. That could be 1X or 2X.
- Other classes of share—Class A and Class B, as an example, get paid back in a waterfall, in descending order.

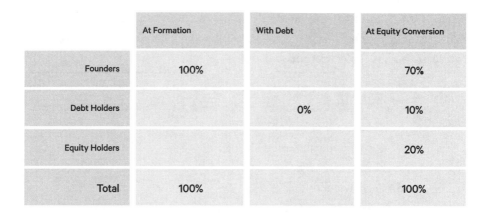

	At Formation	With Debt	At Equity Conversion
Founders	100%		70%
Debt Holders		0%	10%
Equity Holders			20%
Total	100%		100%

- Participation rights—This allows the investors to keep up to a "pro rata" percentage ownership stake in your company for future rounds of funding. So, if they acquired 20 percent now, and you raise a huge round in the future, they can keep their stake up to the 20 percent.

Beware of terms sheets or investment strategies that aren't commonplace in your type of investment. Unusual one-off terms will likely kill future investment in your company. In the case of investments, complex is bad. Besides, you don't want to spend 20 percent of your fundraising round on legal fees. That's wrong and not good for you or the investors.

Also be aware that institutional investors are going to want to acquire 20–35 percent of your company. This allows them to have a significant stake. They will likely have pro rata right (the ability to keep the percentage with additional invested capital) going forward.

Again, review *Venture Deals* or *Secrets of Sand Hill Road* for more details. The big-picture topic you need to understand is that you don't want to get seven-plus years into your startup and have a term sheet to sell the company only to find out that your common shares aren't going to pay off once you settle the preferences discussed above. It shouldn't be a surprise.

HOW TO VALUE A STARTUP

Your startup is worth what you can sell the shares for, or in your case, what you can raise money against as a pre-money value. In general, idea stage (pre-revenue) startups have ranges of acceptable pricing. These numbers are based on market heuristics, not a formula. When you go to raise money for your company there are four basic ways to "calculate" the valuation:

1. Berkus Method—Created by Dave Berkus (quoted above) for a company expected to reach $20 million in revenue in five years, starting from zero:
   a. Sound idea (basic value) +$300k
   b. Prototype (reducing tech risk) +$500k
   c. Quality management team +$300k
   d. Strategic relationships +$200k
   e. Product rollout or traction +$100k
   Total pre-money value $1,400,000
2. Comparable value—Like market comps on a house, this is based on comparable companies. This is useful if you have any relevant comps you can find in recent funding.
3. Discounted cash flow—Is a way of valuing a company over time, based on future revenues and profits. But, for an early-stage startup that's creating profit, it's hard to value.
4. Venture capital method—Based on dilution and average investment size of the fund. A fund may have a target of 20 percent ownership and average investment or check size of $2 million, a post-money value of $10 million. If you're early, they won't invest because your deal isn't in their stage of investment thesis.

Sorry, no crisp formula. I know it can be frustrating.

All fundraising has information asymmetry. In the early days, you know more about the company than friends and family. Even so, they should get the best pricing. That's the reason nonpriced convertible debt is so appealing. In the later stage, the VCs have seen more deals than you have, but only the deals they've done, the ones they've missed, and the ones they've passed on. Even with that, they have a limited data set. Also, what you can sell the company for will be less than what you can raise money for as a future value.

The closer to revenue you get, the more the expectations are going to be based on data, not your opinion or just heuristics. Have you consistently delivered on your milestones? Does the team have a track record of meeting product release deadlines and is sales closing deals? The answer to all three needs to be yes.

Pricing a Round of Equity Funding

Pricing a round of funding is like pricing a unique or vintage car—it's worth what you can negotiate to sell it for at that time. The best way to get the highest price is to have more than one investor in the process, to create competition in the deal. To do that, you'll need to know your "comps" as referenced above. It has to be a realistic comparison, not wishful thinking. So, do your research before you do the deal.

Documentation for this type of funding is much more complex than a convertible note. Though your attorney should start with a standard template (again, no new documents or find another lawyer), it still won't be cheap. The cost to go back and forth between attorneys in the "redline" process can be very expensive. It's up to you to manage the legal expense associated with the deal because you need to intimately know what you're signing. You can't delegate this to your attorney.

Why You Need a Lead Investor

Investors are looking for someone to lead a funding round. That means that individual or team will do the due diligence, price the round, and set the terms of the deal. Expect the lead investor to take 30–60 percent of the round. A small check on a big round isn't viewed as a vote of confidence. The firm will also be writing the term sheet (amount, price, voting rights, etc.) as well as taking a board seat. It's important to understand the legal terms, so engage VCs in discussion and ask why they want the terms they are asking for. It's cheaper than negotiating through the attorneys.

A lead investor will also help you syndicate the round of funding through their connections. They have other investors they've worked with in the past or think may fit the profile of your investment. In addition, they have an incentive to get the deal done, push the deal to other firms, and help you integrate the back-channel feedback from your meeting.

But be clear here, you are quarterbacking the fundraising round. There are a lot of strong personalities in VC, but it's your company. We VCs (and I'm including myself here) think we add more value than we do. The lead is helping to syndicate, but you need to pick the final investors and make sure you get what you want. It's likely to be a negotiation, but you need to keep your opinion front and center.

Meanwhile, in the background, the VCs and angels are likely talking to each other about your deal. As an example, in Seattle we do a monthly call for angels and VCs. These are the kinds of questions they ask each other:

- Have you seen this deal?
- Did you like it or are you going to pass?
- What would you want to see to get you interested in this round?
- What do you think about the CEO and the team?
- What do they think about their traction and numbers?
- What are the total investment amounts and percentage of the deal?
- What do other firms think of the valuation?

If you get feedback that some of your thinking is out of line with the market, take it to heart.

Customer References

As part of the process, VCs are going to want to call your customers. Be aware that multiple firms will ask to make those calls, and it will be time-consuming to your customers. VCs can share due diligence, but many will want to do their own. Given that, you'll want to make sure that you gain customer approval in advance. But you also don't want to risk losing a customer. I mean that if your biggest customers get calls from multiple investors who don't end up investing in your business, the customer might wonder what's wrong with the company. Also, you need to qualify the VCs' interactions and strip out the tire kickers from the investors that will lead. I would suggest sending a qualifying question in an email, like this:

> Thanks (VC name),
>
> I'm happy to provide customer references. Because the process creates overhead for my customers (revenue and relationships), I want to make sure I use those requests only as required. If you receive the positive outcome from the customer call that I expect, is that all that is required for you to lead or invest in this round of funding? If there are other items you require first, let's make sure we knock those off before we do the customer call.
>
> Best regards,

Wow, Dave, isn't that presumptive of you? Not at all. You're looking for your lead investor, and if this fund isn't willing to commit to either leading or a large percentage of the total round of funding, then you don't want them making unnecessary customer calls. You are qualifying your investors just like they are qualifying you.

Time Kills All Deals

There's an old maxim in M&A and venture investing: The lead should pull your deal forward. If you have additional interested investors that require consistent pushing (email reminders, calls to set meetings, etc.), then they aren't going to lead.

Fundraising Seasons

Fundraising has two seasons, at least in the US market. January to June and September to the end of October. The off seasons are the holidays and summer vacation schedule. Ideally, in the windows, you want to prepare and plan for meetings. You can still get individual partner meetings outside of these windows, but getting a fund to have consensus on an investment is hard. Get your preparation done in advance, especially if you're fundraising in the short autumn season. Is it possible to raise outside of these windows? Of course, but it's a headwind you don't need to fight against when you could use good planning instead.

Monthly Updates

In the early days, your monthly updates serve two purposes. They are to keep potential users informed of your progress, release schedule, and shipping. They're also to keep potential investors apprised of your progress against the plan you've outlined in your pitch deck. The more useful the features, the more interested the users will be. The more momentum you have, the more interested investors will be.

Your monthly updates will include three themes with details.

- What we did:
  - Product progress—new features and releases
  - Customer progress—more interviews or type of customers using the product

- What we're doing next:
  - Next features to ship
  - More calls to new customers
- What we need:
  - Referrals to specific customer types, include buyers
  - Talent referrals

As you mature the updates, the investor version will begin to include some traction metrics. These might include number of users, revenue, marketing lead growth, and sales funnel.

Be consistent with your scheduled updates, put them on your calendar, and stick to that. If you don't, people will forget what you're working on.

DOS AND DON'TS OF FUNDRAISING

Do:

- Keep your eye on the ball. You don't want to lose revenue or miss your plan while you're fundraising.
- Run the process like an enterprise sales process, including:
  - Screen investors with qualifying questions.
  - Track progress.
  - Gain commitment (BATN):
    - Budget—Are they currently investing in this size/stage of a round?
    - Authority—Who is involved in the decision?
    - Timing—Where are they in fund life/timing and where are they in timing on your specific deal?
    - Need—Is this the type investment they like/would lead?
  - Quarterback the process. Even if you're new to fundraising, show your leadership.
    - Ask for permission to document the meeting notes in a Google doc and share with the participants.
      - Tag owners of tasks, ask for timelines.
      - Set regular standups or next meeting dates.
    - This includes managing legal expenses (on both sides).
      - Ask for a budget from your firm (or multiple firms) and manage them to that budget. If you're surprised by the price, it's your fault.

- o Create a reason to close and push toward a date that you expect to close.
- Clearly explain the problem you're solving and how your solution helps customers. Investors aren't really quick; you need to make it simple for them.
- Ask for feedback. If you feel like someone is patting you on the head, ask why they aren't investing. You may not like the feedback, and you shouldn't take it personally, but you need it.

Don't:

- Don't hide the ball on bad news. If you lose a key employee or customer or face a legal threat, let the investors know.
- Don't be overly optimistic. We know positivity is essential to being a founder, but there's a fine line between optimistic and delusional. Self-awareness is a great trait for fundraising. It's better to be right on your forecast instead of sandbagging or inflating the numbers. Because the timing is going to last sixty to 120 days, missing the forecast is a bad thing.
- Don't create a reason to wait. Examples include:
  - o I once received an email from a startup declaring an upcoming "major partner announcement." That's great news! I'll wait to invest until I hear the announcement.
  - o I've been told a company is launching a major release. Awesome! I'll wait to invest.
  - o I've been told that a company's pipelines and major customers are signing, so they expect more revenue. Great, I'll wait to invest then.

Things to Avoid During Your Pitch

I've seen a lot of pitches that went off the rails. Here are a few examples of what not to do:

Rhetorical questions

As part of Startup Next, I often provide feedback on pitches, including short ones of just one, three, or five minutes. While these are thoroughly contrived situations, they are also necessary because they force founders to communicate their ideas quickly and clearly. And I'm adamant that you should NEVER fricking begin your pitch with a rhetorical question.

I know some presentation experts disagree with me here, but I've seen count-less pitches and this approach just doesn't work. Why? Four reasons:

1. Don't waste the little time you have, just get right to your statement.
2. By the way, people don't like to raise their hands even if you want the affir-mation during a stressful situation. You're not a teacher giving a lecture to students, you're talking to investors. Don't alienate your audience.
3. A silly question like "How many of you here today drive a car?" is supposed to show that your market is everyone. But we know your market isn't really everyone, so you've failed in the first sentence.
4. If you ask an obscure question that you think is clever or specific to your industry, you risk causing people to nod and smile without having a clue about what you are talking about, which makes them feel foolish. And investors, like most people, don't want to look foolish.

I majored in communications and studied rhetoric. I've blown my share of pitches trying to be clever and left people feeling confused, and I'm sure I even took some consultant's advice and started some of them with a rhetorical question. But I know better now. Just remember the purpose of the contrived pitch is to get you into a real conversation.

Kitchen Sink

I was judging a competition a couple of years ago as two cofounders were giv-ing their pitch. At the end, as if the previous three minutes weren't enough, they described all the additional things they could do in the future like tapping "both the B2B and B2C marketplace by monetizing like Pinterest because of the viral customer growth" or some similar vague claim. Up to that point, I thought I knew what they were doing, but this scattered closing convinced me otherwise. Don't be tempted to throw in things you think investors want to hear.

Buzzword Bingo

This is a silent killer that founders don't pay close enough attention to. Because you understand your industry, and all industries have their own vernacular language, we are tempted to talk to the audience like they know our market. Investors are like most people when confronted with buzzwords. They will commonly nod and smile like they understand what you are talking about even when they don't. But, ultimately, you will need to translate for them if you expect them to invest or if you want them to refer you to friends that might invest.

More Than One Person on Stage

I know you have an amazing cofounder. And yes, she or he deserves the audience's recognition as well. But not on stage during a short pitch. Because what usually happens is the second person just ends up advancing the slides for the speaker while trying not to look awkward. To minimize the risk that it goes poorly, have just one person delivering the pitch.

LAUNCHING/MILESTONES

Fundraising alone isn't the single measure of success. It can be a milestone, but the priority is getting your product launched and in market. You're not through until you ship. It's a bit like writing a book—there is always more you can write, more you can edit. But at some point, you need to get the product in front of the customers and get the feedback even if you don't think it's perfect yet. LinkedIn founder Reid Hoffman puts it this way: "If you are not embarrassed by the first version of your product, you've launched too late." You also need to hit your milestones. Our best portfolio CEOs set milestones and built teams that could hit them over time. Our most troubled portfolio companies never seemed to hit the milestones they forecast.

Deliverables

1. Complete your pitch deck.
2. Complete a two-page executive summary.
3. Complete your email templates that you will use to set meetings.
4. Build out your target investor list in a spreadsheet (Google Sheets) or HubSpot:
   a. Firm
   b. Contact
   c. Title
   d. Email

     e. Past investments

     f. Last communications

     g. Notes

5. Go back to Chapter 6 and rerun your scorecard.

     a. Did you improve on the areas you were weak?

     b. Where are your gaps and how will you address them before you meet with investors?

I would also rank your investors into three tiers. The top-tier group includes your ideal investor profile. They have a track record in your vertical or technology. Second tier should be interested but not as clear a fit. Third tier consists of people you can call on, but only if you have a lead investor. Start your process calling on the second tier. Make your mistakes there and perfect the pitch and get critical feedback before launching to your top-tier group.

PART THREE

Breaking Down Business Models

In this section, I examine the primary business and revenue models in commerce today. Though these models lean toward tech-related companies, they are not exclusive to this group. Like the sales methods outlined in Chapter 9, the nice thing about the list that follows is that you just need to pick one or two options and then test them with your product. Hopefully, your product idea is unique. But how you monetize it won't be.

I once met with a company working on a new way for people to book high-end travel online. The idea was interesting, held promising value for the big cruise companies, and was a convenience to the traveler who didn't feel safe booking a $10,000 cruise vacation online. They also told me they were inventing a new revenue model at the same time. I discouraged them from compounding their risk factor that much. They were already testing for product/market fit, a risky proposition itself. But to try to create an unproven revenue model as well made the risk uninteresting to a seasoned investor. The point is this: If your product is great, you have product/market fit, and your traction is scaling, then you can test a new revenue model. But hit those other milestones first.

As a refresher, business models include three components:

1. The cost of building/delivering a product,
2. The cost of selling the product or the revenue model,
3. The reasonable to unreasonable profit gained in the process.

This section focuses on the fourteen most popular revenue models. I've also tried to address how models have shifted over time. For example, Microsoft used to employ the licensing model almost exclusively. Today, they have shifted to subscription model.

These fourteen models were drawn from a list of 2,600 seed-funded companies originally pulled from CrunchBase in 2013 and that covered the prior eighteen-month window. Our team sorted the companies by B2B and B2C and looked at 2,600 websites, pricing pages, and "contact us" pages until we could determine the models. Where the model was listed as "other," I would contact the company and ask for more details. (And a special thanks to all those companies for their support.) Keep in mind, CrunchBase data is crowdsourced, so the precision and detail can be lacking.

Since that original list pull, we've been able to further track the successes and failures of many of the companies, and I've outlined the research results in the following section.

RESEARCH RESULTS

We tracked the models and plotted them on the chart below based on time from seed round to A round on the x-axis and from A round to B round on the y-axis.

One of the questions we asked was how long it took companies to go from their seed round to A round and from the A round to the B round. In the plot below, you can see that many of the models clustered in the way you would expect. Some models work best at scale, like big data, so they take time to mature for product and investment. The surprise was that combination revenue models matured at a rate significantly faster than singular models—but the data is a bit odd in the chart. The time to raise Seed to A round was extraordinarily fast and needs further research. This runs contrary to the common VC practice of picking a model and staying with it. I'll confess that, prior to this data, I shared that mindset. Having more than one model felt like a lack of focus or a waste of capital. But the data shows that combinations speed the time of investment capital.

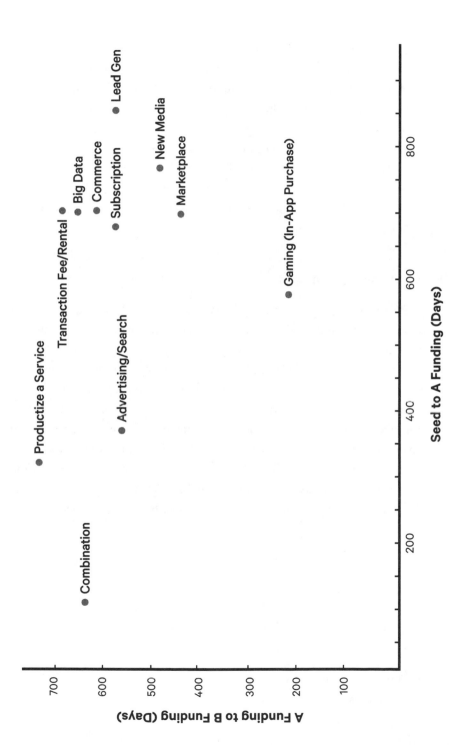

The Surprises

So many seed rounds! When I originally pulled the list, I assumed that companies would have a single or maybe two seed rounds of funding. But seed rounds went from number one to number ten. With rounds being called by a range of different titles, benchmarking was difficult. There were also companies that had been participating in multiple accelerator programs. Big A rounds of funding have become more of an optics issue for the startup companies. In Seattle, it's $8–$12 million; in Silicon Valley, it trends toward $15 million plus. To be clear, the investor seldom cares what you call the round. They have an average check and are looking at a percentage of equity. The perception from the startup is that a big A round is required to get coverage in publications.

Deconstructing the Failures

Deconstructing the failures was a unique challenge that required using the internet archive the Wayback Machine to look at the last cached pages of those companies no longer in business. These findings are anecdotal, as the companies didn't provide any data about why they closed, but they are still revealing. For instance, one thing that many dead companies had in common was that there was no easy way to buy their product or service. Many didn't have a pricing page, or a call to action. So, the lesson is, if a customer visits your page and wants to purchase your product, you need to provide a transaction method and a clear call to action. Even if they have to talk to sales, give them a path! This finding is consistent with the failure data from CB Insights—either the company didn't know its customer, they built a product that their customers didn't want to buy, or they didn't have a clear revenue model.

Key Metrics

There is a general set of key metrics that can be applied to all of the models. You may end up having a specific key metric for your business. That will evolve over time, and key metrics help you tell your story. For now, here are some metrics that can be prescriptive:

- Customer Acquisition Cost (CAC)
- Lifetime Value (LTV)
- LTV: CAC ratio

- Acquisition channels
- Churn—for companies (or logos), the number of customers as well as cash in net dollars
- Organic growth
- Land and expand—percentage of monthly recurring revenue relative to starting month
- Annual Contract Value (ACV) and Total Contract Value (TCV)
- Post-demo conversions
- User engagement
- Average Selling Price (ASP), as well as the trend in ASP
- Customer mix
- Sales Key Performance Indicators, for example proposals, average contract value, and conversion data
  - Year over Year growth, number of reps, sales payback in months

Business and Revenue Models

Business Models 101

Business models are how you make money with your startup. Yet they are often overlooked. In an article on SiliconValley.com, Chris O'Brien wrote: "I am constantly impressed by the crazy amount of energy entrepreneurs spend hatching innovative services, so I have never understood why they seem to spend so little time figuring out their business models." I second that.

People will often wrap a lot of separate concepts into the business model discussion, and I want to break those down for you here. If you're an engineer or have never been on the sales and marketing side of business, you don't yet have a solid understanding of how to take your product to market. This will include marketing methods, sales, and business models. Building the best product isn't enough to be successful.

A revenue model is the way a business monetizes its product or service; it's the system you will follow. So, you are going to end up choosing a system and example to follow from the list of business models below. The marketing and sales metrics we've already covered carry over into the key metrics below.

Fourteen Business Models

I can hear the skeptics now. *Really Dave, only fourteen models? Does that consider all the new companies getting launched?* The answer is, generally, yes. I think we see new models occasionally, but most of the innovations are in more mature companies, which are already at scale instead of launch. Three new business models from the past decade include Groupon, which has an innovative model of selling another company's inventory at a deep discount. The second model is metered services, which takes subscription to a new level as usage goes up. It's slightly different from tiered prices as it is more precise. Think Amazon AWS (Amazon Web Services), Twilio, and Splunk. The third model is the emergence of crypto currencies, and the underlying question of utility tokens versus securities, that the coins and tokens model uses. Because it doesn't have metrics, I've taken it off the list for now.

My goal in narrowing the list of models is to provide some focus for startup founders. Creating a new product should create value. How you deliver that value is the realm of pricing, marketing, sales, and revenue models. Revenue models are not defensible since they aren't trade secrets and they are not difficult to copy. In the case of Groupon, they innovated in a way that enabled literally thousands of competitors ranging from big players (Amazon Daily Deals, LivingSocial) to small, geography-specific daily deals.

Why Revenue Models Matter

A startup is a risky investment for you and your investors. You need to find PMF, and you don't need to take additional risk inventing both a new product and a new revenue model. Trying to do both at the same time compounds your chance of failure. Just pick a primary and secondary model to test.

You don't have to wait for your product to be complete to choose your revenue model. In fact, the sooner the better. How long it takes you to come up with a revenue model can determine the success or failure of the startup. If you pick a primary and secondary and find out you're wrong, that's OK. You can change to a different model.

Revenue models can actually decline and die. For example, take the software licensing model. Not too long ago, you could buy a license for Microsoft Office or their server products, and have that license for as long as you owned your machine. As a business, you might have paid an annual maintenance fee of 15–20 percent, or perhaps paid for an upgrade. But the licensing business was shrinking in 2015 with the decline of PC sales. Microsoft had historically sold all its products through its own channel and didn't allow customers to purchase directly. Their historic model was based on distribution and resellers. The investment in the channel was huge, but they no longer needed to move physical inventory. I'll mention licensing as a model below, even though it's going the way of the dinosaur due to the lumpy nature of its sales cycle and lack of visibility to the customer.

As Forrester senior analyst Frank Gillett said about the shift from licensing to subscription in a *Business Insider* article in 2015, "It's ugly and it's going to take time." Microsoft's estimate was that it would generate 80 percent more revenue per customer. Today, it's difficult to imagine any software company that doesn't want recurring revenue subscriptions. Even the largest enterprises are used to buying their software on demand or with software as a service (SaaS).

Keep in mind, SaaS is a delivery model not a revenue model. Cloud services are similarly a delivery model. But just because something is hosted in the cloud or delivered as a service doesn't mean it's a subscription. Delivery models will continue to evolve. I believe enterprise software will be "free" in the future. The cost will be embedded in the services and supply chain benefits.

I'll reference specific companies in the outlined sections. Many of the models have their own nuances that I will point out. If you find additional models, at the startup stage, I'd be happy to add them to the list. I haven't discovered any new models myself over the last few years.

B2B, B2C, or Other?

Who ultimately writes the check for your product? Or whose credit card is used at your checkout page? Answering these questions will help you figure out the type of business you have. It's not always as simple as it seems. For example, a consumer might use your products, but if you're selling display advertising to businesses to the users, your business model is B2B. Facebook creates value for consumers (people not users) and captures that value through their advertising business model. If you want to grow your company, you will need to find a way to capture revenue for the value you've created.

And then there is business to business to consumer (B2B2C), which is the model that LinkedIn uses now at scale. That isn't the model they started with, however. They started with the new media model, but as it created a significant customer base, it started to monetize by selling access (subscriptions) to recruiters. The final one is business to government (B2G), in which a business sells to government. A dot-com bubble survivor, Onvia, now Deltek, is an example of this type of business.

The Difference Between Launch, Growth, and Scale

There are two models that can kill your startup because they work at scale and not at launch. One is advertising, which isn't a viable business model unless you can get to about one million unique visitors per month. The other is big data, which requires that you have data to sell. There's a third model, marketplaces, that can possibly work at launch, especially if it involves people, but that would still be really difficult. You'll need to have sizable capital backing to get to that point, if that's your only way to monetize your business.

I've used this image earlier in the book, but it makes a point I want all founders to understand. Your business needs are different in the early stages than they are at later stages.

When you launch your startup, you get one primary revenue model. As you grow the business, you can add options from the list below, but you have to survive long enough to get to scale before you get the luxury of having multiple business models. Pick a primary and secondary revenue model, then become an expert in that model with your data.

THE FOURTEEN REVENUE MODELS

The following models are outlined in rough order of complexity. For example, commerce is a simpler model than new media or advertising. However, these aren't hard and fast rules, and you shouldn't pick a model due to its simplicity or complexity, but because it fits your customer and product. Each model in the following chart includes a sample, examples, and use cases. I've also broken down the models by key metrics, corresponding challenges, notes, and other details.

To be clear, my personal experience leans toward technology-related revenue models, and I haven't run companies in each of these categories. I also lean toward B2B rather than B2C. We all tend to gravitate to the models we know. To address the key metrics for each of the models, I've done interviews with entrepreneurs and the VP of marketing and sales in larger organizations to capture their knowledge of the business. You'll find those details in the section below the table summary.

It's OK to pivot revenue models. For example, you may find that a transaction fee works, but a subscription doesn't. If you're an existing business and you already have your primary revenue model, I challenge you to consider adopting a second revenue model as you grow. Is there a way to repurpose an existing product or service to grow your revenue and profitability?

SERVICES/FEE FOR SERVICE

The services revenue model isn't tied to any particular vertical market, including the technology sector. It is the most common revenue model and is seen from consulting businesses to restaurants. Here's what you need to know.

Services are different than product business because as you gain new customers, you need more people to meet the demand of those customers. And unlike a product business, you can't "make money while you sleep." Consequently, service businesses are viewed as less scalable than product-oriented businesses.

On the other hand, it's the easiest model to start because it generally begins with your time. In many cases it can start with a side hustle you are passionate about and that you build up over time such as a catering business or social media services business. It's not a bad revenue model, but the potential margins aren't as high as for product businesses.

Key Metrics

- Gross margin is the percentage difference between bill rate/pay rate, e.g., bill rate of $100/hr. and pay rate of $50/hr. or 50 percent gross margin (GM)
- Balancing bench or nonbillable hours of fulltime employees

Service businesses balance who is selling the business with who is delivering the business. If your GM gets too high, the odds of your employee going directly to the client increase because both the employee and client feel like they are not getting value for the services received. Service business can also include products or goods, as with restaurants. In this case, you have retail pricing less cost of goods (and less spoilage) that determines your gross margin. Software maintenance is another example. Maintenance used to be a 20 percent annual fee that paid for upgrades.

Revenue Model	Summary	Example	B2B, B2C, or Other
Services or Fee for Service	In contrast to product-based companies, what you sell is provided by people. As you add more customers, more people are required to deliver the service. Some of these companies also include the sale of products as part of their delivery of services. This can range from building materials in construction, to restaurant supplies.	Consulting services, construction services, restaurants.	Business to Business (B2B) Business to Consumer (B2C) Business to Government (B2G)
Commerce	The shift from services to product and commerce is the sale of a product. These can be products you resell or products you manufacture. The key difference between commerce and services is that you can scale and grow disproportionately without adding staff.	Amazon and Amazon Basics—some products are manufactured by others, some are manufactured by or for Amazon (directly or under contract). D2C examples are Maui Jim or Tumi.	B2B B2C B2G
Subscription	Subscription models rely on customers paying a recurring (monthly, quarterly, or annual) fee for a product or software as a service (SaaS). This isn't a new model. It started with newspapers and magazine and has been adopted by tech. Investors like the monthly recurring revenue (MRR) model because it represents the truest form of revenue less monthly churn.	Salesforce Spotify Microsoft Office	B2B B2C B2G

Revenue Model	Summary	Example	B2B, B2C, or Other
Metered Service	Unlike simple stair-stepped pricing, metered services charge on actual usage for a period. It aligns usage with the customer's usage. If the AWS bill went up it's because usage was up.	Amazon AWS T-Mobile or Verizon Splunk Twilio	B2B B2C B2G
Transaction Fee /Rental/ Affiliate	A company that charges a transaction fee or rental fee on top of a product or service provided by others. The key here, compared to subscription, is that the fee is not necessarily recurring but transactional.	99designs Kickstarter, Chegg	B2B B2C B2G
Productize a Service	If you're building an enterprise software product, you're likely to start with a version of productize a service. The "whole solution" is going to require a significant amount of work. Non-recurring engineering (NRE) is a method used in billing customers for a combination of software and services.	Guidant Financial, Moz	B2B B2C B2G
Combinations	For example, a subscription with a transaction fee. I used to believe that you could only do combination models at a scaled solution. For instance, Uber's primary model is a market-place, but it also makes transaction fees, as well as lead genera-tion with credit card referrals. You still need a lead or primary model, but the data shows that having a path to combination models is a faster path to fundraising.	NakedWines.com uses a monthly subscription of $40 that includes one bottle of wine. But since it drives you to their site, the average transaction at the site is more than $140 Smartsheet	Favors B2C B2B B2G

Revenue Model	Summary	Example	B2B, B2C, or Other
Marketplace	Marketplaces are difficult at launch because you have to have product/market fit for both sides of the marketplace.	Alibaba	B2B
Products	The good news is that if you build a marketplace, you've built a bit of an intrinsic moat for the business.	eBay	B2C
Services	Marketplaces for services exist in "panels" for companies that connect people with questions with experts.	Toluna	B2G
Lead Generation	Lead generation companies understand how to market to a key target customer cheaper than larger competitors.	Mint.com	B2B
	For life and auto insurance, you'll fill in a form online and your information will then be sold to a large insurance company like State Farm.	CreditCards.com	B2C
	For B2B, these are content-heavy sites like G2.com that help you choose enterprise software.	G2.com	
Gaming	Though a bit like transaction fees, gaming has shifted from a purchase of a downloaded game (commerce) to a unique model of "in-app sales" largely of virtual goods.	King—Candy Crush, and what-ever today's hot game is.	B2C
			So far, businesses and governments aren't buying games directly.
			Look for an enterprise version of "in-app" sales in the future as companies are incented for imbedded services or integrated APIs.

Revenue Model	Summary	Example	B2B, B2C, or Other
Advertising/ Search	When you have a free service, you're the product. This is true of both advertising/search and new media.	Google Facebook	
New Media	New media is really a customer acquisition model that ultimately matures into an advertising model.	Facebook Pinterest WhatsApp	B2C, if the product is free, you are the product.
Big Data	Big data companies need to have a huge data collection before they can monetize it. For example, university or research organizations with big data sets can sell access to that data. That may be in a subscription model.	PatientsLikeMe or 23andMe have large data sets that can be anonymized to be sold. DiscoverOrg sells amended company data.	B2C B2B
Licensing	This is the classic Microsoft model that's in decline but still used. Microsoft was not an early adopter of the subscription model.	Microsoft server licensing	B2B B2C B2G

COMMERCE

Examples: Amazon.com, Grainger Supply. At scale, Amazon has a lot of business models today including marketplaces for other companies' products. But at the start, commerce was the basic model. They were selling other people's products at a margin over the cost of goods (wholesale price of books). Commerce serves both B2B and B2C consumers. Even in the Amazon example, the model works for both consumers and businesses. W. W. Grainger is also an example of B2B or wholesale commerce model. Their historic model was a supply company and catalog business that moved online.

Classic reseller programs created early in the life of the company, like Microsoft, were based on a physical goods distribution model as well as services. Products needed to be distributed via wholesale warehouses (Ingram, Tech Data, Synnex, etc.), and these distributors also took on payment responsibility for product sales, providing manufacturers with fewer customers to invoice directly. This distribution method feels almost quaint today in the era of subscription models (see below).

There are many companies in the transition from a distribution (wholesale/ retail) to a direct-to-consumer (DTC) model. These brands are discovering they need direct customer relationships instead of "being Amazoned." For example, Nike DTC revenue was $9 billion in 2017 and $12.4 billion in 2020.

Key Metrics:

- Wholesale prices or cost of goods sold (COGS)
- Average margin percentage
- Average basket

Commerce usually involves selling physical products rather than virtual goods. These products can be manufactured by the commerce provider or third-party manufacturers. In the case of Amazon Basics, launched in 2009, Amazon started manufacturing their own products so they could provide a better value to their customers, and likely greater margins for itself, rather than selling an HDMI cable with a different brand name attached. They've now copied more than 3,000 popular products. It shows that having the search data for top-ranked products creates margin opportunities. Commerce models can also mature into marketplace models.

SUBSCRIPTION

Examples: Salesforce.com, Spotify. Subscription businesses are B2B, consumer subscription of virtual goods, or hosted software as a service. As mentioned above, SaaS is a delivery of product. When the product was on a CD/DVD or was sold as boxed software, we didn't call the model "boxed," just software. In this case, it's software delivered via the web. The subscription model isn't new. Newspapers and magazines have been using it for years.

Key Metrics:

- Average revenue per user (ARPU), which can be calculated by subscriber (B2C) or seat or company (B2B).
- Conversion ratios of those that register, download, etc., including how many converted to paid.
- Lifetime value (LTV) is the number of months your customer will use your product. Early in your company life cycle, you should calculate the LTV at twelve months, and as you have more usage data, you can extend the LTV.
- Churn is the percentage of customers who cancel per month.
- Sales efficiency, or "magic number," is the incremental profit returned after sales and marketing investment.

> Most SaaS companies operate at 0.8 mark, meaning the business pays back the cost of the revenue and sales expense in five quarters.
> —Tomasz Tunguz

Costs associated with virtual goods are the cost of creating the product plus sales and marketing, as well as the cost of hosting and supporting customers plus the margin. There are also subscriptions to physical goods that have different key metrics but are similar in how they are sold. Examples of physical subscriptions include beauty and makeup companies like FabFitFun or Glossybox. Retail has also made a foray into this arena with Curateur or Nordstrom's TrunkClub.

One of my personal favorites, Dollar Shave Club, sold to Unilever for $1 billion. It started as a three-dollar-a-month subscription that ballooned into a massive list of men willing to save money and have a product delivered to their mailbox. And for physical goods, you're adding the complexity of shipping as well as returns and restocking.

Subscription models have some of the highest enterprise value because they create predictable patterns of recurring revenue. At launch you may take annual subscriptions, paid up front. This will create better cash flow, though you'll need to make sure your revenue recognition is correct from an accounting perspective.

METERED SERVICES

Examples: Amazon AWS, Spunk, Twilio, Microsoft Azure. Metered services are an extension of tiered pricing or subscriptions, as price goes up with volume. The difference is the precision of the pricing. For example, Twilio prices per text message, AWS on actual server usage. There is no "breakage" from overcharging for a bundle that isn't used. This revenue model generally aligns with the customer's objective. This model is prevalent in enterprise IT. The only B2C example is in telecommunications, your mobile phone bill—think Verizon Wireless. That increase isn't necessarily correlated to the customer's business growth.

Key Metrics:

- Registered users
- Average usage per month
- Trend
- Churn

One of the reasons you see AWS and Azure introduce new services is to meet customer requirements as well as drive up usage and revenue.

TRANSACTION FEE/AFFILIATE/RENTALS

Examples: Chegg, Kickstarter, and OfferUp. There are many different transaction fees and rental business models. What they have in common is a fee charged to post or fees associated with transactions. The challenge with transaction fee businesses is that margins tend to be small. This implies a need for both scale and efficiency. If possible, don't start your pricing too low if you're launching a transaction fee business. Note that marketplaces monetize on a transaction fee basis as well as fee to post.

Key Metrics:

- Average transaction revenue
- Fee as a percentage of the transaction
- Number of transactions per month

Craigslist has such a large array of offerings that it can standardize the fee it charges to post. Though free listings make up the bulk of the traffic on the website, it captures value by charging for premium listings regardless of whether the product sells or the job posting is filled.

Chegg rents textbooks for about 10 percent of the retail price a customer would normally spend in a bookstore. It then makes up the profit based on the number of times the book rents in its lifetime.

Tripadvisor earns a fee for every airline ticket or hotel booking they route through Expedia. For example, the average transaction fee for an airline is 15 percent of the booking. The travel industry is one of the large verticals that also uses the lead generation revenue model.

Affiliate models have the same economics. ClickBank is one of the largest affiliate networks on the web. It allows companies to generate traffic to purchase your product. ClickBank promotes your offering to their network in exchange for a percentage of every transaction. As we'll see, this is closely aligned to the productize a service model.

PRODUCTIZE A SERVICE

Examples: Guidant Financial, Moz. Typically, productizing a service involves implementing or building a set of tools that allow you to decrease the cost of delivering the service over time. It can be difficult for companies to make the leap to product as they become dependent on the services revenue and margin (usually 35–50 percent). The gravitational pull of service revenue keeps companies in the service business.

It's hard to move away from the predictable revenue and profit of services. Companies that do make the transition usually move to another model that scales without hiring additional people. They are also rewarded with higher enterprise value. However, you can build a great business with services, it's just not likely to be venture funded.

Key Metrics:

- Revenue per unit sold
- Cost to build or deliver the products/tools
  - Typically, heavy on labor and services
- Positive and negative impact to the product to build one-off versions for a customer, which might be called the impact of distraction

I was working with a local Seattle B2B Accelerator program when this popped up as a new model I hadn't previously found in the research. (Though, ironically, at the time I was on the board of directors for Guidant Financial, an example of the model.) This model starts as a business or consumer service, but the "messiness" of the service is hidden behind a bundled price and an outcome.

Guidant provides their customers (consumers financing a business) with a product that allows them to roll over their 401(k) retirement funds into a self-directed IRA. The benefit is that the customer doesn't have to pay the taxes and fees that would be incurred in liquidating those assets using the traditional method, allowing customers to invest in their own businesses instead. And since finding the right attorney and accountant to do this work is difficult, Guidant also provides this service (filings, incorporation, etc.) as a package product.

Another example is Moz.com, formerly SEOMoz. Moz was originally an SEO consulting firm that built internal tools to serve its customers. The company later made a break from services and launched into a subscription software product, eventually selling the services business off as a different company.

White label is another way to think of productizing a service. If you can, for example, put your logo on my platform for your use—the customer-facing software—I've effectively allowed you to white label my product.

Another example is providing engineering services via non-recurring engineering (NRE) as you build a product for a customer. You will want to make sure that you can reuse this code for your own purposes. Which leads to the next model.

COMBINATIONS

Example: Smartsheet. Combinations blend primary and secondary revenue models. For instance, a subscription and service revenue or productizing a service and adding a transaction fee. Key metrics are pulled from each of the models. The revenue mix, e.g., 25 percent services and 75 percent subscription, are tracked at least on a monthly basis.

The data actually runs contrary to what most venture capitalists will tell you, including me before seeing the data. The historic perspective was to recommend you pick a model and focus on it. Yet the data shows that companies that have a combination model develop at a faster rate than those with a singular revenue model. The maturity is based on fundraising alone and tracked from the time of the seed round to A and B rounds. More important, the takeaway from this learning is that having a primary and secondary revenue model is good for your business.

In the case of publicly traded Smartsheet, for years, 20 percent of its total revenue came from professional services. The primary reason is that its customer required professional services from them as a vendor to implement their solution. Without those services, it would be difficult to use or deploy. Because these services are profitable, and only 20 percent of total revenue, the public market doesn't penalize them for the mixed revenue.

MARKETPLACE

Examples: eBay, Alibaba. These two e-commerce giants represent both the earliest success in online marketplaces (eBay) and the largest (Alibaba), selling everything from lawn furniture to seafood. Unlike commerce, the marketplace model doesn't involve taking ownership or possession of the product to be sold. And it's unique in that it provides B2B, B2C, and consumer to consumer (C2C) sales opportunities (including multisided marketplaces).

Marketplaces for services exist as well. For example, 99designs and Upwork .com provide access to a wide variety of professional contractors for a fixed or variable service fee. GLG connects businesses that have research questions with professionals who can answer them (like an upscale, profitable Quora). Toluna is another example. It makes a global community of experts available for you to survey to test your product. With ten million members, they have a massive list of profiles. Without such a large list, however, you'll have a long timeline to build revenue if you're working within this model.

Key Metrics:

- Average transaction amount
- Commission or fee for transactions
- Number of transactions per month

Marketplaces have a great deal of nuance and can vary widely based on the location of the customers they serve. For example, on a trip to Brazil (or Brasil if it's your home country), I noticed an unusually high percentage of marketplaces pitching their ideas at a Startup Weekend event. That's because, in opaque markets—for example, where pricing data for wholesale auto parts is still not available—marketplaces make that data more transparent. Marketplaces thrive in areas where there is a discontinuity of information, and that information can be in product availability (inventory) or price data.

There are also niche marketplaces like Ruby Lane for vintage goods or websites that let you buy recently used or secondary domain names via an auction process. Gig economy businesses like Uber and Airbnb line up in this category as well. And in both cases, the companies created entirely new marketplaces. The novelty of this approach has resulted in market caps, the total value of the companies, where Airbnb is worth more than the hotel chain Hyatt, without owning a single room, and Uber is worth more than Hertz, without owning any cars.

LEAD GENERATION

Examples: Mint.com, NetQuotes, All Star Directories. This business model applies to both B2B and B2C. Mint provides a free service that is monetized by converting those free users into leads for credit card companies and other vendors. In the case of NetQuotes.com, you're filling out a request for auto insurance. They then sell your information to multiple vendors. In advertising, this is referred to as a cost per lead (CPL), which is different than a cost per sale (CPS) like you'd find in the transaction fee model. These advertising networks get paid based on the results they deliver. All Star Directories built a series of websites that capture leads for for-profit schools, and they sell those leads to nursing and art schools, as an example.

For B2B examples you can look to information sites like G2.com that help enterprises discover big-ticket software. These companies have created massive content farms of information that rank them high on organic search engine optimization (SEO) where they generate cheap traffic. They then sell that traffic, lead, or form data to the software companies.

Key Metrics:

- Cost of generating traffic
- Percentage of traffic-to-form data
- Value of each lead

This market was created when individuals and companies skilled at figuring out the nuances of creating web traffic began selling their expertise to third parties. In many cases, the markets trail the high-value keyword trends from Google Ads, including insurance, loans, mortgage, attorney, credit, and others.

If you are skilled at delivering traffic around specific keywords, vendors in these categories will pay a premium for those leads.

GAMING

Examples: Z2 (purchased by King, the creator of CandyCrush.com). The gaming market has had the most dramatic shifts over the last ten years with the introduction of the iPhone and growth of app stores for Apple and Android.

Key Metrics:

- Downloads
- Percentage of play
- Average in-app purchase
- Transactions per month

There are many challenges in the hit-driven business of gaming. One of the biggest is simply being found in the ever-growing app store. And if users do find and download your product, you hope they actually use it. One of the key metrics in the category is usage in the first twenty-one days after installation. I'm sure you're like me and have apps on your mobile devices you don't even remember installing. The plus side is that the cost of creating a virtual sword that can be sold for one dollar creates amazing margins!

ADVERTISING/SEARCH

Examples: Google, Facebook. I did preface this section by saying the models are listed in order of difficulty. Advertising and search align in the mechanics of monetization by delivering eyeballs in the form of consumers, and companies paying to be found via:

- Display ads (cost per thousand)
- Fixed run of site sponsorship
- Text ads (cost per click)

Affiliate commission models like Clickbank also fall into the transaction fee model.

Key Metrics:

- Traffic
- Click-thru rates
- Average revenue per click
- Clicks per month

Scale is the challenge with this model. You'll need significant traffic, usually recognized to be more than a million unique visitors a month. Google is the category killer in this model, but remember that Yahoo was first, and very few people thought that anyone could dislodge it. Today, Yahoo has been sold at a discount after they identified a breach to Verizon. Who would have guessed that ten years ago?

Sponsorship, a single price point for a set period of time, is an additional model of advertising that is based on an estimated number of impressions on the brand. It's one we often see with professional sports franchises. For instance, in my city, the Seattle Mariners stadium recently changed names from Safeco Field to T-Mobile Field.

NEW MEDIA

Examples: Twitter, WhatsApp, Snapchat. These three new media examples represent the aspirational goal of all B2C products in that they have a viral coefficient that creates a K-factor (explained just below). "Going viral" is more than a throwaway phrase (if only everyone that threw it out actually knew what it meant!). Viral coefficient is the number of new users an existing user created. If the number of converted users is greater than two, it's defined as "going viral." At its core, the mechanic is calculated from a system perspective. The new media model could also be defined by the lack of revenue model in that it defers revenue in favor of near-term hypergrowth.

Externally, what causes something to go viral can involve a funny video (like the one from Dollar Shave Club (see Addendum/Resources) that was viewed more than twenty-five million times), PR stunts, or quizzes that capture your attention and compel you to share them on Facebook. This model works best with B2C, where there is rapid customer growth. B2B companies, however, can have "net negative churn" or great word-of-mouth marketing, but the numbers don't rise to the point of going viral—something we all better understand in the post-COVID-19 world.

Key Metrics

- Customer acquisition channels
- K-factor
- Churn

Viral Coefficient (K-factor)

Let's look closer at how to calculate viral coefficient or K-factor and the growth needed to go viral. Here is the formula for K-factor we'll be using in this model:

- i = invites from new customer
- c = conversion percentage
- $k = i * c$

Total Users (t)	Invitations Sent	Conversion %	K-factor
100	5	20%	1

<1 is BAD (or not viral)
>1 is GOOD

Of course, you also need to address retention because if your K-factor is high but you're losing customers as fast as you're gaining them through churn, you won't win. If you have a K-factor greater than two you have a viral winner. Two other rules of thumb:

- Only track active users, not registered users. If you are tracking registered users, the only person you're fooling is yourself.
- Look at the time required for referrals and begin tracking the trend of that timeline. Is it going up or down?

Want more on how social media companies changed viral economics? Watch the documentary *The Social Dilemma* for the drivers and downside.

Keep in mind that B2B models don't generally go viral—only B2C models do. LinkedIn and Slack are exceptions. The best that most B2B companies can hope for in their marketing is positive "word of mouth," or solid referrals. Let's face it—if your business customer discovers that your product gives them competitive advantage, they aren't likely to refer it to their competitors. LinkedIn created the "upload your contacts" feature early on that allowed a massive list import. Did they get to a K-factor of >2? I'm not sure, but that would be the closest. Also, Slack created viral loops within the enterprise. Like WhatsApp, the network works better when the user base is expanded. If you're a B2B company, you should have a plan to use viral-style marketing. And if you do create a K-factor >2, let me know!

BIG DATA

Example: PatientsLikeMe.com. There has been a lot of talk in recent years about the role of big data in the "internet of things," machine learning, and artificial intelligence. "Big data" implies that you have the massive data required to run regression analysis, or better yet, AI models to find trends, meanings, and patterns where humans can't. Bear in mind that at launch, you won't have big data. So, create a plan to survive to get to that point or find third-party data to ramp the timeframe to scale.

Key metrics are different with this model. For Patients Like Me, they sell the anonymized data to healthcare companies that want to use that data for product development. Obviously, the higher the value of the data set, the higher the price for the product.

LICENSING

Example: Microsoft. Licensing as a business model involves selling intellectual property (IP) via a license to third parties. I referenced the most common practice of licensing above in talking about Microsoft's license model. At the extreme end are patent trolls with patent portfolios or process patents that they have secured for software. They charge a license and royalty fee associated with using that IP. Sadly, they don't offer any value to the business and are a risk factor to your business. In the software market, either the license is sold to third-party manufacturers that installed the software as part of a bundled solution, or the license is sold to a customer in the form of a license agreement.

Key Metrics:

- Cost of legal to secure IP
- Initial license cost
- Royalty

Licensing requires that you've already invested to secure the IP, usually in the form of patents. Patents can take three to five years to receive, and you'll have twenty years from filing to monetize your property. Samsung and Apple lawsuits have become famous for IP violations and cross-licensing.

SUMMARY—THE FIFTEENTH MODEL?

I had considered "coins and tokens" as a new revenue model, but it looks like a passing fad, even though blockchain could still be transformational. Ultimately, if you can't tie some form of key metrics to the model, I would question if it's a sustainable option.

Have you discovered a fifteenth model? Send it to me! I'm not limited to fourteen. Once, when I was a judge at a startup event, one founder soberly stated during his pitch that they were going to have both a B2B and B2C model. He also threw in any number of revenue models and names of several recently funded companies for good measure. They wanted to capture the interest of every investor in the room with this approach. Instead, they looked like complete newbies. When you're starting out, you don't have the resources to execute more than one or two revenue models, no matter how many buzzwords you employ. Stick to choosing your primary and secondary models instead.

PART FOUR
Go/No Go

At every milestone you'll need to make a deliberate decision whether to move ahead with your startup. Sometimes the answer is obvious. Customers are coming on, revenue is growing, the team is hitting milestones. Woohoo! That's easy—double down and grow. Or your biggest customer has cancelled, the team is exhausted, and the market conditions have turned against you. You're out of cash, and your will to continue has evaporated. Sadly, the answer is shut it down. There's also a third, more common scenario: the data is murky, the revenue is lumpy, and the team is tired. You don't see a clear path ahead, and that's a hard time to make a decision.

As we conclude, I want to provide some context for your next steps, both up and to the right as well as winding things down. Where it's possible, I want to help you provide data to drive your decisions. You'll need to work on building a financial model and beginning to track your forecast versus actual monthly performance.

Though you're working on your startup as a solo founder or a small team, you're also part of a larger community.

Increasing Your
Odds of Success

In *Good to Great*, Jim Collins writes about the "flywheel effect." In early industrial age manufacturing, a flywheel was used to increase a machine's momentum and power. Because it was so heavy, it was hard to get it spinning. But once it got going, it was hard to slow down.

When you build momentum in your company, you know you have it. But you don't always know why or what caused it. The same is true when you lose momentum. Since there are so many variables, you need to be systematic in your testing. At this point in your startup you are faced with scarcity. Cash, people, and time are limited. Consequently, you need to prioritize those very limited resources and look for opportunities to amplify things that are working.

This starts with having a hypothesis or position on all your day-to-day decisions. You don't have the resources just to test something for the sake of it. You have to test with a specific outcome in mind. Let me give you a real-life example.

You have two features that will take roughly the same amount of engineering resources to build. One will help you fix some technical debt that's been building up as the system has grown, which your VP of engineering knows is a problem. (Technical debt refers to known bugs or items in the code base that might be fragile or problematic.) But with limited resources, you haven't had the engineering time to do that work. The other feature is customer facing and designed to make user onboarding and self-service easier. This feature would allow you to scale your current customer success (CS) team to more customers. CS is the group that would help sign up new customers after the salesperson (or you) sells them on your solution.

Which feature should you choose? And how should you make the decision? You're wearing many hats at this point, from chief revenue officer to VP of marketing, so should you make the decision just because you're the founder or chief executive officer? No, I think one of the muscles you're building as a team is to get other members to better understand the decision-making process. By involving the key team members, you'll get everyone on the same page for this particular decision. Here's a way to think about the technical debt:

- Risks
  - If you don't fix the technical debt, the application could break at some point as you get more users.
  - You're kicking the can by not fixing it.
- Influences
  - Most builders want to work on the new thing, rather than maintain the old thing.
- Returns
  - Site speed could increase.
  - Frees up engineering for a future feature with fewer bugs.

Regarding the new customer onboarding/self-service consider:

- Risks
  - Customers haven't proven they want it or will pay for it.
- Influences
  - Releasing fast is important to show the company is responsive to customer demand.
- Returns
  - Could allow the CS team to take on about 20 percent more customers.

Here are the hard realities. You don't really know how long it will take to fix the tech debt or build the new features because the data is inconclusive. However, if you keep doing customer development interviews and asking customers for commitments, you'll have some data to inform your decision.

Put some numbers to it. If you make the decision to build the new customer-facing feature and can take on 20 percent more users, how much will that mean in cost savings? Well, if you have two CS team members at $45,000 a year that allow you to go from 100 to 120 customers with an average revenue of $20,000 a year, that math works in your favor, and will continue to benefit the company going forward.

By contrast, what's the cost of a significant outage or downtime? What would be the cost of going down for one day, two days, etc.? Put a number on it. Now, based on that number, someone must decide. But your decisions can't be on a whim as a leader. Your team should understand how you are making those decisions. If you're viewed by your team as a mad scientist whipsawing between priorities, they will grow frustrated over time.

Here are some other examples:

- If trade shows are working for marketing, attend more events and look for new ones. But, if you have a $5,000 budget for a show, travel, and time, make a hypothesis on the number of leads you hope to get from the show. Then track how many leads closed over the year. This way you'll know if you should do the same event next year or if it's just an industry boondoggle. Know how many leads you expect to get.
- But don't only do trade shows. Always test other channels as well. Spend 75 percent of your marketing budget on what's working and 25 percent looking at other channels. Remember, companies that spent 100 percent on trade shows before the COVID-19 pandemic had to quickly pivot—or worse.
- Ask your customer to rate and prioritize features so you know which ones to focus on. This is better than pretending you're smarter than your customers and just pushing them out to the market. To do this, form a small group of customers that will give you critical feedback and make them part of your inner circle.

I'm a big fan of LinkedIn cofounder Reid Hoffman. I think the book he wrote with Chris Yeh, *Blitzscaling*, includes great observations from high-growth companies in Silicon Valley. However, you're not likely at that point yet. *Blitzscaling* is a playbook for tech and web-based companies with capital and resources (people) to accelerate their growth. The theme is prioritize growth over efficiency, and by implication, profitability. Use that playbook when you get Series A funding and beyond.

Scaling prematurely can be a problem. If you have more money and start testing without a thesis, the outcomes will waste your time and money. As you test, you'll begin to outline where you can go from $100 on marketing spend to $1,000 to $10,000 and predict the results with data. How do you continue to build momentum? With persistence, solid decision-making, good habits, and putting yourself in circumstances to win.

Scaling Too Early

Scaling before PMF is a problem because you prematurely spend cash you will desperately need later. I've seen this happen because the leadership has cash and is feeling good after fundraising. So they go on a hiring spree for talent. This includes more engineers, sales and support staff. You can't get too far in front of your financial model and budget. You can invest slightly in front of your forecasted return, but only slightly. If you have to make a pivot because you don't have PMF, you'll end up with a layoff.

Startup Business Mechanics and Compensation

CHOOSING A STARTUP LAWYER

I'm not a lawyer, so take the following as a fellow entrepreneur's recommendations rather than a legal opinion. This is only a primer on the topic with some thoughts on the benefits and drawbacks of each option.

I'll apologize in advance to your attorney cousin, but you need to choose a solid and experienced startup lawyer. Most lawyers charge by the hour at a rate that varies depending on whether it's a senior lawyer, associate, or their paralegal. Some lawyers bill on a per-project basis for tasks that are generally within a predictable scope such as filing a patent or trademark. What you will learn working with lawyers is that because they bill on an hourly basis (in six-minute increments at most big firms), you'll need to be on top of their billing. And since you are a startup, you can't afford to waste money on big legal bills. For example, when you ask about incorporation, you'll be likely to get a long discourse on all your options. I'm not sure if this is because you really need to understand all the options or because talking slowly and in a professorial tone allows them to bill more.

Experienced startup lawyers should have a package price that includes the cost of filing and incorporation as well as a standard document package (see below). Most of these documents contain standard boilerplate language and don't need a great deal of customization, which means it should be reasonably priced for you. Also, be aware that some startup lawyers will talk about how they can help you raise startup capital. That's usually a method to get them a new account. My experience with lawyers making such claims is that they seldom add any real value to the fundraising effort (again, see below for details).

Incorporation

You must choose one of the following options:

LLC—A limited liability corporation is the fastest and cheapest way to incorporate, just know that you will likely have to convert to a C corp later. There are online services to do this, but you'll need both a state and federal ID number. LLCs and S corps are what's called "pass-through" entities, which means that the owner, not the entity, pays taxes based on gains (or losses) on their pro rata ownership.

S Corp—S corporations are the second form of pass-through entity, in which taxes are paid by the shareholders on a pro rata basis instead of paying corporate tax. The benefits of an S corp or LLC in the early days include:

- Credit for losses. Just like shareholders will have taxes on gains, they also have credits on early-stage losses that can be applied to their personal taxes.
- No double taxation if the company is sold.

Drawbacks of S or LLC in the early days:

- Shareholders (investors) will need to wait for you to file your year-end taxes before they can file their own taxes with the K-1 that you provide. Be aware that you will need to pay attention to filing dates.

C Corp—C Corporations are the most common form of incorporation for technology companies planning to take outside investment. This type of incorporation allows you to retain losses and earnings, which means when you lose money your first year or two in the business, you can take it as a discount against future profit.

State of Incorporation—If you're going to raise any significant form of capital, you should seriously consider incorporating in Delaware from the start. Delaware is a non-review state, which means you can do nearly all the filings online. Over time, Delaware has created the most consistent "case law" for incorporation, so large investors know exactly how Delaware will treat investment and legal decisions.

83(b) Election—In the US, when you file for incorporation, you'll have the option to file an 83(b). Your lawyer should provide you with the form. What this does is notify the IRS that you have exercised your option to purchase price of the shares. It also starts the clock ticking on capital gains versus regular income treatment of taxes. No sense paying more tax than you need to.

Supporting Docs

When you choose a law firm and get incorporated, you should be given a virtual folder of standard documents that includes:

- Form of employment agreement for your jurisdiction.
- PIIA is either included in the employment agreement or a separate proprietary information and inventions agreement. This means that the employee or contractor has given their work and inventions to the company in exchange for compensation in the form of cash or equity.
- Nondisclosure agreement.

You can also find terms of service and privacy templates online. At this point, you don't need to spend extra cash on custom docs.

Now, if you still haven't had the awkward founder conversations I outlined in Chapter 7, I strongly suggest doing that before you incorporate so you don't run into problems down the road. Before incorporating, you want to figure out ownership percentages and who is putting money in and who is hoping to take money out. Every member of the founding team has expectations, even if they have never been communicated to each member of the group.

Keep in mind that even though you are going to grant yourself shares at the time of incorporation, I would expect that every shareholder is going to have a reverse vesting schedule or future vesting schedule on options. So, what happens if a year after you agree on percentages of equity, one of the cofounders, who holds 30 percent of the company, decides to take a job with their former employer because they need the benefits? In this case, you don't have any real way to value the company and you don't have money to buy them out. They leave the company but still hold the stock. That is a problem. To avoid this, it's important to discuss those issues in advance. It may be a long conversation, but it's better to do it before you get into that second round of funding.

Initial Employees

We've talked about cofounder's equity. At incorporation, you and your cofounders will determine the percentages of equity and the splits. You will usually set aside an option pool of about 20 percent equity for initial employees. That pool will typically be "leveled up" with each subsequent round of funding. Later stages will only level up to 10 percent for an A or B round of the otherwise non-granted shares.

These initial employees may know that they have 1 or 2 percent of the company. My recommendation is that you talk in terms of absolute shares rather than percentage points. With each round of funding everyone gets diluted, but the enterprise value of the company has grown (we hope), and their stock is worth more, but their ownership percentage will shrink. As cofounders, you'll need to decide on the level of transparency you will want to have with the team as it grows. Most employees don't understand options. That means it's not useful as a tool to motivate behavior. You'll be required to help them do the math as to the value just like any other benefit. Healthcare in the US is paid by the employer as a direct cash savings to the employee. Options are an abstraction. If you're growing a company that you don't plan to sell, for example a family business or a services business, you may never grant stock options to employees. If there isn't a likely exit scenario, options won't be perceived as, or be, valuable. Options are just a form of compensation.

COMPENSATION

Having a framework for early-stage compensation is important. As cofounders you are working for sweat equity. In some cases, you're the only funder of the company. Early on, you have more equity than cash. Your cash compensation will be below market while your stock compensation will make up the difference. This will entice some initial employees to join the team. With each subsequent round of funding, you'll move toward market for cash compensation and move down the amount of equity. By the time you've raised a seed or A round, you'll have a standard offer letter of market compensation and set number of shares. Vesting schedules are usually four years. We see a pretty standard "cliff vest" at the one-year mark, which means the employee needs to be around for a year before any shares vest. After the first year, they vest at 1/36th every month.

"Acceleration at change of control" is a clause in your employment documents that you'll need to address for key employees. What it means is that if you sell the company before the employees' shares have vested, they will accelerate and get paid as if they had completed the vesting schedule. If these employees are key to getting the deal done, you'll want to include that clause. The acquiring company will need to find the right compensation plan to retain them after the sale is complete.

Building the Community You Want to Be Part Of

The startup community must be inclusive of anyone who wants to participate in it.

—Brad Feld

No one owns the community; it is made up of people. Some of those people you will love, some will be tough to tolerate. It's like any community (or family), but make the choice to be supportive of the greater community. The whole is truly greater than the sum of its parts, even the parts you don't like.

I started my first company in 1998 in Seattle. At the time, there wasn't an active startup ecosystem. Some folks who haven't seen the ecosystem mature over the years think it's still pretty weak. Yes, we lack early-stage venture capital. That lack of capital, as well as early-stage angels moving upmarket into that role after the recession of 2007–2009, has pushed many early-stage companies to think smaller than they should. Even so, it's my community.

Your community will have its own idiosyncrasies. Victoria, Canada, for instance, has a population of 325,000 on an island without institutional investors, so they have to travel to Seattle and Silicon Valley to find venture capital. I've been in many international cities that lack an angel infrastructure, and most of their deals look like real estate deals as a result, and that's a problem.

It's true you need to remain focused on building your company. But you should also remember that you are part of a community, and the community needs you before, during, and after your exit. Your type of contribution will change over time. There's a season for mentoring and giving back, and there's a season for investing. By participating at all stages, you make the community stronger. For more ideas, I suggest reading Brad Feld's *Startup Communities*, which offers an excellent outline of ways to support the growth of your local startup community.

There are five components of a startup community ecosystem: talent, density, culture, capital, and regulatory environment. I had the chance to be a minor contributor to a whitepaper with UP Global (now Techstars) and Google. By leveraging the team's experience doing events in 120 countries, and equipped with Google's data, we were able to narrow the ecosystem factors down to these five items. Since we published that in 2015, I wanted to add my own editorial as it relates to current timing, my experience in Seattle, and ways to impact your community while you're building your startup. Let's look at each one in detail.

Talent

Talent, or human capital, is at the core of the entrepreneur community. Even capital follows talent. Having people with the right skills in your community is key. Here are some points to consider:

- In Silicon Valley, 50 percent of startups include one or more immigrants as a key founder.
- We're far from achieving diversity and equity in our industry, but change is occurring. More women lead founders are finding a venture market that is more supportive than ever for funding. Plus, plenty of data confirms that more diverse teams produce better returns. We've moved past the "right thing to do" argument and on to the "best thing for the business" and hopefully now some real change.
- Universities are a source of bright young people looking to use their degrees. Hire them. Don't forget about intellectual property and tech transfer.

- And experience—not all roles require a four-year or advanced degree. Start-ups tend to be more flexible than big companies regarding picking people for their scrappy talent versus a perfect resume. This includes alternative educations programs, like code training programs. I'd like to see those programs start earlier in the education process.

A useful way to contribute to the overall talent pool in your market, even while you're building your company, is to network and support local events as a volunteer, attendee, or panelist. Let's face it, if you're going to grow, then you are always going to be recruiting talent. And the best way to recruit is to have an active strategy for you and your team to be out in the market. Yes, it takes away from building product, but it's an investment, not an expense.

How can you help contribute to talent? I suggest you start with setting aside four hours a month to mentor. You could focus on youth or other startup founders that are a chapter or two behind you in their own journey. My view of mentorship is that it has no direct economic payback to your business; it's something you do for the benefit of the community.

Density

Density, or business clusters, could be part of the reason you located your business in the neighborhood you are in right now. Communities need access to flexible and relatively cheap space. And by flexible, I mean the term of leases. I remember when I was launching my first company and was faced with signing a five-year lease. Though I couldn't predict where I would be in five months, let alone five years, we signed the lease because we didn't have a choice. Today there are more coworking spaces than we could have imagined even five years ago, so you may want to try one before shackling yourself to an expensive, multiyear lease. Density also includes access to mentors, service providers, vendors, education, and public transit. The ideal situation is where you don't need to drive to get lunch.

Culture

Culture varies widely so it's important to take the pulse of where you live. In general, the West Coast, and Seattle in particular, is more supportive of startups, risk-taking, and failure than the East Coast. Other countries lack a culture of risk-taking and have few entrepreneurs.

To contribute to your culture, first recognize that failure is part of success. Seattle's Startup Week runs a series of events on themes or tracks. Tracks include fundraising, women in tech, hiring, etc. We also created a failure track where we talk about startup failures and glean lessons from them. We get together and raise a glass to the companies that have failed in the last year. At the same time, we want to embrace the founders and the teams and encourage them to try another idea.

Capital

There is always a capital gap, the difference between available cash and the demand from startups. You will always be in an unbalanced market. In Seattle, we like to bemoan the lack of capital and VCs. Yet we're not alone. As I travel around the world, I find it's true in every city except maybe Silicon Valley.

But here's the good news: There are more sources of funding today than ever before. Kickstarter and crowdfunding programs continue to open new access to previously unavailable funding. Cities like Portland, Oregon, have a seed fund that coinvests with early-stage capital (though they won't lead a round of funding). In some countries, like the UK, they have a more integrated approach to funding at each stage of growth. And around the world, more communities than ever are coming up with creative ways to address the lack of access to capital.

Helping your own community with capital requires a long-term vision, especially if you don't have enough of it yourself right now. But there are ways for even new startups and founders to make a positive difference. For instance, keep in mind that your investor will be looking for additional investments, so when you see one, pass it along. Or make introductions between investors and entrepreneurs in your area.

I also encourage you to get together with other founders and pledge to give back to your community by investing 10 percent of your exit (when you sell!) in other local startups. This has worked well elsewhere. In Silicon Valley, individuals would continue to co-invest with each other in groups like the "PayPal Mafia" that included Elon Musk, Peter Thiel, Reid Hoffman, and others. Seattle doesn't have a group with that level of success, but we continue to look for ways to invest in the market. Another way to invest is to give 2 percent of your founding equity to a nonprofit.

Regulatory Environment

Over the last few years, I've been more involved in government than I ever expected to be. Not as a politician, but as an entrepreneur with a voice. I don't know that I can change tax policy or influence other policy matters, but I do get to weigh in with my vote and my perspective. I also create opportunities to visit with politicians and express my opinion. You can do the same. Even though you don't have a big company yet, as you grow you will cultivate a new and expanding circle of acquaintances that may include politicians. Be prepared to advocate for entrepreneurs. Have your talking points ready and be crisp and to the point without being argumentative. Provide some valuable education to local politicians and regulators and more questions will follow. Your voice as a founder is more powerful than you may realize. It starts with entrepreneurs being leaders, and everything else will follow.

I've also been in countries where the citizenship fears the police. For those of us who don't see that concern every day, we find it confounding. We know that business is the economic driver ahead of politics—that data is clear. But some regimes fail to recognize that reality.

While you're heads-down building your company, I want to remind you that there are many other founders in a similar situation. They are stressing about the same things you are, like hiring talent, raising capital, and growing customers. If you plug into the community, you will find each other. And you'll learn more from your fellow founders than you will from venture capitalists or investors. You can mentor another founder; you only need to be one chapter ahead of them on a specific topic. If you're good at revenue and they are good at technology, it's a good trade! Share knowledge and support each other. Remember, we're all on this journey together, and I'm glad to be part of it with you! I do have one favor to ask: make sure to also mentor people who don't look like you.

EPILOGUE

THERE IS SO MUCH MORE TO COVER

How do you scale your sales team? How about preparing for an exit? How do you run a board meeting that brings value to you as a founder/CEO? These are additional topics that I've blogged about and will cover in future books. Right now, however, you're on a mission to get to the first big milestone, Product/Market Fit. Once you have that, you can worry about the next set of challenges.

I'll say it again: Startups are hard. I think I've reinvented myself a half dozen times over the years and with each company. I've seldom stayed in the same industry segment. Unicorn outcomes are not the norm. There are more singles and doubles, to use a baseball analogy, than grand slams. What I love about founders is that even after a few hundred pages, you still don't think this math applies to you. I love that about you! Forever the optimist, the glass always half-full. But just in case someone you know needs this advice, let me share a few lessons learned from a couple of deals that didn't go well.

FAILING SMART AND STARTING OVER

As I covered in Chapter 4, deals die for a variety of reasons. Maybe you didn't find product/market fit. Maybe you ran out of cash, or the founding team fell apart. Sometimes outside factors will kill a company and your dream. Who knew a pandemic would strike and change so many things? Regardless of why a company failed, it's still dead.

A couple of years ago, a founder I know was selling his gaming company to a much larger company. During the due-diligence process, the buyer backed out of the purchase. Though they had a breakup fee in the contract, the buyer hadn't placed the money in escrow. It seemed like a redundant thing to do at the time since the deal was progressing nicely. Seeing the lack of cash on the balance sheet and thinking they could get an even deeper discount on the price, the buyer backed out of the deal. The entrepreneur said no. He didn't want his team going to work for someone who would renegotiate a deal at the last minute. Deals are hard to get done. Most deals fall apart because of terms, besides the price. So even when you have a letter of intent, there are still a lot of things to work through.

Avoid the "Zone of Insolvency"

This refers to the point when you realize you don't have enough cash to pay your obligations. This may happen a lot in the early stages. I've sweated over making payroll many times, anxiously waiting for a customer's check to come in the mail. If you get to a point where there is no check coming in, you need to understand what you're required to do next. Your attorney can give you some guidance, though keep in mind that he or she will likely no longer be getting paid for the advice since they are going to be yet another creditor on your list. But at least they can explain the bankruptcy or wind-down process and your shifting duties.

There have been any number of times over my career that I was worried about payroll. Hell, I've worried about payroll when we had the cash to pay it. I was responsible for the families that were counting on that payroll. Rand Fishkin wrote about layoffs in his book *Lost and Founder*. Be careful about taking advice from a millionaire about the amount of severance pay that may be adequate for a member of your staff living paycheck to paycheck.

Take a Break

If things fall apart, take a break and catch your breath before you jump back in. Find a way to pay the bills in the meantime with a consulting gig or work on another project. Give yourself a chance to get some clarity by putting distance between the end of your last company and the start of your next venture.

See You on the Journey!

I can look back now at my successes and failures with less emotion. The scars have healed, but I still get a little twitchy. There are seasons that you'll feel in control riding the wave, and there are seasons with external factors that are completely out of your control. The best you can do is prepare and do the work. If you need a training partner, let me know—I'm in!

"Here's to the crazy ones. The misfits. The rebels. The troublemakers. The round pegs in the square holes. The ones who see things differently. They're not fond of rules. And they have no respect for the status quo. You can quote them, disagree with them, glorify or vilify them. About the only thing you can't do is ignore them. Because they change things. They push the human race forward. And while some may see them as the crazy ones, we see genius. Because the people who are crazy enough to think they can change the world, are the ones who do."
—Rob Siltanen

ADDENDUM/RESOURCES

For a list of all books, blogs, tools, and resources mentioned in this book, go to

www.dkparker.com/books/trajectory-startup

where you'll find links to resources listed by chapter.

ABOUT THE AUTHOR

DAVE PARKER lives in Seattle, Washington. He's a serial entrepreneur and community builder. Over his career in technology companies he's had both successes and failures, though you always learn more from failure. His wanderlust has taken him around the world to meet founders, accelerators, investors, and government officials.

Founders are his favorite.